Beyond Nostalgia

AGE STUDIES

Anne M. Wyatt-Brown, Editor

Beyond Nostalgia

AGING AND
LIFE-STORY
WRITING

Ruth E. Ray

University Press of Virginia

Charlottesville and London

The University Press of Virginia
© 2000 by the Rector and Visitors
of the University of Virginia
All rights reserved
Printed in the United States of America
First published in 2000

Library of Congress Cataloging-in-Publication Data

Ray, Ruth E., 1954–
  Beyond nostalgia : aging and life-story writing /
Ruth E. Ray.
    p.   cm. — (Age studies)
    Includes bibliographical references (p.) and index.
    ISBN 0-8139-1939-8 (cloth : alk. paper)
    1. Autobiography—Authorship—Study and
teaching.   2. English language—Rhetoric—Study and
teaching—Michigan—Detroit Region.   3. Creative
writing—Study and teaching—Michigan—Detroit
Region.   4. Aged—Education—Michigan—Detroit
Region.   5. Aging—Michigan—Detroit Region.
  I. Title.   II. Series.

PE1479.A88 R39   2000
808'.042'07—dc21   99-055852

For May Berkley at eighty-two: friend, colleague, activist, student, teacher, and the best possible role model for living a full and impassioned life at any age.

Contents

Acknowledgments

Special thanks and acknowledgments to:

The Brookdale Foundation for the fellowship that made this research and my orientation to the field of gerontology both possible and pleasurable.

The Wayne State University Office of Research and Sponsored Programs for the matching grant that provided transcribing and travel during the first two years of this project.

The Wayne State University Dean of Liberal Arts and Department of English for providing released time from teaching and committee work for the duration of my Brookdale Fellowship.

Jeff Dwyer, Director of the Wayne State Institute of Gerontology, for believing in, encouraging, mentoring, and promoting me and my work in age studies (both unknown and unproven) from the very beginning of this project; for quick and pointed commentary on every chapter; for office space and financial assistance; and, above all, for friendship and moral support.

Faculty and staff at the Wayne State Institute of Gerontology. The collegiality and professionalism I experienced at the Institute, where I was in full-time residence while researching and writing this book, were essential to the development of my ability to conduct an interdisciplinary project. Thanks especially to Elizabeth Chapleski, kindred spirit.

Tom Cole, Professor, Institute of Medical Humanities, University of Texas Medical Branch-Galveston, for serving as guide and moral compass, especially during periods of doubt, depression, and writer's block. Everyone should be so lucky as to have a friend and mentor like Tom.

Gisela Labouvie-Vief, for signing on as a Brookdale mentor, leading me to the research on emotion and lifespan development, and being a strong female role model in the halls of academe.

Melanie Monahan, Detroit area creative writer and writing group coordinator, for setting me onto the subject of senior writing groups in the first place.

Social workers Kathy Supiano and Leslie Ferrett and facilitators Emily Nye and Helen Hill, for sharing information, allowing me to visit their writing groups, and modeling how to work respectfully with elders.

Judy Saunders, for her outstanding and timely transcriptions, which provide the very foundation of this book. Transcribing is an act of skill, patience, and fortitude, but in Judy's case it was also an act of commitment and genuine interest in the people and groups represented here. I cannot adequately express my gratitude to Judy.

Kathy Hoard, director of the Metropolitan Retiree Services Center, for assistance in creating the Detroit area writing groups.

Anne Wyatt-Brown, series editor for the University Press of Virginia, for her thoughtful and encouraging readings of early drafts of this manuscript.

And, most of all, the members of the senior center writing groups, for their wit and wisdom, so generously shared.

Beyond Nostalgia

Introduction

Feminist Visions and Re-Visions

IT IS A FRIDAY AFTERNOON in early December, one of those Michigan days that portends a long winter. In this Midwestern college town, the semester is winding toward its conclusion. Professors everywhere are surely reading student papers at this very moment. On this tree-lined street, the Geriatric Center Writing Group is holding its final session before the holiday break. We are sitting in the cozy living room of an old house that belongs to Madeline, the eighty-year-old retired English professor who facilitates the group. Present are Mabel and Christine, longtime friends and neighbors in their mid-seventies; Charlotte and Emily, both eighty; Sue, seventy; Phil, seventy-five; and Robert, the "baby" of the group at sixty-two. Actually, I am the "baby" at forty, but I don't exactly count. For the past ten weeks, I have been visiting, observing, and recording these meetings. I am here to learn how older people tell life stories, and the group has graciously taken me in. These are ordinary people, none of them writers by training or profession, yet they gather weekly to share their writings, motivate each other, and learn new ways of expressing themselves.

We balance china cups and saucers on our knees and eat Christmas cookies as we read, listen, and talk. For today, Christine has written about teaching in a one-room school house, a job for which she was paid $25 a month, plus an extra $5 for keeping the woodstove going. What she remembers most vividly, even more than the teaching and the rough country life, is the warmth of the farm couple who boarded her. She smiles faintly at her description of the box lunches Mrs. Nichols made for her: enormous slices of homemade bread and apple, and always cookies—oatmeal. After Christine is finished, Emily reads a piece about her mother's "progressive" beliefs regarding pregnancy and childrearing, some of which still appall Emily to this day. Charlotte describes a little red coat she desperately wanted as a child of four and never got—her first recollection of desire and envy. Phil describes a time during his childhood when he took some volunteer potatoes from a nearby cornfield and was accused by his father of stealing them from the neighbor's potato field. As Phil was undressing for bed that night, his father came into his room and whipped him, the injustice of which has stuck with him all these years. After this reading, the group discusses parental motivations and corporal punishment. Christine suggests, for my benefit, that "it's hard for the younger generation to understand, maybe even for my generation to understand, how those things—'Spare the rod and spoil the child'—were taken for normal. And we know differently now, but our parents didn't."

I am the last to read that day. The group has requested that I participate as a writer, and I have done so as best I can, reflecting on parts of my own life and sharing my writings publicly along with everyone else. I feel nervous. Today I have written about the unfairness I once perceived at my mother's treatment of my twin brother and me. I realize that the tone of my writing is more critical than the others', and I say so up front, apologizing that "this might seem cranky compared to your childhood memories." Everyone laughs, encouraging me to go on. I read about the quiet anger and resentment I developed in childhood when my mother seemed to minimize my accomplishments in an effort to equalize things between "the twins." In concluding, I say that I have spent much of my adult life trying to figure out and fight against inequalities between men and women. This story initiates a conversation among the women about cohort differences and the inevitable conflicts between mothers and daughters (my part of the conversation is given under the name Ruth).

Mabel: It's really interesting to me, now that my children are all pretty well grown, to get their reactions to what their childhood was, which makes me pretty angry sometimes. Which I also let them know. But it is true, the things that you think you've done, they react differently to. Like how you reacted to your mother. I thought, "Oh, horrible—when she was trying so hard to do the right thing, and it turned out wrong."

Emily (to me): It hurt you, though.

Ruth: Well, I didn't say it was the wrong thing. It was just the thing she did. And I had my reaction, which she certainly couldn't control. But these little things do sort of plant seeds that later develop.

Emily: Sure.

Madeline: How did your older sister react to your mother?

Ruth: She has an entirely different set of issues with my mother [group laughter] because she lived my mother's life—early marriage, children—

Madeline: She had a different set of parents.

Ruth: That's right. She did.

Christine: She's a "good girl."

Ruth: Mmmhmm. She is. And she kind of missed the women's movement. She was already married and didn't get politically active. So now in her fifties, she's beginning to question the trajectory of her life. But you're right, that was a different time.

Mabel: I always felt that God in his justice should see that every woman has a baby girl.

Christine: Yes [more laughter].

Mabel: I'm very angry at a couple of my daughters that do *not*.

Ruth: You mean so they can understand their mothers better?

Mabel: Yes, yes. That's the only time that you *can*. I said to a very wise friend of mine several years ago, "How come the daughters have to go through this period of rejecting their mothers? I did it with my mother." And she said, "And I did it with my mother, who died when I was just seventeen, while I was still rejecting her." She said a mother's early death can be more of a problem than if you have gone through life and rejected her and come around again. I think there's some truth to that. If you reject your mother, then you can see her in a different light *after* you have done that.

Emily: I remember when I was just newly married and my mother came to visit, so full of all her great ideas and all her suggestions. You know, she meant them with goodwill, I guess, but I didn't see them that way. I was angry enough to say to myself, "She's got to live a *long* time before I'll be ready to forgive her!" And she did. She lived to be ninety-one! [much laughter]. So I'm glad she hung around long enough.

In this one, small segment of talk, we see a central difference between my generation and that of the women in the writing group. While my writing vividly recalls an earlier self and characterizes a current self still simmering over injustices, the older women display a much broader range of perspectives. Mabel, a mother of six, initially assumes the position of mother and identifies with my mother in the story, recalling conflicts between her daughters and herself. But she also remembers her position as a daughter who rejected her own mother, and she recalls a significant conversation with a friend in which they tried to understand the reason for the oppositional relationships between mothers and daughters. By living and *talking through* these multiple positions, Mabel now interprets a daughter's rejection more broadly in terms of female development over the life course. Emily, too, assumes a number of viewpoints simultaneously. Although she well remembers how angry she was with her mother as a young woman, and how their conflicts carried throughout much of her adult life, these recollections are now tempered with the knowledge of resolutions that came later. Emily speaks with humor and compassion toward both her mother and herself at earlier times in their lives.

From this brief conversation, we learn much about women's development and the nature of wisdom in old age. These women taught me that wisdom is the ability to see from many positions and to empathize with all of them. Women's wisdom most often shows in the ways women respond to others; it is deeply relational. On this December day, my writing revealed an inability to empathize with my mother's position—not unusual, as Mabel asserts, for a woman who has never had children of her own. Mabel and Emily reinforced that adult development requires major change in our orientation toward others. Theories of adult development suggest that a woman must break from her mother to achieve autonomy and independence before she can re-identify with the mother figure, thereby integrating the mother and daughter aspects within *herself*. To move forward toward acceptance and integration, mother and daughter must recognize and embrace their differences. This takes most of us a lifetime.

The very process of negotiating the mother/daughter relationship is fraught with difficulty. As Kathleen Woodward suggests in her speculations on gender, generational identity, and aging, mother and daughter mirror one another, "reflecting each other's surfaces in an infinity of endless reverberations and permutations of familiar and familial proportions."[1] The mirroring is complex—sometimes negative, sometimes positive, sometimes ambivalent. Mother may look at daughter and regret the loss of her own youth, or she may embrace their differences as confirmation of her strength and longevity. Daughter may look at mother and experience fear and rejection of her own aging body, or she may imagine a better self and look to the future with the anticipation of becoming older and wiser. The brilliance of Woodward's essay is her insight that, over time, a woman develops, not just a gender identity based on sexual difference, but a generational identity based on similarity. The latter "has to do with feeling oneself linked, unconsciously if not consciously, to the generations ahead and behind" through caring for others, including the mother.[2] A daughter goes through a period of rejecting and identifying herself in opposition to her mother. In time she comes to re-identify, but this often does not occur until the end of her mother's life, a poignant truth Woodward illustrates with reference to Eva Fige's novel *Waking*: "In this scene the mother and daughter become once again reflecting mirrors to one another. The death of her mother gives the daughter a new place in the lineage of the family. She becomes the mother. . . . Now she understands herself not in opposition to her mother but in identification with her. Age itself has shortened the distance between them. She thinks to herself, 'I am following behind just a few years.'"[3]

If we take the mother/daughter relationship as a metaphor for all relationships between younger and older women, it becomes a defining feature for the development of women's studies in general and feminist gerontology especially. Although rejection of the mother is a classic theme in the psychoanalytic literature, it has been glossed over in the politics of women's studies and completely overlooked in feminist gerontology. Historically, North American feminists have written as if women were a coherent group of change agents, united by gender and patriarchal oppression. In the last twenty-five years of the feminist movement in academe, however, minority and Third World women and critical theorists have seriously questioned this leveling of difference, largely on the basis of race, class, and sexual orientation. We have yet to challenge it on the basis of generational difference and development across the life course. There is much to be done by gerontologists wishing to understand old age from the perspective of difference as well as similarity within and across generations. It is my contention, worked through empirically in this book, that feminists are best positioned to "read difference" in old age and to place this reading at the center of age studies.

Beyond Nostalgia represents my own initial efforts, as a midlife feminist, to get beyond my "opposition to the mother" and to old age itself so that I might "follow behind" more consciously in the wake of the older woman. I assume many positions in this writing. Sometimes, as in this introduction and the final chapter, where I track my own development as feminist gerontologist, I play the role of the challenging, knowledge-seeking daughter, writing from my position in early middle age and openly acknowledging its limits. Sometimes I take the position of the more distanced researcher, listening, asking questions, taking notes. Other times I assume the role of scholar, interpreting elders' talk and stories through the academic discourses with which I am familiar—feminist criticism, gerontology, narrative psychology, sociology, linguistics, rhetoric, and writing theory. Sometimes I do not say anything at all and let older people speak for themselves, as in the life stories and oral histories presented in my "interchapters"—the sections following chapters 1, 2, 3, 4, 5, and 6. These different author-positions—ranging from theoretical reviewer, to empirically based discourse analyst, to oral historian, to autobiographer—represent the many tensions between academic ways of knowing and experiential knowing apparent in the discourse of late-twentieth-century feminism. Some readers may find the mix of voices fragmenting; others (more, I hope) will find it a refreshing change from the conventional academic treatise. I offer this book as one example of the multiple paths available for interpreting age and honoring diverse forms of self-representation.

Taken together, the chapters and interchapters tell a story of adult development through personal narrative. I show how the presentation and negotiation of life stories in writing groups initiates change and personal growth. Through the process of writing life stories and discussing them with age peers, we begin to articulate what life "means," both individually and collectively. The writing group serves as a friendly forum in which participants discuss these meanings with others who may share similar experiences historically but who are also diverse in terms of sex, race, class, ethnicity, and sometimes age cohort. The very tensions created by these differences are what prompt re-visions (as in *re-seeings*) in the ways we represent ourselves and our lives. Writing groups of older adults challenge members to consider, not just cultural influences, but generational effects on the evolving content and structure of their life stories. Groups assist members in processing old feelings and interpreting the events of a lifetime. Nobody is a therapist or pretends to be. They are more like friendly strangers who have come together for the purpose of understanding themselves a little better. Throughout the book, I illustrate exactly what *kinds* of development occur as a result of these group experiences.

The political challenge for feminist gerontologists is to press for social change in the roles and opportunities for men and women across the life course, with special emphasis on improving the image of older women and extending the possibilities for womanhood in old age. To do this well, we need to learn how women make meaning of their lives across the life course. We also need to know how we as gerontologists are implicated in the study and interpretation of old age. How much of what we call "development," for example, reflects our own needs, perceptions, interests, developmental limitations, and biases? How do we ourselves develop through the study of older adults? Besides studying older women and the situations of old age, feminist gerontologists must learn how their personal and professional relationships with older adults affect their understanding of aging.

This self-reflective stance—a hallmark of contemporary feminist criticism in the humanities[4]—has been masterfully exercised by Margaret Gullette in her book-length critique of age narratives, *Declining to Decline: Cultural Combat and the Politics of the Midlife*. Gullette openly acknowledges her speaking position as a middle-aged academic who considers her own development a major part of her scholarly inquiry. She exposes the pervasive and persuasive manipulations of age in U.S. culture through a series of autobiographical narratives. To illustrate her own middle-age resistance to U.S. culture's "age ideology," for example, Gullette examines her personal response to the physical decline brought on by arthritis, her changing relationships with her son and mother, and her reactions to menopause. Gullette's plunge into self-reflectivity is a call to action for all researchers of aging. She asserts that, "in the long run, hope needs a collective critical project that will go on the offensive against the system. Internal resistance, once articulated and theorized, could become collective." Without autobiographical reflection followed by active resistance, we age researchers are likely to remain unconscious *"victims* of age ideology" who "become *perpetrators* in our turn." [5]

I take inspiration for my own study of age narratives from the words of Gullette and the images offered by other strong feminists. One image that I find especially compelling enhances the cover of Ruth Behar and Sandra Gordon's edited collection on *Women Writing Culture*. In the first chapter, Behar introduces the figure of the feminist scholar writing the lives of distant "others" in her description of the cover sketch by Cuban artist Yolanda Fundora. A nude woman in her physical prime looks directly forward, hand clutching a pencil, as a sea of eyes focuses on her back. The woman is a bluish purple; her short-cropped hair, standing straight up, is painted in multicolored pastels, suggesting the surreal nature of her work. A pink horizon above the sea of eyes shows the setting sun, while a tiny, blue moon rises above the woman's left shoulder. This woman, "coming into her moon," is a symbol of great generative power. The clarity of the purple woman's gaze, along with the determined set of her jaw, suggests that she accepts this power and the responsibility that goes with it.

The first time I saw this picture, I was drawn by its blue mood, but Behar's words moved me to tears:

> When a woman sits down to write, all eyes are on her. The woman who is turning others into the object of her gaze is herself already an object of the gaze. Woman, the original Other, is always being looked at and looked over. A woman sees herself being seen. . . . The eyes on a woman's back are also her own eyes. They are everything she has seen in her travels and her return home. They represent the different roles a woman assumes in the various places where she sojourns, each eye seeing her at a slightly different angle. Sitting down to write, a woman sheds the clothes of each of the different roles she has played and lets all the eyes of her experiences come forth as she contemplates her life and begins to put pencil to paper. . . . The sea of eyes acknowledges the different ways in which women look at the world as well as the willingness of women to accept, rather than to annihilate, such a confusing diversity of visions. When women look out for one another, the sea of eyes on our backs is no longer anything to fear. [6]

Five years ago, when *Women Writing Culture* was first published, Behar's message spoke mainly to me and my personal situation: the purple woman represented my continuing struggles for growth and acknowledgement in academe, where I had just begun to research older women's autobiographical writings. The eyes on my back were the scholarly "authorities" to whom I wished to speak, knowing that I was venturing into new territory involving a risky boundary-crossing of disciplines. I felt the naked woman's vulnerability and longed for her clear-eyed vision and broad-shouldered strength. I wanted to grip my pencil with the same determination, clasping it in my fist as if proclaiming great truths.

Today my reading of this picture is more subtly layered and less self-involved. Having spent the intervening years observing and talking with older women and men about their own self-defining, self-proclaiming gestures with the pen, I see Fundora's woman in terms of *their* struggles, too. I know that the older woman, in particular, writes with the eyes of family on her back, aware that daughters, sons, nieces, nephews, and grandchildren are looking to *her* for narratives to sustain them in difficult times. She knows the cultural expectations placed on the older woman. If she is not trivialized or ignored, she is elevated and romanticized all out of proportion. Being an older woman carries tremendous familial and social responsibility.

Fundora's woman also symbolizes a stronger, more powerful self—a self the older woman writer comes to know as she writes the stories of her life. The woman has lived long and traveled widely, assuming many roles. In old age, she comes back home to herself. She takes time to sit and think, often for the first time ever. She sees herself from a different angle and wishes to record this new vision. She joins groups of her peers to assist in this process and finds that their gazes mirror back her own image.[7] Together, in Behar's words, members of a writing group "look out for one another."

Fundora's woman recalls, too, the responsibilities I face in turning from field-work (observing and participating) to interpretation (writing and rewriting) in constructing this story of research. My age (forty-four at the time of writing), race (white), class (middle/educated), gender and sexual orientation (hetero-sexual female), able-bodiedness and life situation (healthy, unmarried, childless, living independently) provide both insights and restrictions as I try to interpret the life stories of older women and men. I do not inhabit the bodies and histories of the elders in senior writing groups. I am an outsider to the terrain of old age. I can learn to be more sensitive and understanding, more alert to ageism and age ignorance in myself and others, but I will not truly *know* old age until I am there, trying to make sense of it in the context of my own life.

Finally, Fundora's woman calls forth the feminist legacy of "re-vision," the responsibility of which haunts every page of this book. In her landmark essay "When We Dead Awaken: Writing as Re-Vision," Adrienne Rich decries the "othering" of women in both culture and text. She notes that most men do not write for women or with a sense of women's criticism, because they see themselves as primary and women as secondary "others." Women, on the other hand, invariably write in *response* to men, "with the inescapable knowledge of having already been defined in men's words."[9] This dynamic of "othering" versus "responsiveness" clearly shapes the life stories of older women. The women represented here surely write with the eyes of *men* on their backs—fathers, sons, husbands, lovers, bosses, colleagues, religious leaders who have influenced their self-concepts, means of expression, even their willingness and ability to speak about themselves. Historically, the relationships between men and women have fostered unequal power dynamics textually, as well as socially, and women have deferred to men's ways of thinking, speaking, writing, and knowing. The life stories of older men and women represent these gender relations at both the individual and cultural levels: they clearly "reveal the canonical rules of the society at a certain time, its mores, behavioral expectations, and taboos; they give a picture of earlier *categorical imperatives*." [10] This is to not say that life stories are predetermined but that we are "coauthors" with history and culture. The role of the feminist gerontologist is to offer strategies for interpreting older adults' narratives—strategies that are sensitive to the categorical imperatives that have affected gender relations, power dynamics, the perception of personal choice, and the possibilities for growth across the life course.

Beyond the analysis of life story, the role of feminist gerontologists is to initiate the kind of "re-vision" that Rich called for—the act of "entering old texts from a new critical direction." The texts of gerontology need to be reread alongside the texts of older women's lives, and we must provide the critical interventions necessary to read all these texts in ways that are sensitive to gender and cultural difference. In her review of strategies for studying women's lives, feminist scholar Abigail Stewart lists seven methods for meeting this challenge based on twenty years of feminist critique in the social sciences. At the very least, we must

1. look for what's been left out in conventional theory and research—what has been unnoticed, overlooked, and unconceptualized—that may be central to women's experience;

2. use the concept of gender as an analytical tool;

3. explore how gender defines power relationships and how power relationships are gendered;

4. identify women's agency in the midst of social constraint;

5. identify other relevant aspects of a person's social position, including race, class, sexual orientation, able-bodiedness, and age, as well as the effects of those positions on a person's sense of self;

6. analyze our own role or position as it affects our understanding of gender and the research process;

7. avoid the search for a unified or coherent self or voice, recognizing that the "effort to organize and structure the different voices and selves must be

understood as an effort to control—literally to impose an order or unity on what is in fact multiple and even disorderly." [11]

The ideology underlying these methods is one that I share and pursue through the pages of this book: "A frankly feminist strategy would help scholars render women's lives with respect for their agency, their complexity, and the constraints under which they [have] operated." [12] The challenge for feminist gerontologists is to balance historical description and affirmation of women's personal expressions with critical interventions into history making and self-articulation. In this book, I take on this challenge by juxtaposing older adults' life stories with gender-sensitive interpretations and critical readings of my own experience as a middle-aged feminist studying old age. My intention is to provoke in the reader a more nuanced understanding of the relationships between age, diversity, and adult development.

My approach to the study of women's development is grounded in observations of older adults' naturally occurring texts and talk in the context of life-story groups. My way of researching and writing has been described by Margaret Gullette as "organic" gerontology in that it "speaks about, on behalf of, to, and *from*" the people studied with the intention to "teach and make a difference." [13] In presenting my research, I alternate between theory and story, academic explanation and older adults' representations of lived experience. Conceptually, this approach falls into the category of "critical gerontology" as defined by Thomas R. Cole, Jaber Gubrium, Stephen Katz, Harry R. Moody, and others. [14] Gubrium argues for the importance of what he calls "critical empiricism," the aim of which is consistent with Stewart's call for specific feminist methods: "To make visible the variety, contingency, and inventiveness in any and all efforts to present life, and on the other hand, to resist the temptation to put it all together into an analytically consistent, comprehensive framework privileging certain voices and silencing others." [15] I demonstrate the social constructedness of older adults' life stories, emphasizing gender and other forms of diversity, and offer a critically informed reading of these stories that challenges and extends the strictly psychological (and normative) readings so common in mainstream gerontology.

The material for this book comes from my observations of and interviews with members of eight writing groups that met in six different senior centers in and around the metropolitan area of Detroit. In the first few months of my study, I observed two groups established through the geriatric center in a nearby college town. These groups ran for ten weeks as part of the center's continuing-education program and drew community-dwelling seniors interested in writing. One group was facilitated by a fifty-year-old social worker and the other by an eighty-year-old retired professor of English. Ages of the group members ranged from fifty-eight to ninety-two, with a majority in their seventies. The two groups represented here are those that met during the fall of 1994 and the winter of 1995. All group members signed forms consenting to participate.

My initial affiliation with the geriatric center led me to a highly select sample of people: predominantly white, middle- to upper-middle class, all high-school degreed and many with college educations. Seeking to expand my horizons, during subsequent months I observed two writing groups in a racially mixed center closer to Detroit. These groups came to my attention through a letter from their facilitator, Margaret, a seventy-eight-year-old woman who had read about my study in a local newspaper and wrote to say how "very exciting" she found the research and to offer her groups for observation. Though not herself a writer, Margaret had been facilitating senior life-story groups for the past five years. Her main agenda was to offer intellectual stimulation to older adults (including herself) through reading and writing. The two groups Margaret facilitated during the spring and summer of 1995 consented to participate, and Margaret became a trusted friend and confidant.

In my effort to better understand the diversity of life experiences among older Americans, during the fall of 1995 and winter of 1996, I developed my own "Write Your Life Story" groups in five urban senior centers—two in downtown Detroit, one on the near east side, one on the near west side, and one on the far north side. These centers cater largely to the elderly poor and the retired working class. They are ethnically mixed, with educational levels ranging from completion of the eighth grade through high school. Programming in the city centers does not go much beyond the basic activities of "bingo and a lunch," since they operate minimally on government subsidies and small grants cobbled together. Classes, where there are any, are provided by volunteers, but it is hard to find people to volunteer; most of the centers are located in beleaguered city neighborhoods with high rates of crime. My offer to facilitate writing groups was a welcome addition to the usual activities. Three of the five urban groups I developed agreed to participate in my study, along with another group I held at a predominantly Jewish senior center in a northern suburb. Although only two of these groups are explicitly described in this book, many individual members are quoted or profiled, and the insights I gained from working with all of the urban seniors inform my interpretations throughout.

My own appearance and demeanor obviously affected people's decisions to join the urban writing groups I developed. As a white woman, I stood out in the inner-city centers, which serve primarily African Americans. The women in these centers were generally cordial and helped me locate rooms and get organized for the sessions. The men joked and flirted and tried to engage me in conversations as I circulated in the activities room, but they did not usually find their way to the writing group. I was keenly aware of my race, age, and sex, as well as the privileges of my social class, and I know the life stories people told me were influenced by the ways they saw me, as well as their interpretations of my reasons for being there. In the urban centers, group participants called me "teacher" and treated the writing group as a kind of English class. In the suburban centers, where writing groups were predominantly white and facilitated by older adults or social workers, members tended to see the group as a more collaborative or communal endeavor with therapeutic overtones, sometimes even referring to it as a "support" group.

Despite these differences, there is at least one element common to all senior writing groups: they are dominated by women, which is why I chose to study them in the first place. All the groups I observed were facilitated by women, three of whom were themselves senior citizens, and the ratio of female to male participation was about five to one, varying only slightly with the community. Of the groups participating in this study, continuing members included forty-eight women and seven men. Senior writing groups, in the words of women's studies scholar Gail Griffin, are "womanly contexts." [16]

Some researchers have suggested that older women gravitate toward life-story writing because it is part of their socially assigned role as "keeper of the family history." Why most older men do *not* get involved in writing groups—aside from the fact that there are only eighty-five men for every one hundred women between the ages of sixty-five and sixty-nine and that this number decreases as age increases—is not clear. We do know, however, that men are underrepresented in senior groups of all kinds. The reason undoubtedly entails a complex interplay of past history, emotions, psychological responses to health and physical status, cultural background, and role socializations. In her anthropological study of a Jewish senior center in California, Barbara Myerhoff interprets the differences between older men's and women's participation in terms of the life-long division between expressive and instrumental goals: women are taught to be "emotional leaders" in the family and community, aligned with what sociologists term the "expressive" dimension of behavior, while men are taught to be goal-directed, problem-oriented, and focused on "instrumental" activities in the physical world.[17] Myerhoff suggests that old age is a time when the instrumental domain contracts and the expressive domain expands; thus, women are primed for an expressive role in old age, while men feel diminished and vulnerable. Additionally, women are used to being socially marginal, which assists them in adjusting to the further marginalizations of old age. For Myerhoff, the distinction between expressive and instrumental goals explains why the women at the Jewish center were more socially active than the men: they had a lifetime of experience in developing and facilitating human relationships. So they naturally volunteered more at the center, participated more in its daily governance, and were more involved in all its classes. They also conversed more freely and wrote more essays, poetry, and stories, despite the strong literate traditions of Old World Jewish males. Myerhoff's description of differences between older Jewish men and women is in many ways applicable to the majority of American men and women born prior to World War II.

If we accept that women operate on the basis of expressive goals, it makes sense that they would choose to express themselves through life story and auto-biography. In her book *Composing a Life*, which details the lives of five pro-fessional women, anthropologist Mary Catherine Bateson argues that men and women operate differently in the world, and that women are more "interested in the notion of reflexivity, of looking inward as well as outward." [18] Certainly women have a long affiliation with diaries, journals, and day books and have used these forms for different purposes than men. In her review of the diary as literature from 1764 to the present, literary critic Margo Culley explains that "many eighteenth and nineteenth-century diaries were semi-public documents intended to be read by an audience. Those kept by men, in particular, record a public life or are imbued with a sense of public purpose or audience. . . . Women diarists in particular wrote as family and community historians. They recorded in exquisite detail the births, the deaths, illnesses, visits, travel, marriages, work, and unusual occurrences that made up the fabric of their lives." [19] With the nineteenth-century split between the public and private spheres and changing ideas of the self, the secular diary became a record of personal reflection and emotion associated with the private sphere of women. Culley speculates that "American men, unused to probing and expressing this inner life in any but religious terms, found, as the secular self emerged as the necessary subject of the diary, the form less and less amenable to them." [20] Men pursued more public forms of discourse, while women pursued the privatized forms, which feminist rhetorician Cinthia Gannett describes as "forms of domestic verbal housework that served the interests of the dominant discourse community, not only by free-ing up males to do other kinds of writing but also by socializing females and males to their very different roles and discursive positions." [21]

There is strong evidence of these socializing roles even today among entering college students: female students are far more comfortable—and accomplished at—keeping personal journals for their writing classes than men. In a survey of seventy-five freshman students at one university, Gannett found that only one of the thirty-five men in the study kept a personal journal or diary on his own, while nearly four-fifths of the forty women did. The young men were also much more likely to evaluate the genre of journals negatively than women. Gannett concludes that young women's interest in journal keeping is sustained by pub-lished models of female diarists (Anne Frank, Anne Morrow Lindbergh, May Sarton, Anaïs Nin) and positive references to diary keeping in the popular cul-ture (a humorous example of which is *Bridget Jones's Diary*, the best-selling fictional account of a thirty-something British woman trying to establish an identity in a world overtaken by crass commercialism, careerism, sexism, and ageism.[22]) There are far fewer published examples of male diarists, fictional or nonfictional, in contemporary Western culture.

It may be, then, that older men consider the personal life story a "feminized" discursive form like the journal or diary and thus leave such writing to their wives, sisters, and daughters. Or it may be that, like the young college men surveyed, older men have had less practice writing about their private lives (as opposed to their public accomplishments) throughout the life course and therefore do not feel confident doing so in later life. It may also be that, for men, writing and talking about themselves *in a group* appears to be a feminized means of expression. Contemporary sociolinguists have demonstrated that both conversational style and group behavior are distinctly gendered: men value autonomy, focus more on the message of their talk, and orient themselves around activity (they prefer to *do* things with other people), while women value involvement, focus more on the metamessage (what might be inferred from what was said), and orient themselves around conversation.[23] Women of all ages may have a greater need than men to discuss their life experiences and to do so in detail. Gail Griffin refers to women's "crying need to put life into words" and claims that there is "something deeply verbal about women . . . talking and talking, driving men to distraction with our need to verbalize and our insistence that they do so." She reminds us that "much of female friendship consists in analyzing and comprehending the world by talking it over (a.k.a. 'gossip'), experiencing events fully only after constructing and shaping them by retelling them (a.k.a. 'inability to keep secrets'), forging human bonds verbally."[24] In short, writing groups may speak more directly to older women's needs than to older men's.

My role in the writing groups varied, depending on the needs and requests of the members. In the two metropolitan Detroit groups, I was an observer only. In the two university geriatric-center groups, I was a participating writer, at the request of participants. In the course of twenty weeks with those groups, I wrote a few of my own life stories, covering a range of topics: early childhood memories, a love relationship, my father's death, a spiritual quest, my love of cats, and my relationships with my mother and twin brother. My participation as writer, of course, altered both my position in the group and members' perceptions of me. On the positive side, it made me appear vulnerable, helping to establish a more intimate connection that carried over to the interview sessions. Those interviews were more interactive and informal than the others: respondents sometimes turned my questions around and asked the same of me ("How would *you* answer that?"). We talked as friends, chatting about food, family, and what was in the news; told each other about books and movies; and exchanged ideas about writing. On the negative side, my multiple roles as writer and group participant, as well as representative of a younger generation, also led to conflicts and one group's decision to withdraw from the study. I tell this story in chapter 7 and address some of the questions it raises about the feminist study of age and adult development.

Even in the groups in which I did not write, I was still more participant than observer. It was never possible for me merely to sit and *watch* in a senior writing group. Group members constantly drew me into conversations and asked for my opinions and commentaries. Some were interested not only in my professional skills as a writer and English professor, but also in my opinions as a woman the age of their daughters. (One suburban group member commented in her interview, "We certainly have enjoyed having you as another person to share with . . . another generation to share with. I guess a lot of us probably think of you as a surrogate child.") I was also extremely interested in their lives and found it difficult to remain silent during the discussions. If I had questions, I asked them, usually positioning myself as a younger woman speaking out of personal interest, rather than a researcher.

The interviews from these groups—those in which I did not write—were also friendly and conversational. We met in the interviewees' homes, and they usually fed me—cookies, sandwiches, soup, coffee, iced tea. After one interview, I left with a plastic shopping bag full of beets, pole beans, collard greens, and peppers from the garden. I felt more like a visiting neighbor or family friend than a researcher. I recorded my impressions in a journal, which reflects my growing affinity for certain people in the writing groups. The following excerpt from my notes, written during the summer of 1995, shows the closeness that sometimes developed between me and the women I interviewed, especially those who had weathered the storms of long marriages. As a divorcee, I respected and admired the intimate relationships they had forged over time with their spouses. In this case, the woman ended our session with a gesture of matchmaking:

> It is a scorching July day. We sit at a round oak table in the kitchen—a family heirloom that one of her sons has refinished. There is a bowl of Michigan cherries in the middle of the table, and we nibble on them while we talk. I turn the tape recorder off several times as she makes iced tea, talks to her husband about who was on the phone, and what's happening with the grandkids. At one point, responding to the urging of her husband, we go outside to look at a bunny comically stretched out in the driveway under the gooseberry bushes, trying to stay cool. In the excitement over the bunny, I knock over my iced tea, spilling it all over the chair and the floor and cracking her good gold-rimmed glass. Her husband gets the mop and cleans things up while she gets me another glass of iced tea. This time she serves it in a heavy tumbler. "It's a good thing you've mellowed!" I say, referring to an earlier comment

she has made about becoming less critical with age. She laughs. A clock chimes in the background. Her husband goes back to reading the newspaper in an adjoining room, but he inserts a comment now and then. "How have you changed over the years?" I ask her. "I've gotten fatter!" she laughs. "And hotter," he calls out. She smiles and tells me that he is always cold, and she is always hot.

Being privy to these daily intimacies makes it hard for me to leave when the interview is over. We linger at the table after I shut off the recorder. She pulls out family photographs and shows me the ones of her granddaughter's recent graduation from the eighth grade. She tells me about every child (she has five), along with their spouses, except for the two boys who aren't married. She is trying to interest me in the oldest son. When she points him out, she apologizes: "He has a funny look on his face here, and he's got those glasses that change color with the light." She mentions a very good restaurant in the town where I live that is owned by a Polish chef. "I'll have to go there sometime," I say. "You'll have to find someone to take you," she hints.

In these interviews, occasionally I shift roles. In one case, for instance, the interviewee (Ginny) had been writing her life stories for several months but had never discussed several experiences she reveals during the interview—unusually easy childbirths, spiritual revelations that altered the course of her life, a personal ethic developed through her childhood association with Christian Science, experiences as the wife of a Unity minister, and her own work as a counselor and substitute minister. After Ginny tells me funny stories about the birth of her three boys, I say, "Well, I hope you'll write about that for the group, because we need some alternative birthing stories that aren't scary to those of us who've never had children!" She replies, half jokingly, that she had decided not to write these stories after hearing about some of the other group members' difficult experiences: "My kids came so easy, I thought everybody else would be mad at me." In this case, I acted overtly as a feminist researcher, intervening to assure Ginny that her lived experiences mattered to me as a *woman* and that, from my perspective as someone who wanted to know more about women's lives, she had been censuring some of the most interesting parts of her life story.

My interviews with all the group members were undoubtedly richer for our earlier experiences together in the writing group. An interview takes place in a social context, and the writing group established an overall positive environment through which most members came to feel more comfortable disclosing aspects of their past. In the interviews, which I always conducted after the eight- or ten-week writing groups were over, I had the opportunity to ask for clarification and elaboration of stories I had heard in the sessions. This process of combining writing group observations with interviews provided me a deeper understanding of the individual's ways of telling than I could have gotten through interviews alone. Linguist Charlotte Linde argues that the life story is, in fact, a discontinuous speech act that occurs over many tellings on a variety of occasions to different audiences. For her, the most significant life stories are those that have "extended reportability" across time and place.[25] Feminists have also argued that narratives told in academic interviews typically reflect a narrow aspect of the life and represent a very specific genre of life story. Marie-Françoise Chanfrault-Duchet suggests, for example, that the oral history interview commissioned by an academic elicits a narrative focused on the social self viewed in relationship to its past, rather than an inner self viewed in relationship to its own desires and needs.[26] In collecting life stories through both the writing groups and the interviews, then, I was in a better position to determine which stories had "extended reportability" in both contexts, as well as to compare how the writers represented themselves to their peers and to me individually.

Beyond Nostalgia includes seven research-based chapters and seven "interchapters." Chapter 1 reviews current theories of social construction, adult development, and the discursive self, focusing on the narrative theories of Kenneth Gergen, Jerome Bruner, Gary Kenyon, and William Randall, along with selected works of feminist criticism. I argue that to gain fuller understanding of change over time, each person's life story must be read with an eye toward gender and other forms of diversity and cultural influence. Chapters 2 and 3 provide my own readings of older adults' life stories in terms of age, race, class, and gender differences. I provide excerpts from writing-group conversations and individual interviews to show how cultural scripts influence how older adults narrate the self, as well as how they interpret each others' narratives. In chapter 4, I look at the relationship between memory and "truth" in the life story, drawing on Donald Spence's distinction between narrative and historical truth and showing how memory is influenced by family scripts that are often heavily gendered. Chapters 5 and 6 examine writing groups themselves as social environments or interpretive communities that operate on the basis of group norms for telling and responding. I show how older men's narratives, in particular, change in response to older women's requests for more talk about emotion. Chapter 7 relies on examples provided throughout the book, as well as ongoing discussions in narrative studies, to emphasize the profound connections between life story and adult development. I take a reflective turn in this chapter to consider the effect of my position as middle-aged feminist on my understanding of women's development. The interchapters offer first-person accounts of older women talking and writing about their lives. They are intimate self-portraits that illustrate the ideas in the research-based chapters and exemplify the great diversity among older women.

ONE   # Language, Narrative, Self, and Adult Development

> The writer's greatest act of creativity
> may be self-creation through language.
> —Barbara Frey Waxman

TWO CURRENT INTELLECTUAL MOVEMENTS inform my analysis of older adults' life stories: social constructionism and feminist criticism. These movements are based on critical theories and empirical practices that cut across many disciplines in the humanities and social sciences and function as critique and corrective to approaches that are less sensitive to gender and other forms of diversity. In this chapter, I briefly review the central ideas within social constructionism and feminism in terms of their relevance to my study of life story and adult development.

Social constructionism is actually a constellation of theories articulating the belief that mind, thought, self, and reality are largely products of history, culture, and language. The world—and the self within it—are not taken-for-granted entities warranted through objective observation but constructions or creations achieved through socially agreed-upon methods of seeing, naming, and interpreting. In the words of psychologist Kenneth Gergen, "from the constructionist position the process of understanding is not automatically driven by the forces of nature, but is the result of an active, cooperative enterprise of persons in relationship."[1] From this position, language and narrative are central to human relationships and the creation of meaning. Rhetorician James Berlin explains that "all truths arise out of dialectic, out of the interaction of individuals within discourse communities. Truth is never simply 'out there' in the material or the social realm, or simply 'in here' in a private, personal world. It emerges only as the three—the material, the social, and the personal—interact, and the agent of mediation is language."[2] In other words, we understand ourselves and our world through interpretive frameworks we have adopted from living and interacting in specific communities at particular times in history.

Although social constructionism has its roots in the philosophical traditions of Kant, Nietzsche, and Spinoza, as well as the more recent theories of William James, Lev Vygotsky, Jürgen Habermas, and George Herbert Meade, it is currently associated with the writings of Richard Rorty in philosophy; with those of Thomas Kuhn in the philosophy of science; Peter Berger and Thomas Luckmann in sociology; Kenneth Gergen in psychology; Peter Cushman, Jane Flax, and Arthur Kleinman in clinical psychology and psychiatry; Clifford Geertz and Victor Turner in anthropology; Hayden White in history; a host of contemporary scholars of English, including Kenneth Bruffee and James Berlin; and the majority of researchers in women's studies. Literary critic Stanley Fish notes that social constructionism "is not an isolated argument; in fact, today one could say that it is the *going* argument" among U.S. academics.[3]

Yet theories of social construction, particularly those that foreground language practices and discourse communities, have had little influence on the making of gerontology as a field, largely because the field remains rooted in scientific empiricism and the study of the aged individual, rather than analysis of the social conditions that establish the meaning and significance of age.[4] There are notable exceptions, however, and these represent promising directions for the kind of interdisciplinary approach I pursue here. I am referring especially to work in the area of "critical gerontology," including that of social-economist Carole Estes; sociologists Jay Gubrium, Mike Featherstone, and Mike Hepworth; the British sociolinguists Nikolas Coupland, Justine Coupland, and Howard Giles; and historian Thomas R. Cole.

Critical gerontology forces us to examine popular trends and assumptions about aging. Carole Estes, for example, has demonstrated convincingly that many of the social "problems" in old age are actually *created* by social and economic policies that perpetuate a "crisis" mentality directed at a younger public anxious about its own future. The segments of the older population that inevitably suffer most from this mentality are women and minorities. Gubrium's studies of the nursing-home environment and the social construction of dementia illustrate that loss of cognitive status is not merely a biological phenomenon but a socially constituted one as well; family members interpret Alzheimer's disease largely on the basis of the individual's behavior in the social world, as well as through cultural messages and media images that provide socially valued ways for family members to respond.[5] Featherstone and Hepworth argue that shifts in public perceptions toward the positive side of aging have been significantly influenced by representations in popular and consumer culture that coincide with the institutionalization of retirement planning. In their analysis of retirement magazines, they describe how the "soft sell" works by recommending consumer goods and services while simultaneously providing information and advice about enhancement and empowerment in later life.[6] Thomas R. Cole also analyzes public images of aging but does so within the broader context of cultural history. In *Journey of Life,* Cole argues that people's understanding of the life course is deeply embedded in cultural images that are historically contingent. In describing popularly accepted versions of the life course from the sixteenth century through the twentieth century, Cole, in effect, summarizes the social-constructionist perspective as applied to aging: "Aging and old age are certainly real, but they do not exist in some natural realm, independently of the ideals, images, and social practices that conceptualize and represent them. Growing old cannot be understood apart from its subjective experience, mediated by social condition and cultural significance."[7]

So far, very few scholars have taken on the challenge of examining the social construction of age through specific language acts. The linguists mentioned above (Coupland, Coupland, and Giles) acknowledge this point in the first chapter of their *Language, Society, and the Elderly,* a pioneering book that merges insights from social psychology and discourse analysis. Their work reveals what they call "social ageism" through explicit analysis of older people's talk with each other and with younger speech partners. They argue that definitions of "the elderly" in any society are constituted through social consensus, which can be identified through patterns of linguistic interaction. Specifically, they find that "older conversationalists frequently have their interactional roles, and key aspects of their life-span identities, constructed *for* them by younger people" in the course of everyday conversation.[8]

The relevant insight from theories of social construction is that age is socially negotiated. Similarly, the aged individual, the older "self," is socially constituted. The social constructionist does not look for a "true identity" or an "authentic self" but examines instead how identity is created through social interaction. In the words of psychologist Edward Sampson as he sums up constructionist critiques of the traditional psychological self as internally contained: "There is an essential interpenetration . . . of society and the individual that warrants our approaching with scepticism any view that makes the individual a transcendent entity. We do not begin with two independent entities, individual and society, that are otherwise formed and defined apart from one another and that interact as though each were external to the other. Rather, society constitutes and inhabits the very core of whatever passes for personhood; each is interpenetrated by its other."[9] Not only does society constitute the self, but individuals constitute themselves within social interaction. Individuals have different perspectives on themselves, depending on the context, as Kenneth Gergen explains: "Attempts to define or describe oneself inevitably proceed from a perspective, and different perspectives have different implications for how a person is treated. One may indeed feel that it is legitimate, from a certain perspective, to define oneself as

American, Irish, or mixed in nationality—that from a certain vantage point one is masculine, feminine, or androgynous."[10] Thus, personal identity is not an essence but a social manifestation that is created and recreated through language acts, social patterns, and human relationships.

The specific study of the self inscribed in language—"the discursive self"—is best reflected in strands of psychology and literary criticism concerned with self narratives. By *discursive* I mean simply *suggested by discourse*—words, phrases, sentences, whole texts, either spoken or written. From this perspective, to know the self one must analyze the ways the self interacts with others verbally. According to psychologist John Shotter, our self talk "is constituted for us very largely by the *already established* ways in which we *must* talk in our attempts to account for ourselves—and for [our experience]—to the others around us. What we think of and talk of as our 'intuitions' about ourselves are 'forced' upon us by the ways of talking that we must use in justifying our conduct to others (and in criticizing theirs). And only certain ways of talking are deemed legitimate."[11]

In contemporary psychology, one of the best-known proponents of the discursive self is Jerome Bruner. His research on language, cognition, and identity, informed by the humanities as well as the interpretive social sciences, emphasizes the "symbolic activities that human beings [employ] in constructing and in making sense not only of the world, but of themselves."[12] For Bruner, one of the most "ubiquitous and powerful" symbolic activities is the story form. He contends that narrative is crucial to life: we are understood as individuals not just by what we do, but also by how we *tell* about it. Everyday narrative, such as life-story telling, is not only a form of accounting but also a rhetorical performance. It functions in certain environments for specific audiences, and it serves many purposes: to justify, flatter, deceive, entreat, challenge, question, resolve, teach. As such, the subject of autobiographical narrative—the self—exists in a transactional relationship with others; it is "dialogue dependent."[13] This is why the study of writing *groups* is important to our understanding of adult development through narrative. Bruner himself has recently begun to study written autobiographies in order to see how a person articulates the self in a particular cultural-historical context. He defines autobiography, not as an accurate historical recording of one's life, but a rhetorical account of "what one thinks one did in what settings in what ways for what felt reasons."[14]

Other psychologists who have theorized about the discursive self include the growing contingency responsible for the promotion of "narrative psychology," especially Donald Polkinghorne, Roy Schafer, and Donald Spence. In his *Narrative Knowing and the Human Sciences*, Polkinghorne characterizes the discursive self in this way: "We achieve our personal identities and self-concept through the use of the narrative configuration, and make our existence into a whole by understanding it as an expression of a single unfolding and developing story." [15] In a similar vein, psychoanalyst Roy Schafer describes the self as a "telling" and sees the function of psychoanalysis as a kind of story session: the therapist assists the client in retelling her story so that new insights into the life occur and change seems possible.[16] Psychoanalyst Donald Spence examines the function of memory in self-construction and makes a distinction between "narrative truth" and "historical truth." He argues that the purpose of psychoanalysis should be the creation of "narrative truth"; that is, a story that gets at the basis of the client's trouble but that may deviate from material or "historical truth." A client's narrative represents a necessary compromise between "what is true and what is tellable" and serves a therapeutic purpose larger than the strict recounting of "facts." [17]

In an intriguing extension of the literature on the discursive self, psychologists Hubert Hermans, Harry Kempen, and Rens van Loon encourage us to see the self as an *imaginative* construct as well as a social one. Influenced by the work of literary critic Mikhail Bakhtin, they argue that the self is established, not only in dialogue with *real* people, but also through *imaginary* talk. They interpret these imaginations as "real" in terms of their influence on a person's overall sense of self. "Imaginal dialogues play a central role in our daily lives: They exist alongside actual dialogues with real others and, interwoven with actual interactions, they constitute an essential part of our narrative construction of the world. Even when we are outwardly silent, for example, we find ourselves communicating with our critics, our parents, our consciences, our gods, our reflection in the mirror, the photograph of someone we miss, a figure from a movie or a dream, our babies, or our pets." [18] The self, then, is a dialogical construct, a multiplicity of selves or "I positions" interacting in both real and imaginary conversations, fluctuating among different and even opposed positions like characters in a novel. Each character (the wounded child, the rebellious teenager, the good citizen, the jealous spouse) speaks with a different voice, and "the 'I' in one position can agree, disagree, understand, misunderstand, oppose, contradict, question, and even ridicule the 'I' in another position." [19] The self is complex, multivocal, multipositioned, and capable of multiple shifts and changes throughout the life course.

Feminist criticism is most instructive in terms of its examinations of diversity as *central* to our understanding of the discursive self. The fundamental purpose of feminist criticism, in fact, is to theorize difference. Feminist scholars work to legitimize what has been ignored, marginalized, and disdained in their efforts to bring about social change. From the start, feminist criticism has been an "outsider" discourse, born of the experience of women's marginality in a patriarchal society and therefore acutely "attuned to issues of exclusion and invisibility." [20] Literary criticism of the 1960s and 1970s pursued gender differences as represented in texts, textual criticism, and the construction of canonical ideas about the characteristics of "great literature," while feminist critics across the disciplines worked to expose the gendered nature of history, culture, and society. In this process, Susan Bordo reminds us, "the category of 'human'—a standard against which all difference translates to lack, insufficiency—was brought down to earth, given a pair of pants, and reminded that it was not the only player in town."[21] The challenges of feminist criticism to the prevailing belief systems are summed up by Elspeth Probyn: "Who speaks for whom, why, how, and when?"[22] Marginalized groups are now demanding to speak for themselves.

In the last twenty-five years, feminist criticism has become more self-reflective, deconstructing its own categories and establishing that, just as the universal "man" did not account for all human experience, neither does the universal "woman" or "feminist" account for all women's experience. The critiques of feminist criticism by feminists themselves, especially lesbians and women of color, have highlighted the fact that first- and second-stage feminisms (the women's suffrage movement of the early-twentieth century and the 1960s women's movement in the United States and Britain) were established and promoted by educated white, middle-class, heterosexual women. In response, third-wave feminists now refer to "feminisms" in the plural rather than the generic "feminism," and current feminist criticism explores differences *within* the category of woman. Literary scholar Lillian Robinson describes the new identity of feminist criticism as founded on the notion that "the difference of gender is not the only one that subsists among writers or the people they write about. It may not always be the major one. Women differ from one another by race, by ethnicity, by sexual orientation, and by class. Each of these contributes its historic specificity to social conditions and to the destiny and consciousness of individual women."[23] New texts and narratives have arisen that give voice to the "subaltern" (subordinate and excluded) within the category of woman, including African American, Chicana, Native American, and Third World, as well as lesbian and transsexual standpoints.

Feminist critics have developed a large body of literature on gender differences as represented in oral and written discourse. The nature of the self, as well as the relationship between life and text, physical existence and its discursive formation, are major themes in contemporary autobiographical criticism. Along these lines, literary critic Janet Gunn postulates that, since the "self" can know itself only in communication with others, language plays a crucial role in self-realization, a fact best revealed in the autobiographical act: "It is by means of language (*graphie*) that self both displays itself and has access to depth; it is also through language that self achieves and acknowledges its *bios*. . . . When the autobiographer brings a life 'to language,' he or she always adumbrates a perspective from somewhere—namely a world whose meanings and codes and even whose burden of unintelligibility serve to locate and ground that perspective." [24] Self-knowledge, then, is "always grounded in the signs of one's existence that are received from others, as well as from the works of culture by which one is interpreted." [25]

In terms of questions about the self, literary critics, influenced by constructionist theories of contingency and multiple truths, are particularly interested in the tensions between narrative coherence and fragmentation in self-representations. Feminist critics have noted that men's writing more often takes the form of a continuous, public narrative or "autobiography proper," while women's writing takes the form of private diaries, letters, notebooks, journals, and memoirs — discontinuous forms consistent with the fragmented, interrupted nature of women's material lives. [26] Although literary critics differ in the degree of significance they place on language, all agree that the self is at least partially discursive — that autobiography or life story writing is in some sense "a narrative artifice, privileging a presence, or identity, that does not exist outside language." [27]

One of the most elegant considerations of the play between self and language is writer Carol Shields's description of an eighty-year-old woman's life review. In *Stone Diaries*, Shields's Pulitzer Prize–winning fictional autobiography of an "ordinary" woman, the narrator explains the protagonist's late-life ruminations:

> All she's trying to do is keep things straight in her head. To keep the weight of her memories evenly distributed. To hold the chapters of her life in order. She feels a new tenderness growing for certain moments; they're like beads on a string, and the string is wearing out. At the same time she knows that what lies ahead of her must be concluded by the efforts of her imagination and not by the straight-faced recital of a throttled and unlit history. *Words are more and more required.* And the question arises: *what is the story of a life?* A chronicle of fact or a skillfully wrought impression? The bringing together of what she fears? Or the adding up of what has been off-handedly revealed, those tiny allotted increments of knowledge? She needs a quiet place in which to think about this immensity. And she needs someone — anyone — to listen. [28]

Shields's emphasis on the relationship between words and life is characteristic of the literary fascination with the discursive self. In an interview in which she talks about the creative impulse behind *Stone Diaries*, Shields elaborates on the importance of language to the creation of identity, particularly for women. She has created her fictional world on the premise that women of the protagonist's generation were often "erased from their lives," mostly for societal reasons, but also because they did not have words to speak the self. And without words, women of any generation are unable to "claim" their lives as their own; they will always be spoken *for*. [29]

On the other hand, there is much of life and the self, too, that is unsayable. Sometimes language does not suffice—there *are* no words—and a person is struck dumb in the face of lived experience. The inability and unwillingness to "language" the self is also of interest to literary critics and creative writers, as evident in numerous works on silence, mutedness, lack of voice, and coming to voice. Writer Lorrie Moore, reflecting on her resistance to constructing a nonfictional account for the *New Yorker* of her baby's traumatic hospitalization, has this to say about the inadequacy of words and narrative to represent the chaotic flux of emotion and lived experience:

> How can it be described? How can any of it be described? The trip and the story of the trip are always two different things. The narrator is the one who has stayed home but then, afterward, presses her mouth upon the traveller's mouth, in order to make the mouth work, to make the mouth say, say, say. One cannot go to a place and speak of it, one cannot both see and say, not really. One can go, and upon returning make a lot of hand motions and indications with the arms. The mouth itself, working at the speed of light, at the eye's instructions, is necessarily struck still; so fast, so much to report, it hangs open and dumb as a gutted bell. All that unsayable life! That's where the narrator comes in. With her kisses and mimicry and tidying up. The narrator comes and makes a slow, fake song of the mouth's eager devastation.[30]

Moore, like other creative writers and literary critics, makes a strong distinction between the I who lives in the material world and the I who constructs that world through story. She allows for the fact that the narrating I is severely constrained by the language and discursive conventions available to her. Contemporary writers like Shields and Moore "question any easy relationship between discourse and the speaking subject, particularly the assumption that *experience* produces a *voice*—that, for example, *being woman* means speaking in a *woman's voice*."[31] For this reason, literary critic Betty Bergland, in her analysis of the autobiographies of Jewish immigrant women, deliberately separates the three subject positions represented in the narratives: the experiencing subject, the speaking subject (the I who writes the story), and the subject of the narrative (the I who is created on paper). In contemporary literary criticism, the discursive self exists somewhere in the tangle of these subject positions.

The various formulations of the discursive self, as well as questions about the possibilities and limitations of languaging the self, have been widely influential within the disciplines discussed, yet they have had little impact on gerontological studies, including most research on reminiscence and life review.[32] Robert Butler, who introduced the concept of "life review" in a 1963 article based on clinical observations of geriatric patients, originally argued that an overall recounting and assessment of one's life in retrospect is a healthy, adaptive response to aging and an important stage of human development. Informed by Erik Erikson's theories of adult development by stages, Butler defined life review in terms of its "essential" human elements, rather than its social situatedness, using phrases like "a naturally occurring, universal mental process" most often "prompted by the realization of approaching dissolution and death, and the inability to maintain one's sense of personal invulnerability." [33] Butler is widely acknowledged as the first in psychiatric medicine to interpret frequent reminiscence among the elderly (previously considered a form of pathology) as a desirable and *to-be-expected* occurrence in late life—indeed, an inherent aspect of late-life development. Although Butler has since acknowledged that life review also occurs at earlier ages, he holds fast to his belief that, from a psychological standpoint, it is most significant (developmentally) in old age.[34] Gerontologists studying this claim have concluded that conducting a life review, especially in groups, increases self-esteem and motivation. Especially in older adults, it initiates an increased sense of personal power and importance; a recognition of past adaptive strategies and their application to current needs and problems; reconciliation with the past; resolution of resentments and negative feelings; a greater sense of meaning in life; and an ability to face death with a feeling that the person conducting the review has contributed to the world.[35]

Given their basis in the positivist tradition of the sciences, however, gerontological studies of life review and reminiscence emphasize emotional and psychological outcomes and typically ignore the influences of language and narrative patterns. This is because, from the positivist position, language is unproblematically representational, a mirror of ontological reality. This position stands in direct contrast to discursive theories, which interpret language as a richly complex screen through which perceptions of self and reality are continually filtered. From the discursive position, "language cannot be a transparent, passive, or neutral instrument. Language is not a simple matter of putting the appropriate labels on objects. Each of us is born into an ongoing set of language games. We must learn these games to be understood by and to understand others. In acquiring linguistic skills we take on a way of life and enter into specific circuits of power." [36] Thus, to understand how life review works socially, as well as individually, we must analyze life stories as linguistic artifacts influenced by time, place and the cultural scripts available for articulating one's self. This introduction of discourse analysis greatly complicates any conclusions gerontologists might make about direct connections between life review and an older adult's "stage" of development.

In *Beyond Nostalgia*, I rely on theories of social constructionism and the discursive self to understand older people's life stories. I illustrate, through discourse analysis of talk and written texts, how older people narrate their identities in groups of their peers. I show how they explore various "I positions" and respond to others' stories from these positions. In conducting this analysis, I mean to promote the narrative approach as central to a culturally informed understanding of life review, reminiscence, and adult development. From my position as a feminist, life stories are rich examples of gender negotiations; they are language acts that make visible the different ways men and women woman "write the self" in old age. They also illustrate the different paths of development available to men and women across the life course.

My own approach to studying adult development occurs at the crossroads of narrative theory, feminism, and gerontology. While most gerontological research on life review and reminiscence takes its cue from empirical studies in cognitive and clinical psychology,[37] I pursue knowledge of the self through *story*, or more accurately, the contingency of multiple, ever-shifting stories that older people tell about themselves. I see development as a narrative construction and an interpretive process dependent on "the backward gaze of recollection," as much as the "forward-looking arrow of linear time."[38] Narrative psychologist Mark Freeman explains this position further: "The concept of development, despite its customary connotations of moving forward in time, can only be predicated backward, in retrospect, after one is in the position to chart the trajectory of the past. . . . [T]he concept of development is itself fundamentally inseparable from the process of *narrating* the past."[39]

A narrative conception of adult development advances on the premise that life stories play a key role in the construction and understanding of individual growth, that "the stories we tell of our lives reveal and *define* the developmental and affective challenges of adult life."[40] Most significantly, life stories reveal that identity formation occurs throughout life and well into old age; "individuals are constantly writing and revising their stories to create 'unity' and coherence in their lives, as well as to define a generative 'purpose' that moves them beyond themselves."[41] Thus, it is not just the stories that are important, but also the changes that occur in the tellings over time, as well as the interpersonal processes of sharing and negotiating their meanings with others.

Along with other narrative theorists, I believe there is a complex interrelationship between language and life. Language and symbol are *constitutive* of human belief and behavior, not mere reflections of underlying beliefs and behaviors. The life story in some sense *constructs* reality: interpretive or narrative change in a story provides the foundation for actual shifts in attitudes and behavior.[42] To some extent we can "write ourselves into being," and by reinterpreting and rewriting our life stories, we can *change* our ways of being. Anne Ruggles Gere and other composition theorists support this view, drawing evidence from the ways texts created through writing groups actually change the quality of personal relationships and the conditions of writers' lives.[43] As one example, from her study of early-twentieth-century women's autobiographical writings, rhetorician Karyn Hollis has concluded that "better lives are possible through writing." Her rationale is this: "Both text and subjectivity have a dialectical relationship with material conditions in which they occur, and both respond to and influence these conditions in the culture at large."[44] The fact that the texts Hollis examined were *written*, rather than spoken, is significant, for writing may have more heuristic power than talk. That is, it motivates more thinking and interacting (as well as more writing) than talk, which is to say that it generates new conditions for growth and enhancement. Narrative psychologist George Rosenwald confirms the importance of such generativity, claiming that the best way to determine adult development through life story is to consider what the stories make possible—the personal updates and innovations that are pursued, in addition to the new cycle of stories that is initiated.[45]

Becoming aware of interpretive strategies is therefore an important first stage in an individual's developmental process through narrative. We will see that as older adults write their life stories, they come to see them in light of other possible stories; to consider the influences that have shaped them (history, culture, language, cohort, family); to decide whether and how they might assimilate or resist these influences; and to write new and expanded stories. In the words of Freeman, development or growth is evident when "'I' am able to do something new with the words bequeathed me, thereby enlarging the scope of my self and my world."[46]

Narrative theorists have determined that certain conditions must be present for development to occur through narrative. First, a person must be willing to tell stories about herself and listen to others' tellings. In the process of the telling, writing, listening, and responding, the person must become increasingly aware of the content and form of life stories (that is to say, that they are structured in certain ways and convey certain themes). And finally, having come to this awareness, the person must begin to choose narrative events more consciously; to construct stories more deliberately; and to revise his or her stories in order to enlarge meaning, understanding, and experience. As Gary Kenyon and William Randall explain, adult development occurs in the process of bringing the stories of one's life more in line with lived experience and assuming a more assertive role in constructing these stories. A mark of individual growth is the deliberateness with which one writes about one's self, moving beyond positions in which one has been "storied" by others to positions in which one reflects, reconsiders, adjusts, modifies, rewrites, and "restories" one's self. Narrative development requires that the teller of the life story discard those stories ("storyotypes") that no longer fit current and arising concepts of the self, understanding that "stories are never locked in," but "always made up of facticity *and* possibility."[47]

Within this narrative framework, "authenticity" is not a matter of being "true" to some inner self but a matter of becoming aware and taking ownership of one's life story. In the apt words of Gary Kenyon, "what is important for a storied being is whether I am participating in the unfolding of my story or only drifting along, having it written for me."[48] As we will see, older adult writers assist each other in the move toward authenticity by making various cultural scripts and interpretive frames (especially those for race, class, gender, and age) visible to one another and therefore subject to "re-vision." These re-visions (in the sense of re-seeing one's self and the possible meanings of one's life) constitute emotional and psychological development.

Within narrative studies, "maturity" and "wisdom" are not so much cognitive processes or emotional states as stances or interpretive positions. A person is truly "wise" when she is able to see life as an evolving story and to create some distance between self and story by reflecting on it from multiple perspectives. "Wise" people watch themselves tell life stories, learn from others' stories, and intervene in their own narrative processes to allow for change by admitting new stories and interpretations into their repertoire.

Narrative development, of course, is not unique to old age, and can be spurred along at any time during the life course. I take this point up more fully in my final chapter, but for now let it suffice to say that development through narrative is a lifelong challenge and opportunity, and that it includes, among other things, becoming aware of what Margaret Gullette calls "age identity." Gullette argues, for example, that conventional scripts for age are essentially decline narratives based on the assumption that the life trajectory after the age of fifty (or even earlier) is one of decreasing effectiveness, gradual loss, and limitation. It is thus our developmental task as tellers of life stories to promote counternarratives that overturn these ageist assumptions. Gullette proposes that we begin by challenging the assumption that age identity is normative and fixed—that one "comes into" identity or "finds" an identity at different times in life. She considers this metaphor "powerfully ageist," because it "implies that once we 'find' an identity, like a found object, it will stay essentially the same," when, in fact, personal identity is constantly under construction.[49] Gullette urges us all to join in writing a particular kind of life story she calls "critical age autobiography," in which we examine and challenge the culture's dominant age ideology and discard identities that have "come to seem false." Says Gullette, "I am proposing an active concept of aging as self-narrated experience, the conscious, ongoing story of one's age identity. Once we can firmly distinguish between the culture's aging narrative and our own versions (particularly if we do so within a collective formed for that purpose), we learn that its threats to being and becoming are resistible."[50] In chapters 4 and 5, we will see how older-adult writing groups function in just this way, although not in the overtly critical or political mode that Gullette has in mind.

Gullette makes an important contribution to narrative studies of adult development because she identifies and critiques the cultural forces that attempt to story our lives, especially in terms of age, throughout the life course. As a literary scholar, Gullette also understands the powerful revisionist potential of life-story *writing*. Although life itself initiates restorying in the form of transitional events (career changes, marriage, divorce, births, deaths, illnesses, accidents), the very act of writing the life story heightens self-consciousness and makes the life "visible" to the extent that an individual becomes more open to revisionist possibilities.[51] Sharing this writing in groups of one's peers extends these possibilities even further.

The narrative approach is unique in several ways from standard gerontological approaches to life review and adult development, and these merit brief discussion. Narrative scholars tend to emphasize difference rather than similarity; they promote the study of development within specific social and cultural contexts over the scientific study of individuals apart from these contexts; they consider what older people themselves say about development, rather than looking exclusively to established theory for explanations; and they are more likely to take into account the role of the researcher in the assessment and interpretation of development. These methods are consistent with the feminist approaches outlined earlier in this chapter and in the introduction.

Psychologist Kenneth Gergen has best articulated narrative scholars' challenges to the conventional approach to adult development, namely, that of Erik Erikson. Erikson's theory predicts that stages of development are universal and ontological. *Development,* as defined by Erikson, constitutes a progression upward toward higher-level competencies (these being integration and generativity in his hierarchy). Low-level performance on psychological tests of these competencies is taken to mean lack of development. Gergen considers Erikson's theory overly general and normative and offers instead an aleatory account of adult development—one positing that biology establishes limits, but that the sequence, quality, and extent of development over the life course are indeterminant.[52] History and culture, not innate tendencies, are the primary influences on change and development. By way of support, Gergen cites research on the development of individuals in various times and cultures, offering Glen Elder's study of the effects of growing up in the United States during the Great Depression as a telling example of the ways history shaped the development of this particular cohort in terms of education, job selection, marriage, childbearing norms, economic values, beliefs about the future, attitudes, and behaviors. Citing gerontologist Matilda White Riley, Gergen concludes that "there is no pure process of aging" and "the life course is not fixed but widely flexible," depending on opportunity and other factors.[53] Gergen considers the individual an active agent who consciously reacts to and interacts with the social and physical worlds, rather than passively responding to biological and psychological imperatives. The aleatory account focuses on variation across the age spectrum, favoring the illustration of difference in adult development over the search for general patterns.

A second feature of the narrative approach is its emphasis on individual development within particular sociohistorical contexts. Narrative scholars study how people in certain groups develop according to the demands and expectations of their culture, family, and peers, as well as the historical period in which they live. An emphasis on social context leads us to privilege accounts of development that are descriptive and pluralistic over ones that are normative and prescriptive. Raymond McDermott and Herve Varenne explain: "As a pattern of institutions, a culture produces a wealth of positions for human beings to inhabit. Each position requires that the person inhabiting it must possess, and must be *known as possessing*, particular qualities that symbolize, and thereby constitute, the reality of their position to others. . . . People are only incidentally born or early enculturated into being different. It is more important to understand how they are put into positions for being treated differently."[54] In the interchapter "Negotiating Normal," I take up the issue of opportunity and differential treatment through a description of the subtle changes that occur in members of a writing group for cognitively impaired, emotionally and developmentally disabled elders. In their own way, McDermott and Varenne counter "stage" theorists' methods of isolating, testing, and analyzing individuals by insisting that development be studied as it occurs naturally through human interaction in real-world settings (such as writing groups). They call for developmental studies that are "based on the possibility that all people make sense and develop fully, albeit in accord with the particulars of the situation."[55]

A third feature of the narrative approach is an interest in people's assessment of their own development. Narrative researchers are likely to ask respondents of various ages whether they have changed over time and what meanings they make of these changes (or lack thereof), assuming that people's *perceptions* of themselves are an important aspect of their growth and development. For example, anthropologists and ethnographers—who have always collected life histories—typically study adult development through interviews and participant-observations of people interacting in their communities. They define "change" and "development" by observing people's behavior over time, following the anthropological view that "the world is likely not available on only [the researcher's] terms and may be more difficult to see and hear than [the researcher] had thought."[56] As a research method, ethnography attempts to "gain access to other minds and other ways of life so as to represent what it is like to be a differently situated human being. Its practitioners are people willing to hazard border-crossings in pursuit of differences that make a difference for the way lives are lived, developed, and experienced, and for the way competence, excellence, virtue, and personal well-being are defined." [57]

Finally, increasingly more narrative researchers, primarily those informed by postmodern theories and feminist criticism, recognize that they, as human beings, affect their own studies of adult development. We thus strive to be self-reflective in our scholarship. When conducting research we intentionally reveal "the underlying epistemological assumptions that caused the formulation of a set of questions in a particular way, the seeking of answers to those questions in a particular way, and finally the presentation of the findings in a particular way." [58] Narrative researchers look at themselves studying others and consider the effects of their differences in terms of age, race, class, gender, ethnicity, able-bodiedness, sexual orientation, education, social position, political beliefs, and other aspects of identity. The image of the mirror is thus common in narrative studies of autobiography, biography, and life story. The crucial question for all of us who study age is this: to what extent can we hold up a mirror to the aging individual (ourselves as well as the "other" being observed), gaze at the reflection, and personally identify with the image enough to break the cycle of ageism? [59] A self-analysis on the part of the researcher in terms of her own feelings and attitudes toward aging may help counter the persistent (and largely unconscious) "middle adulthood prejudice" that Kenneth Gergen finds in most stage theorists' assessments of adult development, where middle age is typically found (by middle-aged researchers) to be the period of greatest "maturity." [60]

Having briefly reviewed the critical theories that inform my analysis in future chapters, I now turn to the actual work at hand—presenting and interpreting older adults' life stories in ways that are sensitive to gender and other forms of diversity. I begin with the social construction of age narratives.

Catherine

CATHERINE is a member of a University Geriatric Center writing group. Her essay "Know It When You See It" appeared four years ago in a special issue of a feminist Christian magazine. Says Catherine, "I kept getting this magazine and reading and reading, and there was never anything about older women in it. So I wrote and complained, and apparently someone else had, too, so they decided to do an issue, and they asked me to submit something. So I did, and this is my one thing that I have published. I got twenty-five dollars for it. How about that!"

Know It When You See It

In this country sixty-five is regarded as the onset of old age. You could say I, now sixty-four, am on the brink of old age. Genetically there's every possibility I will live at least another twenty years. My mother lived to be eighty-four, her mother eighty-three, and her sister eighty-four. My father's mother was ninety-six when she died.

On the one hand, I work at my profession. I continue to study and learn. I am mother, grandmother, friend. I continue to set goals, and life is full. On the one hand, I noticed a different me looking back at me in the mirror about twenty years ago. And this seems to happen again and again every few years. The arthritis I noticed in my right index finger at fifty has made its way to my left elbow. Retrieving names of people and recalling what I had for lunch yesterday takes a little longer. And my energy level is not quite what it was at thirty-four.

But why would these few changes in me and in others my age cause people to treat us differently? This treatment ranges from a patronizing attitude towards us to trivializing our activities, disregarding our opinions, and ignoring our presence. It angers those of us who are recipients of it. My anger flared up when a nephew asked my sister's grandchildren why they were eating their dinner at the "old folks' table" at a recent family get-together. As if we would not possibly be interesting to little ones. It flares up when a salesperson looks past me at younger people in line when I am the person being waited on. It flared up a few months ago when our local newspaper featured an article about our state lieutenant governor, a remarkable woman who happens to be in her seventies. She was referred to as "a crotchety old woman who walks slowly, is hard of hearing, and is opinionated."

And does it surprise you to know that younger women are often the perpetrators of such discrimination towards older women? This insidious injustice is called ageism, and like racism and sexism, we need to know it when we see it. As I become older I identify more and more with the insights of Barbara McDonald, as she writes on aging and ageism. McDonald is a seventy-eight-year-old woman whose book *Look Me in the Eye*, coauthored with Cynthia Rich, is reviewed elsewhere in this issue. Comments like those below and suggestions that McDonald makes in an open letter to the women's movement have made me aware of the unconscious ageist attitudes I find in younger women: "When you speak of the women's movement, do white younger women always come to mind? Or do you envision women of all ages, of all races and cultures, as part of the women's movement? When you compliment an older woman by indicating that she is different from other older women, more fun, more gutsy, more interesting than, do you realize how patronizing this is? And if she accepts your compliment, she is in a sense rejecting some older women. When you talk about your mother or grandmother, don't limit her value to the fact that she sacrificed for you. Tell people who she is now. Better yet, let her tell us who she is now."

Just as my faith-life is a journey, so is my physical, mental, and emotional life. I am in the process of becoming who I will ultimately be, and it is exciting. McDonald speaks of her hope that more and more older women will talk and write about the process of aging in a world that negates them and denies such an aging process. This is my hope as well. I would like young, middle-aged, and old to really look at this injustice, to know it when we see it or hear it, and to confront the source of it. I suggest you carry a little notebook with you for a week or so and jot down situations you observe involving older persons. What facial expressions did you notice? What words were exchanged? What attitude was expressed? How did the older person respond? Then jot down your own feelings about the experience and go from there. Awareness is the beginning of change.

TWO   Age and the Life Story

OVERHEARD at a senior center:
   "When is middle age?"
   "From forty until you get really sick."
Everyday experience tells us that life stories are marked for age. Typical
conversations give many clues about the assumed and desired identities of participants, including their age identities. In a study of teenagers' personal narratives, linguist Carolyn Baker found that adolescents distance themselves from
childhood by simultaneously deferring and deferring *to* adulthood. She considers
this narrative strategy a means of "doing adolescence" through talk.[1] We expect
the same kind of age-marked narratives from other groups; in fact, we consider
it abnormal when narratives do not resonate with our beliefs about age identity
and criticize these storytellers for not "acting their age." Charlotte, an eighty-
year-old woman in my study, disapproved of the narrative strategies of a sixty-
two-year-old male member of her group because he sometimes included gestures
and sound effects in his oral renditions (standing to salute when reading a segment about his navy duty, for example). Charlotte described these readings as a
"regression" to "kindergarten show-and-tell." Clearly, she was operating on certain assumptions about how a "mature" man is supposed to represent himself to
other adults. The interesting question for age researchers is not merely how age
is reflected in the telling of everyday life stories, but also how it functions developmentally. How might age-inflected stories push storytellers and their audiences
in the direction of change—emotionally, intellectually, and socially?
   Although very little research has been done on age-inflections in everyday
narratives, we do have clues that indicate that there are strong cultural expectations for self-representation in later life. Sociolinguists who study spoken discourse have determined that young people regularly "overaccommodate" their
talk to older adults, targeting their speech not to the individual per se but to the
social persona of an "elderly communicator," whom they generally characterize
as incompetent, slow, old-fashioned, and inflexible.[2] Other research along these
lines has determined that younger women (in their thirties) often expect and
encourage older women (over seventy) to talk about illness and adversity, as
opposed to the more positive aspects of their lives.[3] Feminist scholars, too, have
also noted that young women expect older women to play the role of mother or

grandmother in their speech and behavior, offering advice and historical perspective to the younger generation. Older feminists have exposed the ageist and limiting assumptions underlying these beliefs, arguing that to romanticize the older woman's past is to ignore her present and future. Barbara McDonald, herself over sixty, admonishes younger feminists on this point in her "Open Letter to the Women's Movement": "Don't talk about your grandmother as the bearer of your culture—don't objectify her. Don't make her a museum piece or a woman whose value is that she has sacrificed and continues to sacrifice on your behalf. Tell us who she is now, a woman in process. Better yet, encourage *her* to tell us."[4] In that same collection of essays, contributor Cynthia Rich unveils other limiting assumptions concerning older women: they are to be subordinate, meek, and accepting; if they are feisty, they are to express it in a "cute" and nonthreatening way; and they are never to be outraged or outrageous.[5] As a response to these stereotypes, a group of older British feminists has published a book in which, as they tell their life stories, they advocate resistance to the norms of docility and respectability and champion the subversive value of "growing old *dis*gracefully."[6]

We could surely make a strong case for life-story telling itself as an "age marked" behavior. As a person ages, she is more likely to be approached by friends, family members, and associates to tell about the past. In her dialogue on aging, Maggie Kuhn, founder of the Gray Panthers, acknowledges and celebrates these requests: "Old people ought to have a sense of history. They must be encouraged to review their own history, valuing their origins and past experiences. With rapid technological change we are made to feel that our experience is useless. If we could stimulate a life review, we would see what we have lived through, the ways in which we have coped and survived, the changes we have seen—all of this is the history of the race."[7] Kathleen Woodward makes a similar argument from the perspective of feminist studies, naming the older woman as "a figure of knowledge who represents the difference that history, or time, makes, a difference that she literally embodies."[8]

Aside from these cultural imperatives, older adults are likely to have their own reasons for offering up a life story—reasons that are often rooted in family dynamics. As sociologist J. Brandon Wallace notes in his study of near-centenarians' life stories, there are significant social rewards for being a good storyteller: "If telling a humorous anecdote about an early childhood experience routinely elicits laughter from grandchildren, it is probable that the story will be told often. Add to this the elderly's frequent lack of other resources (e.g. money, education, physical abilities) and it is understandable that personal experiences of the past might become an essential part of their contribution to present social interactions."[9] In short, older adults are more socially motivated to tell their life stories than younger adults. And this is true also for *writing* life stories. During the first meeting of a writing group I conducted at a Jewish senior center, a woman, aged about seventy, asked, "Do you have to be *old* to write your auto-biography?"—and then proceeded to answer her own question with a story. She told the group about going to see writer John Grisham speak. After the lecture, she commented to him that she was writing her autobiography, and his reply was, "I'm not old enough to write *my* autobiography." Grisham's response mo-tivated her even more to write her own life story. She felt for the first time that she might have something unique to offer as an "old person" that even a famous writer said he could not deliver.

Grisham's response evokes the passage of time and its significance. Simply put, older adults have less time available to them, are more aware of the passing of time, and tend to make better use of the time they have; they strive to live "in the center of the moment." [10] Many, particularly those in writing groups, are compelled to use their remaining time to reflect upon and to *language* the mean-ing of their lives—to view the past through the wider lens of old age in order to see its larger significance beyond the daily and the mundane.

The Meanings of Age

Through their life stories, older writers offer an "insider" understanding of age in its many varieties. Individually and collectively, they overturn the common perception among younger people that *age* is a singular and unified concept, and the category *senior citizen* or *the elderly* represents a homogenous grouping. In fact, as we will see, the category *old age* is wildly heterogeneous. Sociologist Bernice Neugarten makes this evident in her separations of the "young old," "old," and "old old," and Peter Laslett urges age researchers to consider the vast differences between adults in their "Third Age" (a late-adult period of creativity and personal fulfillment) and the "Fourth Age" (a period of decline, dependence, and death). [11] Sociologists Jay Ginn and Sara Arber make even finer distinctions, arguing that theories of aging must acknowledge at least three different meanings of *age* and the ways each is socially constructed: chronological age, physiological age, and social age. [12] These differences are not just academic abstractions; they structure much of the talk in older-adult writing groups and underwrite many of the life stories.

Chronological age is biological; it is a person's age in years. Chronological age affects a person's structural position in society and therefore constrains par-ticular social behaviors, such as drinking, driving, working, voting, marrying, serving in the military, and collecting retirement benefits. Individuals whose at-titudes, moods, and behaviors are affected by "milestone" birthdays (twenty-one, thirty, forty, fifty . . .) are being influenced by cultural expectations for chronological age groupings. In senior centers, a writing-group member must have reached the chronological age of fifty-five to make use of the services and to participate in center-sponsored writing groups.

Physiological age is medical; it refers to how the body is aging physically in terms of bone density, muscle tone, strength, energy, organ functioning, and so forth, as well as the body's functional abilities and impairments. Physiological age is socially constructed in that it varies considerably according to gender, class, race, and ethnicity, as well as generation. Ginn and Arber focus specifically on the gender differences in the prevalence, type, and onset age of disabilities (such as heart disease and diabetes), as well as mortality (men's tendency to die younger than women). These differences, in turn, give rise to gender imbalances in later life, including the lack of male representation in senior writing groups. Physically, older women are more likely to suffer functional impairments that affect activities of daily living, but are less likely to have a spouse living in the home to provide care. They are therefore twice as likely as men to enter a nursing home. Interestingly, sociologist Bryan Turner argues that the physical body is also a *collective* experience; that is, various health movements popular in different historical periods produce distinctive body types recognizable by members of the same generation. As an example, many would consider the representational woman's body in the United States of the late-twentieth century to be the type found in Nike commercials: young, medium height, thin, and athletic-looking. Today's cultural image of the old body in Laslett's fourth stage is typically toothless—a direct result of widespread lack of access to professional dental care and the practice of pulling bad teeth rather than preventing tooth decay. In Turner's words, individuals experience "the process of aging in relationship to the maturation of their body, and also in relation to their collective generational body-image." [13] Humorous conversations sometimes arise in senior writing groups around the generational contrasts in sex symbols; the voluptuous pin-up girls and square-shouldered, meticulously groomed leading men of 1940s Hollywood have given way to the tousle-haired, T-shirted androgynous look of the 1990s. And the body weights women once considered "normal" are now considered "fat."

Social age refers to the social attitudes, values, and behaviors considered "appropriate" for a certain chronological age. It also includes subjective impressions (how old a person *feels*) and ascribed age (how old other people *think* a person is). In some cases, social age may have little to do with chronological age, as in the case of Barusch's study of poor and homeless women, some of whom were in their forties and fifties and yet described themselves as "old." [14] Social age entails age-based norms that are apparent in people's self talk: "I'm too old to go back to school," "It's too late for me to change jobs," "people my age shouldn't overdo it," "I'm doing pretty well for my age." Social age, too, is significantly affected by race, ethnicity, class, and gender, although comparatively little research has been done to determine the specifics. Ginn and Arber do point to a few gender differences in social aging. We know that, due to women's reproductive roles, their working lives follow a delayed path compared with men's, but they are still considered "old" when they have passed their childbearing years. Men, on the other hand, are not socially evaluated in terms of biological reproductivity and are therefore considered "young," or at least productive, much longer than women. While older workers of both sexes are discriminated against in the labor force, women experience discrimination earlier than men. Social age norms have changed significantly in the twentieth century with improved health and longer retirement periods, but Ginn and Arber remind us that "the rosy scenario of a Third Age of self-development, autonomy, consumption, and youthful lifestyles [in retirement] is essentially a bourgeois option, unavailable to those who have low incomes and poor health." Thus, age-based norms "may still exert powerful pressure to 'act one's age,' especially among less advantaged groups." [15] Life stories—and the group talk around them—are most clearly marked for social age.

In terms of social aging, differences play a major role. What it means to "act your age" is very much affected by the time, place, and social circumstances under which we age; "Aging is a dynamic process produced by the collective behavior of individuals who live within historical and social contexts." [16] For sociologists, cohorts encompass a more specific time frame than generations and may be determined by birth (all Americans born between 1925 and 1929); by the time members entered into significant life events (all people entering the job market between 1930 and 1940); or by shared historical events (people who were children during the Great Depression or who fought in World War II). Sociologists have identified four factors that influence how a cohort experiences and expresses the aging process: (1) the composition and history of the cohort when it arrives at old age (its size, racial, and gender composition, education, family and marital history, religious experiences, and so forth); (2) the organization of society over the life course of the cohort and the resultant opportunities and limitations created by social institutions, such as family, work, and retirement; (3) technological developments, especially changes in medical and health technology that alter survival patterns and functional abilities; and (4) the cohort's linkages with other cohorts occupying different life stages, such as middle-aged children or grandchildren, who may or may not be in a position to provide social and economic support. Given these generalizations, we also must acknowledge that cohorts are diverse in terms of gender, race, ethnicity, social class, and family status and are thus comprised of many subcohorts (upper-middle-class black females, for example, or working-class immigrant males).

Cohort analysis is central to our study of life stories and the developmental tasks they accomplish. Through cohort analysis, we can understand how particular historical events affected people occupying different life stages when these events occured, as well as how the events are likely to be represented in life stories. As one example, the cohort born between 1925 and 1930 had a different experience of the Great Depression as children than the cohort born between 1905 and 1910, who were adults seeking employment at the time. Similarly, the cohort of women born between 1955 and 1960 experienced the *Roe v. Wade* decision (1972) differently from the cohort of women who were beyond childbearing age at the time. Sociologists Uhlenberg and Miner explain the impact of these differences: "Women in cohorts arriving at adulthood after 1960, compared to those who preceded them, are more likely to have attended college and to have pursued work careers throughout their adult lives. With respect to childbearing, they have had more children out of wedlock, but fewer births overall. And these women have tended to marry later and divorce in greater numbers than did the mothers of the baby boom cohorts." [17] A very real outcome of these differences is that baby boomers like me, unlike our parents, will not be able to rely on the caregiving resources of spouses and adult children in our old age. In terms of life-story telling, baby-boomer women will be less likely to structure their narratives around marriage and family and more likely to promote female independence and autonomy through stories of single parenting, career advancement, and self-development. I take this issue up again in chapter 7.

An understanding of cohort characteristics is necessary to our study of older adults' writing, as well as the social dynamics of writing groups, for members of a cohort share the same cultural norms for structuring and telling life stories. Usually writing groups in senior centers attract adults from the same birth cohort—typically, in this study, those born between 1920 and 1930—but include many subcohorts. Sometimes groups encompass different birth cohorts, however, as was the case in a metropolitan Detroit group I observed. Members included a middle-class Jewish woman of eighty-four (Helen) and a middle-class black woman of sixty-four (Cecille); Cecille's parents were the same age as Helen. Cecille and Helen sometimes conflicted in their values, beliefs, and patterns of speech and writing. Cecille spoke openly and critically of her parents, which seemed disrespectful to Helen. In the course of my interview with Cecille, she mentioned the differences between her and "one of the ladies in the group" (later revealed to be Helen):

> One of the ladies in the group when I first joined got very angry with me because I criticized my father. And she's the same age he is, and she did not like that at all. And she said to me one day, 'I hope my children don't feel about me the same way you feel about your father.' And I said, 'Well, maybe

your children didn't have the same experiences with you that I had with my father. And I am not going to temper the way I feel because it upsets you.' So we've gotten friendly since then, but she always asks me about my father.

The conflict between Helen and Cecille illustrates how group members identify with their own birth cohorts and consequently hold different values concerning how a person is "supposed" to talk about their parents in a life story.

Age Talk in Groups at Senior Centers

On a daily basis, older adults function largely in terms of social age. In the senior-center writing groups I observed, talk of chronological age occurred periodically, but it was not central to group interactions. Members meeting for the first time did not ask or tell each other how old they were. Actual age did not seem to matter much to the group, although individuals did sometimes ask me about *my* age, particularly in the groups I facilitated. In the following exchange during the early weeks of the group at the Jewish senior center, two members speculate about my age identity:

Rose (to me): We don't know that much about you.

Samuel: I'm guessing you're married and you have two or three kids.

Ruth: No, I'm not married, and I have no children.

Samuel: Well, see there, sometimes I'm wrong.

Rose: You're young.

Ruth: Well, not that young. I'm over forty.

Rose: I wouldn't have guessed it. Your hair is so pretty. You don't tint it, do you?

Ruth: Yes, I color it. It has a lot of grey in it.

Samuel: Yeah, I would have guessed late thirties or maybe over forty.

Rose: Well, you're a young forty!

To Samuel, age specifies life stage; he expects me, at my age, to be deeply involved in marriage and parenting. He is surprised to hear that I have not followed the traditional woman's path. Having little else to go on, since I have not revealed much of myself in the writing-group sessions, Rose judges my age by physical appearance but is somewhat inaccurate because I do not "look my age." As facilitator for this group, I tried to stay in the background as much as possible in an effort to foreground elders' experiences, but group members subtly raised the topic of our differences by providing historical context for my benefit or making reference to "our generation" and "your generation." They instructed me each week in the many differences that age makes.

As the example with Samuel and Rose shows, younger people's chronological ages are more often the subject of discussion than group members' ages, for older adults typically identify themselves in terms of generational contrast. Discussions about younger adults are common, as in the following exchange between facilitator Margaret,who is seventy-eight, and group member Arlene, who at fifty-eight is the youngest member in the writing group and whose eighty-five-year-old mother has Alzheimer's:

Arlene: It's interesting because there's a lot about me that [my children] don't know. They're in their—well, my son is thirty, and my daughter is twenty-three. And we talk a lot, but they're not really into what I was like as a child growing up. I throw that in every once in a while, and of course they say, "Yeah, right, we know you grazed with the dinosaurs" [she laughs].

Margaret: This is normal. I think every one of us who has any offspring or whether it's your nieces or nephews or whoever, I think that up to a point— and we do the same thing. I mean, we weren't interested up to a certain point, and then all of a sudden, you get to a certain age, and you say, "Now I want to know more."

Arlene: Right.

Betty: They will want to know, too.

Arlene: Yeah, right. And I guess the reason I'm doing this [life story] is because I so regret not knowing anything about my mother, when she was growing up, or even what she was like. . . . And we don't know anybody who knew her. None of her contemporaries knew her. We know people who knew her in her early twenties when she got married, but nothing at all of her teenage years. And yet I see her now, and I wonder, what were the forces that developed her as she was?

Margaret: And it didn't occur to you when you were younger to ask?

Arlene: No.

Margaret: We can't fault this generation, because we did the very same thing.

In this session, members are using chronological age to distinguish youth from old age and to invite instructive comparisons. The example also reveals how mention of chronological age evokes a more meaningful discussion of social aging: Arlene initially identifies her children by age and their attitude toward age ("We know you grazed with the dinosaurs"); Margaret immediately normalizes the stance taken by Arlene's children in terms of life-course development ("This is normal . . . we weren't interested up to a certain point"), and Betty confirms Margaret's point that the children will eventually change their attitude toward family history, just as members of the writing group have. The fact that Arlene's mother has Alzheimer's disease adds another dimension to the making of meaning: Arlene regrets her earlier lack of interest in her mother's life, for much information about her mother's identity is now lost to her.

Once during a meeting of the geriatric-center group, chronological age talk ensued about group members themselves, but this occurred around an unusual coincidence: four members, including the facilitator, were all turning eighty about the same time. "Is this a landmark birthday for you?" I asked rather innocently during a discussion of this coincidence. "Oh, yes!" two members said, simultaneously. Later that afternoon, one of the other soon-to-be-octogenarians mentioned that she was trying not to think about turning eighty and had even had trouble mentioning it until recently. "But my grandchildren just love it," she said. "They tease me all the time." Her comment suggests, again, that age meanings are very much interrelated: chronological age calls forth social-age norms. In an interview several weeks later with one of the women, she informs me that turning eighty affects the way she thinks about the future and structures her time now: "I'm impressed enough with my birthday to feel I'm in my last decade, and if I want to write I better do it now, do it now. And also my age, my age cohorts left and right, something happened to somebody, something happened to my sister—cataracts—my brother had an embolism down his leg and lost his leg, and one thing or another. So it's all the more to the point to keep this rolling as long as I can."

In one of the metropolitan Detroit groups, there was occasional talk about chronological age, but it always served a social purpose. Margaret, the seventy-eight-year-old facilitator, made the effort on more than one occasion to remind me that age cohorts are different—that a sixty-year-old cannot be compared with an eighty-year-old, especially if the older person is living in a nursing home. In Margaret's groups there was much talk that reflected these distinctions. Often the discussions occurred in the context of women's talk about their mothers. In the following brief exchange, Cecille, sixty-four, and Lorraine, seventy, refer to their mothers, who are, respectively, eighty-four and ninety-four:

Lorraine: I find my mother boring. Do you find your mother boring?

Cecille: Not just boring, annoying. When she starts in on that reminiscing . . . and it doesn't help to say, "I've heard that many times." She'll say, "So I'm going to tell you again."

Lorraine and Cecille are not only raising chronological differences, but social ones, as well, by separating themselves from the talk and beliefs of their mother's cohort. Later, Cecille laughingly tells about her mother (who still keeps her own apartment) distinguishing between herself and "those old people in senior-citizen apartments." Ginny chimes in with an anecdote about her mother-in-law: she lived to be nearly a hundred in a nursing home and continually referred to "those old people" around her. These stories reflect how older adults use social age as the primary means of categorizing one another and, by implication, self-identifying. They also reveal how necessary is language—in this case group talk—to signifying the meaning of "old age."

Sometimes social marking was done for my benefit as a younger observer. In a conversation after my first visit to her group, Margaret mentioned the ages of her group members but did so in the context of describing all the activities and organizations in which they were involved. She was, in effect, alerting me to the fact that chronological age is irrelevant to social and intellectual functioning. She wanted me to know that the oldest member in the group—Helen, eighty-four—is "highly intelligent" and dozed in class that day only because the medication she takes makes her sleepy. "See, this is not an old folks' group," Margaret informed me.

In a group session the following month, Helen is absent, and her chronological age is brought up in the context of her social and physiological age. Group members know that she has "health problems," but most do not know the extent of them: diabetes, congestive heart disease, recent treatment for skin cancer, and a lumpectomy last year, among other things. The discussion occurs in the context of talk about who will be returning in the fall:

Margaret: Helen will be coming back, and of course Selma, and—

Lorraine: She was nodding off yesterday when they were singin' the blues [at a musical program].

Margaret: Was she?

Lorraine: Yeah.

Margaret: And you know, she—

Lorraine: She didn't look well yesterday to me.

Ginny: Helen?

Lorraine: Yeah.

Ginny: Yeah.

Margaret: She is so wonderful. This is a wonderful woman. This is—

Lorraine: Yeah, she is. She's exceptional.

Ginny: She overdoes. I mean, she's so busy taking care of everybody else that she doesn't take time for herself.

Lorraine: With her precarious health, if she does anything, it's overdoing it, really. Beyond her own personal care.

Eileen: How old is she? How old is Helen?

Several: Oh, eighty some—?

Margaret, as others make guesses: Eighty-four?

Ginny: In the middle eighties.

Margaret: A couple of weeks ago, she drove up to Lansing for a whole day with somebody else to go to a—umm, diabetic seminar.

Eileen: Oh, a diabetic . . . 'cause they had a conference on aging there just recently, too.

The excerpt shows how and when chronological age becomes relevant to a writing group. It is significant here because it confirms what an "exceptional" person Helen is: despite severe health problems, she is still socially active well into her eighties. Generally group members know much more about—and talk more about—each other's social aging, as compared with their chronological and physiological aging. My work in nursing homes, on the other hand, suggests that this may not be the case in the context of a long-term care facility. There, residents are more likely to differentiate among themselves in terms of chronological and physiological age, especially cognitive status and ability to communicate with others.

One effective strategy for determining a person's social age is to talk about work, both paid and volunteer. A member of Margaret's group, Gilda, seventy-three, several times raised the point that she is still working four days a week. Typically, this fact came up in discussions of group scheduling, at which point Gilda reminded Margaret that she would not be available after September 1, when she had to return to work. The following exchange illustrates both Gilda's pride in still working and the group's affirmation. Margaret has asked her if she could get off for a Thursday afternoon to attend the writing group, and Gilda has said she doesn't think so, even though she has "an excellent boss":

Margaret: Yeah, I know you said that he was so good.

Gilda: He's a great boss. And he still wants me to work—

Margaret: You must be doing a good job. And he knows if he gets some young person starting out, he'd be in trouble. And he's a manufacturer's rep?

Gilda: Yeah, he's never in the office. Well . . .

Margaret: You probably talk to the customers and the manufacturers and so forth.

Gilda: All the time.

Margaret: Very nice. I've been in that business. I know.

Gilda: As long as he wants me, I'll stay [Margaret laughs]. When he tells me it's time to go, I'll leave. He said when he retires, I can retire.

Margaret: How old is he?

Gilda, to group laughter: About fifty-five. I told him I don't think I'll be around that long, and he says, "Well, if you're not, I'll come up to your coffin and tell you to get up and go to work" [more laughter].

The significance of this dialogue is its revelation that age identity is *situational* and *value-laden*. Gilda negotiates with her younger boss through language (retirement talk) and behavior (duration of work) about just when she is to be considered "old"—in this case, "too old to work." The fact that Gilda's boss does not think she should ever retire is rare enough in the working world to be reportable to the writing group. Margaret's comment further serves to establish the importance of older workers compared with younger workers, suggesting that older workers are more personable, thereby increasing sales. Margaret lends credibility to her own assessment of Gilda's importance by noting that she herself has done similar work and "knows" the business practices of a manufacturer's representative. When Gilda directly quotes her boss joking about her death, she is demonstrating that the two have a close and informal relationship that is not affected by a near twenty-year difference in age.

In a later group meeting facilitated by Margaret, members again negotiate the relevance of chronological age, including Gilda's. In the following excerpt, they are responding to the life story of a woman (not a member of the group) that Margaret has just read aloud:

Margaret: This is kind of a note at the end. She said [reading], "I just read through my writing and realized I have left out so much. These are some of the highlights of my life. I am now eighty-four years old, and I realize that in the last year, I have become an old lady."

Eileen, interjecting: Oh, that's nonsense!

Margaret, with a loud laugh: I love you. I love you.

Gilda: I feel that way [old] now.

Margaret (to Eileen): You could write that today you had heard about some-body who said that she turned eighty-four and she realized she's become an old lady, and you said, in the classroom, "That's nonsense!"

Helen: Well, I'm almost eighty-five, and I'm not an old lady yet. I'm a mature person.

Margaret: That's right. Yeah [she laughs].

Gilda (to Helen): Good for you. I feel like an old lady, and I'm a lot younger than you are.

Helen: I certainly don't.

Margaret (to Gilda): Oh, well, you hang around with us, and you won't feel like an old lady [Gilda laughs] But [Margaret returns to reading] she says now in closing, "Everything seems to be an effort for me, but that's what happens when you get to be my age" [Margaret again addresses the group]—See, we don't feel that way.

Margaret, continuing her reading: "I just hope I'll be able to take care of myself as long as I live and not be a burden on anyone. If and when I feel up to it, I will try to continue to write some other stories." I just brought—you know, [here Margaret names the woman who wrote the life story] is going to come in around three o'clock [to talk to us] just because she feels good about the fact that she got this out, and I wanted to show it to you.

Margaret and the group are here negotiating the finer distinctions between chronological, physiological, and social age evoked by another's life strory. In responding to Eileen and Helen, Margaret is affirming that chronological age need not be a significant factor in one's self-representation; rather, how you *feel* (social age) is what's important, and a person need not feel "old" just because she is eighty-four.

This message is repeated many times in various forms throughout Margaret's sessions. As a member of the Gray Panthers who has read extensively in geron-tology, Margaret would especially like to instill in her group members a positive attitude toward aging. This goal is apparent in the way she talks about her own aging. Margaret is talking about a discussion with a former group member:

Margaret: And she said, "Did I write that? I don't remember." And from Ester I didn't expect it.

Gilda: Well, at ninety-two, you know, there comes a time in everybody's life when things change.

Margaret: I tell you, I'm reading a book that was written at age ninety. Bernard Baruch, the famous, you know, the man who—

Gilda: I don't think I want to live that long.

Eileen: Well, my mother lived to be ninety-six.

Margaret: I do! I just made a comment to Helen the other day.

Helen: You did?

Margaret, to group laughter: Don't tell me you forgot, Helen!

Ruth: You'd better write these things down.

Gilda: Yeah, write 'em down.

Margaret: Helen, I made a commitment. You said you were gonna celebrate your hundredth birthday—

Helen: Oh, yeah, she wants to come to my hundredth birthday.

Margaret: And I said, "I'll tell you what I'll do" [she laughs]. I said, "I'm gonna help you"—I didn't say I wanted to—I said, "I'm gonna help you celebrate it."

Helen: I'd forgotten already.

Ginny (to Margaret): Is she ninety-six?

Margaret: No, no, she's eighty . . . [turning to Helen]. You couldn't be eighty-five?

Helen: Yeah, I'm going to be in two months.

Margaret (to Ginny): In two months she's gonna be eighty-five. And she wants to live to be a hundred, and I said, "And I want to be there to celebrate. I'm going to be there to celebrate."

Age Talk and the Life Story

While chronological age is occasionally a subject of talk *around* life stories, it plays little part in the life stories themselves. What is most apparent in all the writing groups I observed is the value of *social* aging. Life stories—and the group interactions around them—are particularly rich examples of age identity as established through generational affiliation. Sociologist Barry McPherson defines a generation as a group of people born during the same period who have experienced and reacted to particular social, political, and historical events *in a similar way*. The events shared by a generation lead members to think and behave in ways that distinguish them from other generations.[18] Any writing group that gathers together people of the same generation makes prominent what anthropologist Katherine Newman calls "generational culture" and highlights the relative salience of this culture in the creation of individual identity. Generational culture draws members "into a cocoon of shared assumptions and moral vocabularies, as well as a source of division, for the intensity of the integration is paralleled by a feeling of separation from other generations."[19] Generational identity relies on the collective memory of major national events such as wars, revolutions, and natural disasters that create a break in the normative life course and bind otherwise unrelated individuals together. Some generations are "stronger" than others in their identity and cohesiveness, and individuals vary considerably in the importance they ascribe to the generational culture in the formation of their own personal identities.

The generation of American adults born just prior to or during the Great Depression seems an especially strong one in terms of its national identity. The senior writing groups I have observed make this generational identity visible and therefore subject to discussion, analysis, and possible critique. It may be that individual group members can come to understand certain aspects of their personal identities only in the company of peers from their own generation. It is worth quoting Newman at length on this point:

> Generational identity is subject to reformulation, nostalgic elaboration, even rejection as subsequent experience modifies the meaning and centrality of this special bond. Indeed, for most people, the most powerful aspects of generational culture are those which emerge in the process of collective retrospection. Living through a war, a depression, a collective nightmare of any kind absorbs the energies of its "victims" in the practical problems of survival. Hence, an important developmental task of later adulthood may well involve coming to terms with the rupture and the collective meaning it has for those who were at the center of the experience.[20]

There are very few cultural settings in which collective retrospection of this kind naturally occurs, aside from specifically organized events (reunions of a war's veterans, for example). Senior writing groups thus provide a unique opportunity for members of the same generation to see how diverse others experienced the same events. Members also have occasion to negotiate the multiple meanings of these experiences and to consider their salience to individual development over the life course.

In his classic longitudinal study *Children of the Great Depression*, sociologist Glen Elder begins with the premise that a generation shares a unique orientation to the world: "Each generation is distinguished by the historical logic and shared experience of growing up in a different time period, and by the correlated activities, resources, and obligations of their life stage. Particularly in times of rapid change, individuals are thought to acquire a distinct outlook and philosophy from the historical world, defined by their birthdate, an outlook that reflects lives lived interdependently in a particular historical context." [21] Elder considers "interdependence" to be a particular characteristic of the generation that experienced childhood and adolescence during the decade between 1929 and 1939 and early adulthood during World War II (the generation most widely represented in the writing groups) "since major crises generally produce experiences that are widely shared." He goes on to say that "collective experience is revitalized when problems are interpreted within the framework of a national crisis, an emergency of such proportion that it threatens the common way of life. . . . Americans were drawn into the nation's struggle for survival in both crises; the struggle became their civic obligation and their personal hardships part of the nation's experience." [22] The effects of national crises extend throughout the life course, leading to a generally shared social and political consciousness. While acknowledging differences in the Great Depression experience according to race, class, ethnicity and gender, Elder claims that working-class and middle-class whites whose families were deprived during the depression do share common characteristics: they assign priority to finances and material possessions, valuing economic gain and security in adulthood; they tend to be prudent and self-sacrificing; and they place considerable emphasis on the family. In the latter case, family life is defined first in terms of the value of children and secondarily in terms of the interpersonal benefits of marriage.

The gender differences Elder finds in this generation help us interpret older people's life-story telling, for boys and girls growing up during the depression had very different experiences. Girls were expected to take responsibility for all domestic duties, while boys worked outside the home, often from an early age. As a result of this socialization, the girls became women who led contingent lives, largely dependent on others (husband and children) for success and happiness. Of the 167 people represented in Elder's data, all but two of the women married: 32 percent married before the age of twenty; 45 percent married between the ages of twenty and twenty-two; and 23 percent married after twenty-two. If they had career goals, women sacrificed them completely or delayed pursuit of them until after marriage and the primary childrearing years. Elder reminds us that "an occupational life for women, apart from the family and its economic needs, was contrary to public opinion throughout the Depression decade; a woman's place was in the home, not in competition with men for scarce jobs." [23] Characteristics of women deprived in childhood during the Great Depression include consciousness of self and others, a longing for peer acceptance, and willingness to sacrifice personal freedom for security. Characteristics of men who were deprived in childhood include preoccupation with matters of economic support and occupational role, early vocational focus and commitment, strong desire for mastery and recognition, emphasis on job security, and reluctance to change jobs. Although they valued family life, men valued work more. Thus, there is not only a specific *generational identity* operating for older adults who lived through the depression, but also a specific *gendered identity.*

Generational Identity

The life stories of those who experienced the Great Depression are a rich source of knowledge about that generation's social aging. Life stories are both explanations of and justifications for individual choices and behaviors, as well as transmissions of cultural history. They reveal what the narrators "held as significant in the past, and how they have perceived and interpreted this through the ideological blueprints that they have internalized." [24] A particular trend in the tellings of all the writing groups I observed was an effort to maintain a generational identity distinct from that of parents and children. Group members tell many stories that contrast the values, beliefs, and ways of living in the past and the present, and that therefore provide opportunities for negotiating complex feelings about changes that occur over a lifetime.

An important function of a writing group is to offer a safe place for members to discuss what happened "then" and how they feel about it "now." At one meeting, Elizabeth reads about her first airplane ride, which happened when she was thirteen or fourteen years old. She prefaces the reading by saying, "I still get chills when I think about it." Her father had bought three tickets, one for each of the children, to take a ride with a barnstorming pilot. Elizabeth found the ride frightening; it appeared to her that the propeller stopped, and the pilot had to reach out and get it started again. She has been afraid of flying ever since and wondered for many years whether her father was trying to get rid of his kids because of the strain of raising them during the depression. In the story, she notes that years later a psychiatrist helped her address these fears and choose a more positive interpretation: her father loved them so much he sacrificed his own ride so they could all go together. Group discussion after the reading is rich in generational perspective: Phil, a former World War II pilot, offers some details about piloting a small plane during that time and conjectures what the pilot might have been doing other than getting the propeller started, which he considers unlikely; Mabel lends support for the emotional aspects of the story, saying that she, too, had "special fears" during the Great Depression; and Christine comments wryly, "nowadays, you could sue your father for that anxiety."

Most older writers begin their life stories with a description of their parents and sometimes their grandparents. Often this writing, as well as the talk surrounding it, functions to distinguish (either negatively or positively) between the writers' generation and that of their parents. Writers talk about parental beliefs that they never shared, including superstitions (one member of the geriatric-center group wrote about her grandmother's odd rituals) and folk healing (a member of the Jewish senior-center group wrote about his mother's faith healing within the shtetl, which he considered "a lot of baloney"). A frequent theme in this writing is the conservative and even secretive nature of the parental generation, particularly regarding "family skeletons." Gilda's stories of a missing grandfather and a shady aunt and uncle are a good example. The occasion for telling about her grandfather is another group member's reference to her parents' "scrappy" sixty-five-year marriage:

> *Gilda:* Well, in those days when you got married you stayed married, unless the father disappeared, like my grandfather. My grandmother told me he went to the bear pit and got killed by the bears. Then we found out later he just left [she laughs]. He never came back.

> *Helen:* Yeah, you hear about a lot of that, in that age group.

> *Gilda:* In those days, I just think they didn't want to face it, so they just left, they never got divorced or anything, they just disappeared.

> *Ruth*, laughing: She probably *wished* he'd gotten clawed by the bears.

> *Gilda:* Yes, that's what she, yeah, that's what she was hoping, I guess. That's what she told all of her grandchildren, that's what happened.

Gilda goes on to further separate her values from those of her parents, explaining that she talks openly to her own children and is writing her life story for them "because my mom, my parents *never* talked about their *parents*. And so I know nothing, absolutely nothing. I can't tell my children anything about them. For some reason, if we ever asked, we never got an answer, it was side-tracked."

In another session, Gilda reads a long, revealing passage about various people in her husband Jerry's family, including his alcoholic father (a Russian furrier who was unhappy with his arranged marriage and who could not make "a decent living" in his cleaning and tailoring business) and her husband's Aunt Ann:

> *Gilda* (reading): "Aunt Ann married Al, and they were very good to Jerry. She bought him his first bicycle and just about everything else he had as a child. She took him to the World's Fair once and was always buying him treats, as she never had children of her own. Then Aunt Ann and Uncle Al moved to Chicago. That was a long time ago. And Uncle Al became a member of the Al Capone gang. And Aunt Ann became a madam [exclamations of surprise from the group].

> *Margaret*, with happy emphasis: I've been waiting for these stories to come out.

Gilda: All of these secrets that my children don't know about—but I guess they're gonna find out. OK . . . [she reads]: "Sonny had a sister, Henrietta, who's a very nice lady, and she always told me, 'Do not believe these stories about Aunt Ann and Uncle Al.' But after I became a member of the family, she said it was really true. Time passed, and I guess Aunt Ann and Uncle Al made lots of money while she was a madam and he was a member of Al Capone's gang, because they moved to California and they would come to visit often. Aunt Ann was a lot of fun, and she always played poker with Jerry and his friends. But she would always cheat so Jerry would win, and his friends never realized it . . ." [group laughter].

Gilda goes on to say that she has many other things to write about Aunt Ann, who was "a riot."

Margaret: It sounds as though you have a lot of wonderful stories.

Gilda: Oh, too many, I guess. Lots of 'em I don't want to tell. But they'll come out, I guess, eventually.

Margaret: Yeah. You know, there are so many families that—none of these stories are unusual, they just haven't come out. It happens to so many—

Gilda: Yeah, but that doesn't mean. . . . These things can happen to anybody.

Margaret: I mean it's absolutely fascinating. Absolutely fascinating. I mean, I think of families I know who, you know, are supposed to be so—whatever. And then I find out that the uncle is one of the guys from the Cleveland gang who was sent out to Las Vegas. You know? One of the original dealers out there. . . . But I mean all these kind of things happen. My father . . . told me once about my mother's, about a brother who committed suicide. My father said that he threw himself in front of a train. And he blamed my mother's older sister for it. Of course, I never talked with my mother about it. *Nev-er.* It never came out. And now when I talk to my cousins who are the children of my mother's sisters, nobody knows exactly because apparently none of the three sisters said anything.

Later on in that session, the group has a discussion about Gilda's finally "breaking the family pattern of silence," and Gilda acknowledges that, although she is ambivalent, she thinks it should be done: "Because my daughter said to me, 'If I could get grandma back here, for just two hours, I would ask her so many questions, because she was so wrong in never telling us about [things].' You know? And it's true. It's true. She was."

On the brighter side, some writers use the act of writing about their parents to offer a little social history for the edification of their grandchildren. A case in point is Emily, a member of the geriatric-center group, who has written several stories about her parents, both of whom were influential public figures in the early 1900s. Her father was a politically active lawyer, a member of the "X Club" (a group of New York intellectuals and activists that included philosopher John Dewey), and, at one time, park commissioner for the borough of Brooklyn. Emily's mother was a "forward-looking" woman and a member of an elite woman's study club founded in 1898. As Emily explains in her writing, her mother met Margaret Sanger and "became a lifelong follower, devoting many volunteer hours to the Brooklyn Maternity Center and later to Planned Parenthood and the Margaret Sanger Research Institute. She even went to an international conference in India when she was 81." Emily goes on to say that her mother "enthusiastically marched . . . in parades for women's suffrage both before and after the first World War." She also "did not hesitate" to drive their first car alone "in spite of high spirited shouting, 'Look at the lady driving an automobile!'" After Emily has finished reading, Charlotte comments that she's written "a lovely bit of social history," and Emily replies, "Well, I want my children to know about my parents' lives, and it's very interesting, but I don't want to bore them either."

Later, in my interview with Emily, I learn more about her feelings toward her parents' lifestyle and progressive beliefs, which have influenced Emily's own life course. For one thing, she has "always had a hang up about money, because we were better off than many of my friends, and I was embarrassed to bring a new friend home. They'd say, 'Oh, you live in a BIG house,' and I felt, 'Don't blame me.'" Although she is proud of her mother's early contributions to the women's movement (Emily herself is former chair of the local Gray Panthers and a member of the League of Women Voters), she does not agree with many of her mother's childrearing practices, which included the following: shutting the children in closets and once putting Emily out of the car and driving off in lieu of a spanking (neither parent believed in corporal punishment); giving charge of the children in the 1920s to an authoritarian French governess, who was ultimately dismissed on the grounds of emotional abusiveness; and sending the children to a series of progressive schools, "just because my mother jumped from one idea to another," which made Emily feel like a "guinea pig" and a perpetual outsider among her schoolmates.

On the punishment issue, Emily, at eighty, still feels strongly: "I think it's rather appalling to think that my high-minded, broad-minded, liberal-minded parents would—well I guess they thought they were way out in front because they didn't believe in corporal punishment—but these other punishments were maybe just as bad, but . . . it was the state of the art at the time. I think that [story of the car incident] has historical significance as well as my own personal shock." Partly in response to these personal experiences, as well as to the times, Emily married, focused exclusively on childrearing when her children were young, and never finished college or pursued a career, despite the fact that she was extremely bright and had much potential. "When I was in college it was marriage versus career, this was the choice, and I felt, 'I know I want a family.'" However, Emily ends our interview on a positive note that speaks to her mother's role in shaping her life: "I've been fortunate that I had a courageous mother who nothing daunted her, and I was brought up without fear. In those days, there wasn't as much to fear as today. . . . I've been a very fortunate person."

Members of the writing group also use the gathering to articulate—often with great humor—the unique identity of their own generation. A wide array of topics are likely to evolve both in and around life-story writing, including generational differences in entertainment, childrearing, language practices, and attitudes toward sex. Many writers told how they amused themselves during their childhood, describing simple games like dress-up, hide-the-thimble, marbles, jacks, hopscotch with a flat stone, roller skating, hide 'n seek, and paper dolls. The purpose of these stories is often to celebrate the imaginative make-do elements of a depression-era childhood and the value of "being happy with what you have," as opposed to the buy-me-something-new and I'm-never-satisfied-with-what-I-have attitude of today's children. One of these stories, which Margaret's group liked so much they asked the writer (Eileen) to read it again because I had missed the previous session, begins: "No TV? No computer? No Nintendo? No roller blades? No two-wheeled bike? Gee, Grandma, you never had any fun! Not true, my dear, we had loads of fun."

A writer in another group (Catherine) described to me the impulse that led her to write a life story she called "Playing in My Day": "Not to compare it to the kids today, 'cause I certainly have no idea—maybe they will be much richer imaginatively and emotionally and so on. I don't know. But I wonder about it. And then also the fact, I guess, that there are so many kids that don't have anything. And to see kids with tons of stuff, why, I'm a little bothered by that. But I'm not going into that in the article." Her comment is generally representative of most older writers' feelings: they want to express the values of their generation for the possible benefit of grandchildren, but they don't want to be heavy-handed about it, and they don't want to come across as simply "old-fashioned" or "out of touch." This requires a delicate balancing act. For women, especially, writing about such topics as childhood games is an indirect way to have a say in family childrearing practices. When I ask Catherine if there's anything she would share with the writing group (her own generation) that she would not share with her children, she says, "Oh, umm, well maybe something like I just said . . . about toys. Probably things that my kids are doing now that I would never say anything to them about. You know, I wouldn't criticize them personally, but things that I'm not feeling great about."

Eileen's story about childhood entertainment also includes a section on radio programs, which generates a humorous discussion about how naive and trusting her generation has always been. In talking about her piece, Eileen mentions a time she went to see the program *Inner Sanctum,* broadcast from the Fisher Building in Detroit. Seeing how the sound effects were made "really spoiled everything."

Lorraine: Was *Inner Sanctum* the one that started with the squeaky door?

Eileen: Squeaky door—yes! yes! And they had that, you know, just a little piece of something that they manipulated to make the squeaky sound.

Selma: Well, you remember *The Breakfast Club?* "Round and round the breakfast table"?

Eileen: Yes. Yeah.

Selma: I went to Chicago, and this was in the forties, and I couldn't hardly wait to go to this broadcast. And here I went 'cause I had these visions of people goin' round and round the breakfast table [group laughter]. There was no breakfast table. There was nobody [loud laughter]. It was so disappointing.

Ginny: Yes. On radio, they can fool you.

Selma: All the things, you know, all the things I had imagined in my mind. I used to like to listen to that, and they'd sound so happy.

Eileen: There was another program. What was it? *One Man's Family?* It was kind of—all about the characters in the family and what they did every week, it was a continuous thing every week. And—

Selma: But, remember, you know, listening to radio, how you used to listen to tap dancing and whatnot? Remember that *Amateur Hour?* . . . And you would just sit there and imagine this talent performing and decide who should be the winner. And I heard one of the comedians talk about, "How stupid can you be?" he said, "*listening* to tap dance?" [loud laughter].

Lorraine: They could have been doing it up there [she makes a tapping sound on her head, to loud laughter] for all we knew.

Eileen: But then we developed our imaginations.

All: Yeah, that's right.

Generational identities become obvious when group members discuss their feelings about sex and sexual talk. In one group meeting, a discussion ensues about "how much to tell" in a life story. Several say that they do not want their children to know "everything," and they justify their reticence by noting that neither do they want to know all the intimate details of their children's lives. Two women discuss how their mothers never openly talked about sex and how they never dared to *ask* because of unspoken rules about propriety. One of the women uses her daughter as an example of the current generation's frankness about sex: "She's taking fertility drugs, and she asked me how I got pregnant so easily and whether all my pregnancies were planned. I never would have asked my mother those questions." She says she feels comfortable answering them herself, though, "because I'm a retired nurse."

Unless directly questioned, most members of older writing groups are reluctant to offer intimate details about sex, pregnancy, or childbirth. In one group, a writer (Gilda) broaches the subject of sex through veiled references to her honeymoon and the early months of her marriage. She reads to the group: "We went on a honeymoon for three days up to Charlevoix, rented a log cabin, and we have many pictures in the big book of our honeymoon. We went to live with my mother because it was the only place we could go, as we knew Jerry would soon be leaving for the war. Being very young and innocent and no one to talk to, my cousin Ella took me to her doctor, and he showed me what to do to keep from getting pregnant. Right? Okay" (group laughter). She goes on to say that "apparently I was not doing what the doctor told me to do the right way," because she got pregnant fairly soon after the wedding. Gilda tells the group that she did not think her children should be able to read the letters Jerry sent her during the war, so she threw them all away after Jerry died. "I feel those were all personal, and I don't think that your children should read those letters," she says. "And [the children] kept saying, 'Well, that isn't right!' And I said, 'Those were personal letters to me only, and the three of you weren't even born yet.'" Margaret confirms that she did the same thing with her war letters. Gilda's comments speak to the difference between an older writer's need to tell, and a younger generation's desire to know: especially in regard to sex and romance, parents may need to tell much less than their children want to hear.

Group members are quite aware that the sexual values of their generation seem antiquated to children and grandchildren. During a discussion of sex education, a writer in the geriatric-center group mentions a 1934 article she cut out of *Ladies Home Journal* when she was fourteen years old entitled, "Any Girl Can, But the Smart Girl Doesn't Have To." She found it and sent it to her daughter and sixteen-year-old granddaughter, "so they could get a chuckle out of it."

During one session of Margaret's group, which on this day is attended by only two members and myself, a lively discussion occurs around sexual values and explicitness in language. All the participants in this discussion are white, middle-class women, and two are Jewish. Prior to the following excerpt, the group has talked about a recent television program on *Prime Time Live* in which children ages four, five, and six reveal considerable knowledge about sex and the use of sexual language. Ginny comments that she did not even know those words as a young woman, even though she worked in a filling station "where there was a tire man and a brake man" and served in the navy. The word they are referring to in particular is what Margaret calls "the four-letter *F* word." The following discussion begins with Lorraine mentioning that there is something she wanted to write about but "didn't want it on paper." She tells the story aloud instead:

Lorraine: I've talked about my cousin Charlie, who I always had an affinity with. I told him I would like to go to a burlesque show. I must have been, maybe nineteen or twenty, and I'd never been to one. And my cousin Charlie took me. I hated it, and we left after maybe five or ten minutes. I couldn't stay. We were talking about how naive and sheltered our lives were when we were young. And I think that was an example. We—certain words were never said out loud or never seen in print. There are certain words that I still have difficulty saying, and I'm not talking about slang or dirty words. I'm talking about regular words that are acceptable that I have trouble with.

Margaret: Give us . . . [with her hands, she invites Lorraine to say more].

Lorraine: P-E-N-I-S [she spells the word out] I have a lot of trouble with that word.

Ginny: Mmmhmm.

Lorraine: It's very hard for me. As you can see (group laughter). I had never until maybe two or three years ago, I never heard that word out loud.

Ginny, nodding: Yeah. Yeah.

Lorraine: Or seen it in print. It's in the newspaper everyday.

Margaret: Did you see the outline of—when I say outline what I'm talking about is a drawing. Where did I see that? They explained exactly how the prostate—

Lorraine: I saw that, that was an ad in a magazine I saw.

Margaret: Is that it? Yeah. And it showed the penis, it showed everything, it showed exactly how it was. And I thought, "This is good. This is good." To have the body become—to take the mystery out of it.

Ginny: Yeah.

Lorraine: I'm not saying that it's bad, I'm saying that I have trouble with it because of my background. It was never, never said.

Margaret: I understand.

Ginny: Believe it or not, my father took me to [laughing] the French Quarter in New Orleans [group laughter].

Lorraine: Oh, really?

Ginny: He was, there was a convention. I guess I was eighteen 'cause I must have been just out of high school. And he was a Shriner, and they were having a Shriner convention in New Orleans. Well, my mother didn't feel good, so she stayed home. And I went with the Shriners to [laughs] the French Quarter.

Lorraine: And what did you see there?

Margaret: Yeah, I mean, you look embarrassed [laughs]. Why are you embarrassed?

Ginny: Well, it was a striptease. They didn't strip as far as they do now. All I can remember is the gal had—

Lorraine: Tassels?

Ginny: Tassels that she could swing around [group laughter]. Two different ways.

Lorraine: Yes, I saw—

Margaret, laughing: Remember that?

Lorraine: I saw that once in Chicago, but I was a married woman with a child already by then. And I still wasn't comfortable with it.

Ginny: Yeah. Grown men can act so childish [she laughs].

Lorraine: I don't think that's childish, I think it's male. I think men are just very sexual beings.

Ginny: Yeah. Yeah.

Margaret: That's interesting that you're saying that, because you read more and more now about women being more open, too. Young women being more open.

Lorraine: Yes, yes that's true.

Margaret: It's a different kind of thing. You don't have the younger women today, the women up to, say, I would say up to fifty—the women from the 1960s on, those who lived in the fifties and so forth—

Ginny, extending Margaret's sentence:—that were young then—

Margaret: It's a whole different—I don't know how to say it. There's a whole different attitude. What is the word I want? It's not attitude. It's a whole different brain process.

Ginny: Yeah, a whole different outlook on life, really.

Margaret: That's right.

Lorraine: The inhibitions aren't there anymore.

The three women go on to talk about attitudes toward dating and living together before marriage. Margaret tells a story about a woman in her hometown who dated a local man ("a good catch because he was an orthodontist") and who had a "terrible reputation" because "everybody talked about how she was sleeping with him." Ginny responds that "now they don't get married unless they've lived together for a year or two," and Margaret replies, "Yeah, and I don't want to pass judgment one way or another. I think that's fine. I think it should be that way." Lorraine counters, "I think it can be that way for anybody except my granddaughters," which draws a big, approving laugh and a round of applause.

Clearly, the level of sexual explicitness in language raises many conflicts between social values "then" and "now." Louise Harris McBroom, a former member of a writing group I observed, expressed her concerns about language and value changes in a book of life stories she printed at her own expense. Published when she was eighty-nine, *Bits and Pieces of Eighty Years* includes one "experimental" chapter among the more conventional segments on childhood memories, schoolteaching, marriage, family, friends, and retirement. "The Author's New Book" is a piece of short fiction written in the third person. It is an acerbic commentary on the inappropriacy of language and values in currently published books. The narrator of the chapter describes the character John Jones as a down-and-out writer who has not sold a book in ten years. Jones conducts some research and discovers the formula for today's best-sellers: no plot, pasteboard characters, but lots of sexually explicit language. In the narrator's words, "The key to their success was the vocabulary used and the sexual behavior of the people in the story. In the first chapter of one book, he counted fourteen 'fucks' and twenty 'shits.' In the next chapter, some homos and bisexuals were introduced and there were hints of more titillation to follow." Jones, of course, follows the formula and publishes quickly and successfully: "The press was unanimous in praise: 'The best writing he has ever done, an amazing comeback; he writes for the "now" generation.'" Jones even garners the approval of academics: "Professors of English began mentioning his name and assigned papers such as, 'Comparison of the style of this author in the sixties with his most recent work.'" The concluding lines of the fictional chapter introduce a new character, lacking in education, who nonetheless has a better understanding of "good literature" than Jones, the critics, and the academics combined. The unnamed man skims through Jones's book, using criteria learned in high school from "an inspired teacher of English" and puts it down in disgust, pronouncing, "This book is nothing but trash; it isn't worth reading." Although I wasn't present in the writing group when Louise composed and read this chapter, I heard about it subsequently from more than one group member who considered Louise extraordinarily creative and courageous for writing it.

Gender Talk and Generational Identity

Gender differences abound in writing-group talk. Most of the examples I have given in this chapter reflect older women's central concern with human relationships—how people interact within and between generations and what the writers choose to reveal about themselves and their attitudes toward others through their life stories. Although male group members may enter into these conversations, they do not typically initiate them. The men are more likely to talk about how the *physical* world was different in the past. Robert, for example, describes the various features of cars he drove; pranks his father's generation and his own played on Halloween ("Remember that this was before McDonald's had metal detectors to find razor blades in children's candies"); and life during World War II ("Gasoline and food was rationed. Meat, fats, and butter were scarce. We recycled tin cans, newspapers and cardboard, car batteries, and almost every type of container. Papers and leaves were usually burned. There were Victrolas, seventy-eight rpm records, and theaters with war movies on Saturday afternoons"). Phil describes unusual foods he ate as a child (bean sandwiches, which he was ashamed to take to school); the many places he lived and the schools he attended while his father changed jobs; planes he flew during World War II; and the particulars of air force life. Bill describes his early school years in Greece, where his parents were missionaries; his passage to the United States at fifteen with his brother; small-town life in Scranton, Pennsylvania, during the Great Depression; his status as conscientious objector during World War II, and his civilian work as a translator for the war effort.

Daniel, eighty-four, devotes one of his writings to describing a "preventorium" for tuberculosis, where he lived between 1920 and 1921. While Daniel describes the details of daily life at the preventorium, it is the women in the group who comment on how different family relationships were then, as neither parents nor health-care officials apparently considered the *emotional* effects of institutionalization on a ten-year-old boy. In another writing, Daniel includes a small drawing of the cardboard sign provided to families during his boyhood to signal the iceman as to the pounds of ice needed. Daniel mentions after reading this piece that his childhood home and neighborhood have changed physically, and he wants to write about them now because "it seems wrong to me that there's nothing to show where I've been." Daniel, like most of the other men, marks his place in the world in terms of his physical impact on it.

Older men tend to focus their life stories around the theme of overcoming difficulties in the physical world. In the following excerpt from the group at the Jewish senior center, Samuel reads a story about fixing a car during the depression. Introducing the piece, he says, "I wrote about something that I've done, and probably I can call it a successful accomplishment." His story prompts a discussion about technology and adapting to technological change:

Samuel, reading: "During the Great Depression, this was about 1932, I bought an old Cadillac for fifty dollars. I bought it more out of curiosity of what I could do with it. It was a challenge. I had hoped to repair it and make it look as beautiful and useful as it was when it was new. I spent many hours laying on the ground fiddling around with its underside. I took the engine apart. What I didn't know about its engine would fill a book. I read the book of repairs and followed the instructions, how to and what to, and why do the things that the book instructed. Part of this self-study course entailed the purchase of tools and parts. Reading the instructions, I would make my own changes. I assumed sometimes that I knew more than the engineer who wrote the book. The car ran well enough when I bought it, but I wasn't satisfied with it. I knew it needed new piston rings. Today's automobiles never need new piston rings. The rings last longer than any other parts of the car. To install new piston rings, you have to have a special tool to squeeze the piston rings into the slots where they are supposed to be. I manufactured a piston ring squeezer out of things I found in my ashamed-to-throw-away box." That's [turning to the group] as far as I went. I could go on and on about the whole thing. But after I fixed the car and the car ran, I found out that I didn't need any piston rings [laughter].

Ruth: Oh, great.

Rose: You learned the mechanism of a Cadillac car.

Samuel: The mechanism of a Cadillac car is like any other car.

Rose: Really?

Marvin: They were very simple compared to today's cars.

Samuel: Yeah [several voices chime in].

Marvin (to me): Before radio came in, which you don't remember that, they used to make transistor sets, like.

Samuel: I used to make my own radios.

Marvin: Remember? [several voices].

Samuel: I used to wind the lines around the tube. And you can have it any form, a box or whatever. And then you can have a sliding thing to slide along and touch any part of the coils to give you different stations. We learned it in high school.

Marvin: What year was that?

Samuel: Oh, I can't—it was . . . [he laughs].

Marvin: In the twenties? Early twenties.

Samuel: Yeah, it was in the early twenties. I remember taking that box that I made the radio on, it ran on the roof of our apartment, on the Lower East Side of New York. We used to spend a lot of time on the roof. I had installed an antenna, a slant rise from the floor to the roof up to the chimney, and attached it to the radio. And we sat around, and we had earphones, sat around. It was an amazing thing. I heard Herbert Hoover speak. Such a loud and clear voice, Herbert Hoover.

George: In those days, you had a radio, not TV. Radio people would have antennas on their houses for the reception. And in Canada, we had, it was a tax on radios. So when they came down to check if you had a tax, if you had an antenna on your roof, they automatically knocked on your door and asked for your radio license.

Ruth: Ahh.

George: And they got a lot of people that way. If you didn't have an antenna, you could get away without a license.

Ruth, laughing: But then you couldn't get any stations if you didn't have an antenna.

George: Well.

Sylvia: They had rabbit ears. Rabbit ears worked.

Ruth: They worked pretty well?

Samuel: I remember the old radio that I made, I'd bring it into the kitchen, and I had the wire going through the window to the antenna on the roof. And the whole family would sit around the table. And I got, we had a copper bowl, a fruit bowl. I polished the inside of the copper fruit bowl, and I put one ear piece in the bottom of the fruit bowl. That magnified the sound so that everybody around the table could hear it [group laughter].

Ruth: Oh that was pretty smart.

Marvin: It was local stations that you got.

Samuel: Yeah, right. Local stations.

Marvin: If you got anything out of town, it was the talk of the town. If you got Cleveland or Chicago.

Rose: I remember tuning in Dempsey fights.

Several voices: Yeah.

Rose: And they had, for people that couldn't hear it, that didn't have radios, there was a loudspeaker at the corner of our street. And all the neighbors came out to hear the fight. You know?

Marvin: I went to school with a fella, I think I mentioned before, his name was Harry Amison, who when Jack Dempsey was barnstorming, he was in the ring with him. Harry Amison was his name. . . .

Samuel: To me it was unbelievable that you could turn the radio on and hear something that's coming from so far away. *Several voices:* Yeah.

The men carry this discussion, and they are quite animated. Marvin, whom directors at the senior center believe has Alzheimer's disease (although neither he nor his family has confirmed this) is more talkative than usual. The discussion provides an occasion for the men to display their knowledge about an earlier time and to take collective pride in the resourcefulness that has carried them through to old age.

All of the stories repeated in this chapter confirm how age identities are socially constructed—how they surface and are negotiated, in this case through talk among members of the same generation. We see how "elderliness" is manufactured and modified in sequences of talk and how an elderly "identity" is unstable and shifting, depending on the circumstances.[25] Establishing an "age identity" through generational affiliation serves complex social and psychological functions, and it can be emotionally satisfying and affirming, as we have seen.

Life-story telling that is based on generational affiliations can also be a way of expressing what psychologist John Kotre calls "cultural generativity," or the passing on of values. Extending Erik Erikson's theory of adult development, Kotre defines generativity as "a desire to invest one's substance in forms of life and work that will outlive the self,"[26] including written life stories. Although the impulse for cultural generativity occurs throughout life, it is probably most predominant in the period following biological reproduction. Kotre looks to anthropology to explain why:

> From an evolutionary point of view, this post reproductive period is an anomaly. What function could it possibly serve for the survival of the species? . . . One answer offered by Margaret Mead is that it promotes the

survival of children and grandchildren through social instead of biological mechanisms. Old people, for example, might be the only ones who know where to find food and water during a drought because they were the only ones alive during the last one. A related answer is that the post productive period of life ensures the transmission of culture, which is vital to human survival.[27]

By "culture," Kotre means the set of symbols used to interpret existence and to give a sense of meaning and place to a group of people. Through the telling of life stories and other generative acts, "the individual weaves an aspect of himself into a tapestry of meaning that has extension and continuity. He becomes the voice of a tradition larger than himself, and the tradition flows through him to the young. In this way culture carries on."[28] Obviously, writing groups for older people provide a context in which members reflect on the traditions their generation shares and collaborate on how best to represent themselves in terms of these traditions to younger generations. They also provide a context in which to question life stories that construct social limitations on the basis of chronological age, as illustrated in Margaret's response to the writing of the woman who considered herself "old" at eighty-four.

To what extent is reliance on the narrative constructions supplied by culture and generation beneficial and to what extent might it be detrimental to development in later life? On the one hand, identification with our cohorts gives us a sense of continuity and purpose; we can speak on behalf of a whole generation that has helped shape our identity and define our place in the world. Such identification has strong emotional appeal, as can be seen in many of the writing-group conversations. In articulating a generational identity (as opposed to a strictly individual one), we are poised to question and challenge aspects of that identity that no longer seem warranted in the contemporary world, as seen in the metropolitan group's discussion of their generation's trusting acceptance of "reality" on the radio. In such cases, we might say that social aging is subject to narrative revision. On the other hand, overidentification with cultural and generational narratives, particularly those informed by chronological and physiological scripts, can limit the possibilities for both life story and personal development. This is a lesson that Margaret emphatically reinforces to the members of her writing groups, and it underlies interactions in most of the writing groups I observed. All writers, at some point, must identify how their lives diverge from the lives of others in their generation, and find the courage and imagination to create alternative stories.

Alice

ALICE, a member of the East Side Senior Center, submitted this life story to a Detroit area writing contest for senior citizens and received an honorable mention.

Child Labor Law and I

I, Alice N _____ , at the age of ten lived with my Armenian parents in the borough of Manhattan of New York City in an apartment in the middle on the fourth floor of a five-story building. Each floor had two two-bedroom apartments in the middle, and two two-bedroom apartments in the front section. My brothers Sarkis, George, and Mesag (Michael) and I lived in this three-room apartment heated with a small coal stove, plus we cooked on it too. We had an overhead tank on our toilet. The kitchen had a big sink. Next to it was a large bathtub with a big porcelin cover and an old ice box. Father made a sette from lumber with a seat on hinges. When night came, it was used as a spare bed. My school was between 27th Street and 2nd and 3rd Avenues. There I enjoyed our once-a-month assembled performances, alternating with dancing class and classical music class.

We were a happy family. Our building had a nice group of ethnic people: Italian, Armenian, Greeks, Germans, and many more. My father sold hot dogs and lemonade, pushing a very heavy wagon with wagon wheels in summer, spring, and part of the fall. In winter, he'd roast chestnuts and peanuts in his baby buggy converted with a small coal stove. I have not had delicious chesnuts since 1939. This was the end of his life.

New York City is a fashion area where work was brought home to make or sew. Every year, July through October months, home work was brought at this time to be ready for Christmas for gift items. Task #1: Two men's hankies were made into someting like a pajama top. Task #2: Ladies' hankies were made into aprons with ribbons and bands and put into a box. Then there is the task that really got me involved with the child labor law. We were doing faggoting, making a binding to match the color of dress material. This would be basted onto heavy brown paper with a design on it and eventually hemmed in silk thread. My mother would split the work and earnings with her neighbors. This not only brought neighbors closer to each other; for us children it was fun, too, to listen to their stories. My job was only to rip the basting stitches out.

As a child, I used to miss school days. Whenever I had a cold, it would last a long while. This day my brothers had been napping. Mother said, "Aghcheegus yeas bede shuga yertam. Yehbar ner it hok dar." Translation: "Daughter, I'm going shopping. Take care of your brothers." I was at the table thinking to myself, "Now is the time to put to use what I learned and observed that I was doing fine." My brother was stirring about during his nap to wake up. A knock on the door was what came to his attention. His thoughts were, "Mother is here," so he opened the door. To our surprise, in walked a lady. I found out later that she was a truant officer asking, "Can you do the work?" I, being proud of myself, bragged, "Yes, I can." Mother's surprise came days later. Mother received a summons to appear in court. My mother contacted her friend Lucy. "Why am I getting this? Why must I go to court? Why! Will you go along with me?" Lucy replied, "Ayo hadid gartam nice hotir." Translation: "Yes, I go with you, don't worry."

Court day was mother's first experience and her first time. Mother explained through her interpreter Lucy: "Your honor, Mrs. Tokatlian only had asked her daughter just to rip the basting stitches away from the brown paper off the finished product. Mrs. Tokatlian didn't realize that her daughter was that inquisitive to learn by looking over Mrs. Tokatlian's shoulder." The judge was very understanding. "I know your daughter shows talent but don't have her miss any more school days. This time I'll excuse you that you had no knowledge of child labor law."

Recently in the *Detroit Free Press* newspaper column on Saturday, October 2, 1995, I read an article ("Market Pays Child Labor Law Fine") I enclose: "Westborn Fruit Market on Woodward paid a fine exceeding $16,000 after the U. S. Labor Department found numerous violations of child labor laws, the agency's Pontiac office announced. Federal investigators turned up 23 instances in which children ages 14 and 15 years old were baling scrap paper, operating meat grinders and working later in the day than the law allows." People that migrate from Europe, Asia, think not of child labor law. Twelve-year-old children are taking on minor jobs, such as mopping and minor cleaning around shops. People send their children to jewelers, tailors, hoping that the child will learn the trade. This is one way of keeping a child's mind busy and receiving a minor amount of money. There should be some type of task to keep our young generation "crime free." Busy minds and hands keep a child out of trouble and out of jail.

Annie

THIS EXCERPT from Annie's life story is based on an interview at the East Side Senior Center in Detroit.

What really matters to me, and what I would *love* to have, is to have those kids of mine straighten up, be decent types. What matters to me mostly is my grandson. I want the best for him, and so far, he's sort of living up to my expectations. I just hope he don't get discouraged in any way. You know, it makes his mother kind of help keep him on the straight path, to know that I would like that for him. Because so many things happen. And he's the only one out of the grandchildren that I know. The only one out of *all* that I have. So that's what really matters to me most, that he be taken care of. I just hope he don't have to fall into hands or have to be adopted or whatever.

That's why I'd love to be a hundred years. I could try to keep helping him and talking to him. I took him away from my daughter one time and just kept him. He didn't want to leave me, he just wanted to stay there with me. So I kept him as long as I could. And I turned him back over to her when I could give her something to do instead of running the streets. I figured she needed some responsibility anyway. But I'm still trying to watch over him and her both, because I think she—I don't know, it's just a hunch or feeling I have that she's—you know, you can tell when people aren't thinking right, the way they laugh and the way they talk. Sometime when something's up, something is not right, I call her and talk to her. And bless his heart, my grandson calls me everyday and want to know how I'm doing. He don't have nobody but me and her, 'cause all my family ·is gone, except my sister, and she's in a nursing home in South Carolina. So I would like to be there for him until he gets old enough to do for himself and work and take care of himself.

I'm glad to know that I could add a little something to the story that I'm trying to tell, that the kids would sorta understand. If they would understand and know how I have come through life, they would make a change. Because see, I have worked all my life. Kids now won't work for just the minimum wage. They say, "I'm not doing this, that, or the other." They'd rather get fast money. A lot of people's kids would rather get out there and sell dope and get on dope and steal and rob rather than get out there and work. They're lazy. And the parents now, they'll sit down and won't even teach the kids to work. You've got to start the kids off at an early age.

I'm trying to influence my grandson. If I can just keep it sinkin' in, and if my daughter don't turn back, saying, "Well, I'm gonna get him this, or that, and the other." I'm trying to teach him the value of a dollar. Trying to teach him to save. He's been pretty good at trying to save, 'cause when he come over, I might give him maybe four dollars and tell him, "That's your allowance, now keep it." And he's got a little bank pass chuck full of money at my house. He'll put the money in there pretty good. So, well, I have a couple of CDs in the bank for him, in case anything happens to me. But the rest don't know that, 'cause money's gonna mean something in life later on for these kids, and they don't understand it.

It do make me a little angry sometime, when I see people not wanting to work, and every time they have a baby they want to put it on the welfare. I hate welfare. For some people, it's necessary. But some of 'em, they're double-dipping and using two and three social security cards and two or three different names. That's not nothing but bleeding the system dry. I mean, I really detest that. I'll be frank about it. If you can work, get out there and work. I worked for 10 cents an hour. Uh-huh. I didn't make a whole lot of money. The only time I got started making money was when I came to Detroit in '43. I think the first time I took home a paycheck, it was for eighty-two dollars, jumping from six dollars a week. I thought I had plenty of money! Thought I'd struck it rich. And even that seemed to fade away, 'cause I know I have had a lot in my life, and I have had nothing in my life.

As kids, we lived off of nothing. Just made us an onion sandwich with mother's biscuits and put salt and pepper on that onion. But it was good. We was full. Here now, they want the best of everything. I never seen kids like this in all the days of my life. And they'll go snatching gold off people's necks and things like that, got me afraid to wear it. If you got something, a fur or whatever, you're almost afraid to wear it because you don't know when it's gonna get snatched off your body. I have seen it. Getting on the bus, a woman had on a fur, and she was sitting right there in the front seat where they have that little bar there. When a fellow got off the bus, he carried that fur on off with him. And I have known a woman got her ring cut—her whole finger cut off to get the ring. They're starting out young for that, really too young for that. I do wish these young people would change.

But I think parents have a lot to do with it, too. If you got a child bringin' in a big wad of money, and you know he's not working nowhere, now you good and well know where he got it from. Steal it or selling dope for it, one or the other. But the parents go ahead and *use* that. When I was a child, if I happened to bring home something I didn't have no business having, my mother would beat me all the way back to the store or wherever I got it from. I had one grandchild that would steal. When he'd go out, if you weren't careful, something's going out with him. If it ain't nothing but a pocket handkerchief or a pin, there's something going right out the door. But I love him still. I don't hate him. I just don't want him around. Don't want him around.

But I'm gonna hold on, 'cause that's all I've got—my hope and my faith. I'll keep on hoping that things are gonna change.

THREE   Social Scripts for Gender, Race, and Class

ALTHOUGH MOST PEOPLE are keenly interested in their own lives, they do not usually write about them. For some reason, the act of *writing* a life story, as opposed to telling it, is most prevalent among middle-class white women, who perhaps feel a greater need to mark their place in the world *textually*, largely because they have the resources and opportunities to do it. The minority elders at the urban senior centers I have visited are mostly concerned with getting through the day and are not inclined to write about themselves or to dwell on the past. Those few who do join writing groups were often good students in school, but many had to drop out because of work, illness, or pregnancy. Even for these elders, most daily events take priority over the weekly writing sessions. To understand the larger social context of the urban writing group, consider these aspects of life for the elderly poor in the inner city:

· Most women at the East Side Center wear fanny packs under their sweaters and sweatshirts, having long abandoned the shoulder bag because it makes them more vulnerable to attack. Many of the women have been accosted on the street, and some of the men, too. Malcolm tells me before one of our sessions that recently a young man tripped him in the mud and pulled out a screwdriver. "I grabbed his arm," Malcolm, who is in his sixties, says, matter of factly. "I might not be sittin' here if I didn't. I don't like to fight. I'll walk away first, unless somebody's tryin' to kill me. And he was tryin' to *kill* me."

· Izzy, in her eighties, tells me about her neighbors, who have stolen just about everything in her house, including all her electrical appliances. She thought they would stop when they had cleaned her house out, but then they broke in and took the moulding from around the doors. "All I got left is an old, sick dog, too tired to move, just like me," she says. Annie nods in recognition. Her house has been robbed three times, and she has been attacked on the street. "Nowadays, I feel like knockin' on my own door when I come home and sayin'—'Anybody in there?' It's enough. All my life, people tellin' me 'Be nice, be nice.' Well, when's somebody gonna be nice to *me*?"

· A woman in her late fifties at the Central City Center is between jobs—and houses—since hers recently burned down. She has a mental illness, which makes it hard to keep working. Sometimes she comes to the center dopey with drugs. She has a college education and once wanted to be a freelance writer. She joined us for a group session once, but she was unable to concentrate. She left.

· A woman at the same center carries the weight of a heavy past with her. In her writings about childhood, she alludes to sexual abuse endured from 1934 to 1942 while living in Detroit with "the aunt from hell." Abuse and low self-esteem have dogged her ever since. At sixteen, she married a verbally abusive man (to get away from the aunt), who convinced her she was stupid. Eventually she divorced him, but she has not been able to complete her general education diploma, despite repeated efforts to return to school.

The city centers themselves speak of hard times and struggle. Most of these facilities occupy a section of an old building in a bad neighborhood. The West Side Center, for example, takes up the gymnasium, adjoining offices, and kitchen of a former junior high school. Iron cages are bolted onto the first-floor windows. The grounds have been overtaken by weeds and litter. Across the street is an abandoned gas station and a store plastered with signs: "All new, fully stocked. LIQUOR. Daily lotto. FOOD STAMPS. No returns. We cash checks." As I pull into the parking lot for the first meeting of the writing group, I notice a young woman in a modest grey car that boldly advertises its armored alarm system. She is a nurse, come to draw blood for health cards. She carries a black case with stenciled letters, WE CARRY NO DRUGS. Inside the center, I am approached by a frail-looking woman. "See this pen?" she says, holding it out to me. "It's from my church. Got the name of the pastor and everything. I want you to have it for a seventy-five-cent donation." The print on the pen is worn: the first *t* in *Christ Covenant* is missing, and part of the pastor's name is gone. I fish around in my briefcase for change (I don't carry a purse either, and hardly any money). "I can always use a pen," I say. She gives me a bit of philosophy in return: "Nobody knows what you want unless you open your mouth and say it!" The cost of a state-subsidized lunch at the center is seventy-five cents.

· The director at the West Side Center is a thirty-something white woman whose salary is less than $20,000 a year. Most of the seniors there live on social security and food stamps. The center's mission: Keep people independent. The director has recently spoken at the funeral of a member who hung herself. "Many of these people are not just poor, they're alone," she says. She points to a tiny black woman with sunken cheeks playing dominoes. "She's ninety-two. Two years ago she had a stroke, and nobody knew it, including her. She came in here slurring her speech, and I took her to the hospital. She has no family, but she's always saying to me, 'I signed up for a hundred years, and I'm going to be here a while yet!'" The director does not think she herself will be here much longer, though. The job is too stressful. Directors in the urban centers rarely stay more than a year or two.

Getting to the writing group prepared and on time is sometimes too much to ask of these urban elders. Many forget to bring their notebooks, so they scribble on the backs of flyers and envelopes. Just about everything takes precedence over writing: going to the bank, getting a flu shot, going to any free event sponsored by the center. What I consider "modest" goals for the group—a few pages of a handwritten life story—seem to many of them overly ambitious and optimistic for an eight-week session. They keep coming back, though, and each woman reads aloud and writes at every session. Everyone is very proud when we are finished.

I open this chapter with these observations because I want to highlight the unseen influences on the writing of an elder's life. Socioeconomic class is often treated as a simple "variable" by scientific gerontologists. Yet class, along with age, race, gender, ethnicity, and able-bodiedness profoundly affects the shape and quality of a life; it is the subtext underlying most of the life stories written by urban elders, and it intersects in complex ways with race and gender. There are well-established social scripts for writing about class, particularly for the poor and working class, just as there are conventional scripts for gender and race. Middle-class white women, for example, typically tell relationship stories, and when they tell achievement stories, they interpret them in terms of relationship. Black women tell relationship stories, too, but they are more largely framed in terms of race and class, and their stories are often survival narratives that focus on personal strength and agency, along with assistance from God, in overcoming life's challenges. Middle-class white men tell achievement stories, with secondary reference to relationships, and the working-class Jewish men in my study are more likely to tell survival stories in socioeconomic terms. These differences are significant, ultimately, because they exemplify the narrative and cultural influences on the older adult's life story—influences that many are unaware of prior to sharing their stories in groups.

The excerpts I use throughout this chapter to illustrate these social scripts are drawn from my observations of seven writing groups and interviews with thirty group members, ranging in age from sixty to ninety-two. Quoted here are thirteen white women, four of whom self-identify in terms of ethnicity (Jewish, Polish, and Armenian); seven black women; five white men, two of whom self-identify in terms of ethnicity (Jewish); and no black men (only two were in the writing groups, and both of them declined to be interviewed).

Collectively, the seven writing groups reflect the heterogeneity of the older adult population, although each group individually is more homogeneous, at least in terms of race and class. Four of the groups—one from the university geriatric center, two metropolitan Detroit groups, and the Jewish center group—are primarily white and middle-class. The two urban Detroit groups from the East Side Center and the West Side Center are primarily black and working class. The locations and resources available to these centers vary drastically. The university center is situated in a modern geriatric complex that offers medical services, social services, counseling, and an extensive educational program. Writing groups either meet in a clean, well-lit, climate-controlled room at the center or, for an even cozier atmosphere, rotate among members' homes. Everyone has private transportation and feels secure driving around the university town alone; no one expresses any reservation about visiting a "stranger's" house in any part of town. The two metropolitan Detroit groups always meet in the same room of the senior center around long tables pushed together. The center, which has a large educational and social program, if not an extensive budget, is situated in the middle of two high-rise apartment buildings, subsidized for seniors by the government. Some of the group members, and the facilitator herself, live in these apartments, which are modest but well-maintained. The Jewish center group meets at a senior center located in a Detroit suburb, once primarily Jewish but now racially and ethnically mixed. Still, many of the seniors have raised their children in the neighborhoods surrounding the center, and they share long associations with local people and places. The center itself is associated with the suburban city's recreation department and is large and active. Its educational program reflects its constituency: high-school equivalency and self-help classes are more common than the "enrichment" classes (including college-level literature courses) offered at the university geriatric center some thirty-five miles away.

The two urban centers are the most impoverished in terms of location, facilities, and services. As already noted, these facilities occupy corners of other buildings—a former junior high school in the case of the West Side Center, and part of the first floor of an old four-story YMCA building on the East Side. They are not even identified by a sign out front. The East Side Center is located at a busy intersection across from the Living Truth Temple and the Living Truth Feeding Center. The parking lot behind the building is surrounded by a chain-link fence with barbed wire on top. It overlooks the United Missionary Baptist Church ("Come unto me all ye that labor and are heavy laden and I will give you rest"). Nearby neighborhoods are battle-weary: burned out buildings, unpainted houses with broken, rag-stuffed windows, and cars abandoned in various states of disrepair. There are bright spots, created by urban activists to uplift people, like the mural painted on the side of a three-story building across the street, entitled "African Amalgam of Ubiquity." A scroll in the hands of a muscular black male reads, "Behold! My people arise, stand strong and proud, for ye come from pharaohs, emperors, kings and queens." He is surrounded with the faces of Rosa Parks, Jesse Jackson, Malcolm X, Martin Luther King, and others, and two black hands hold up a new baby encircled in light.

It is important to keep in mind that the interviews I conducted in these places are simply *moments* in a lifetime of tellings. They are mediated by time, place, and purpose—in this case, participation in an interview with a much-younger researcher who is white and educated. I know that the race and sex of any researcher significantly affects interview responses (and the life stories people tell), especially in regards to questions about race and sex, and that older adults may be even more affected by interviewer characteristics than younger adults.[1] It is because of these facts that oral historian Gwendolyn Etter-Lewis argues, "Although matching interviewers and interviewees by gender and race does not guarantee a bias-free interaction, such a match is more likely to create an empowering environment for the narrator and a more reliable finished product."[2] Still, Etter-Lewis acknowledges that a "clash in cultures" is not an inevitable feature of cross-cultural encounters, especially if the researcher has taken the time to learn about the interviewee's culture and is sensitive to difference. How my own presence and persona affected elders' responses—in combination with the structure, sequence, and perceived relevance of my interview questions—is an open question.

My generalizations here should be read as suggestive interpretations, rather than objective "findings," informed as they are by feminist theories of autobiography and my own interests. The following excerpts are not "proof" of difference so much as illustrations of a particular reading strategy that reveals the enormous impact of social difference on the storytelling patterns of people from the same generation. My intention in this chapter is to illustrate the rich diversity in older adults' narratives and to suggest some cultural reasons for it.

Cultural Scripting

Contemporary autobiographical criticism has taught us that we all have many selves, each of which has many stories to tell. Some of these selves are inconsistent and competitive with one another: the good soldier competes with the rebellious young man; the self-sacrificing mother competes with the independent career girl. Which self prevails in the telling of a life is up to the narrator, but certain selves are more or less likely to be represented, given material conditions and the historical and cultural context of the telling. The life-story teller is constrained by lived experience (although the girl dreamed of independence, she stayed home and raised a family); by cultural scripts defining the "appropriate" ways to live and tell about a life; and by the limits of memory, consciousness, and desire. There are also rhetorical demands on the telling itself, as well as considerations of audience and purpose: the story must present a coherent and unified version of the self-in-retrospect, and it must "make sense" and "sound like" the person whom others (family members, friends) have come to "know." In other words, the life story must be a persuasive version of the self in terms of authenticity and truth-value (although the contested nature of these terms is taken up in chapter 4).

Culture, to some degree, writes our life stories *for* us. Autobiographical critics Sidonie Smith and Julia Watson remind us that narrators take up culturally available models, as well as narrative templates that structure experiential history.[3] Our culture teaches us how to read our lives, as well as how to write them—what to see in ourselves and how to interpret and convey its meaning to others. Narrative psychologist Mary Gergen explains that these cultural models typically function below the level of consciousness: "We use these forms unwittingly. . . . [Therefore,] 'know thyself,' a seemingly timeless motto, loses clarity when we hold that our forms of self-understanding are the creation of the unknown multitudes who have gone before us. We have become, we are becoming because 'they' have set out the linguistic forestructures of intelligibility."[4]

The recitation of a life story is also embedded in local community contexts that offer their own models for the shape and content of the story. Smith and Watson, for example, list some of the stories we are expected to tell in particular institutional settings: religious confessions and conversion stories are told in church; psychological trauma stories in the therapist's office; stories of social victimization and economic impoverishment at the social-service agencies; medical histories in the hospital; and stories of political oppression at the immigration bureau. These settings also have expectations for what is *not* tellable: "Only certain kinds of stories need be told in each narrative locale. Only certain kinds of stories become intelligible as they fit the managed framework, the imposed system." The self recitation is, then, to some extent "prepackaged, prerecited."[5] Religious conversion stories are not generally told to the doctor unless they fit within the framework of a medical history. The center for senior citizens, too, is a social context with its own unspoken "rules" for telling the life story, a point I discuss more fully in chapter 6. For the moment, let us say that life stories are expected to conform to a set of social norms; there is an unspoken dictum, for instance, against telling explicit stories of sexual pursuit. Life stories are also expected to provide hope and inspiration to others. Stories of unmitigated complaint or resentment without resolution (or at least awareness of the need for resolution) are poorly received at the senior center.

It is the creative and developmental task of every life-story teller to negotiate the culturally available scripts and decide how much to adjust a story to the local setting. A counternarrative is always possible, but that would lead to a renegade status at the senior center, which is extremely unlikely among the people in my study. Those with unconventional narratives or resistant tendencies usually self-select to leave writing groups. This was the case with a ninety-six-year-old African-American woman in one of my writing groups who came twice and then stopped attending when the group began to write about adult years, marriage, and childrearing. She pulled me aside after a group meeting and said, "I'm a lesbian, and I don't want to write about that here. I've discussed it in other places, including a book on older lesbians that I was interviewed for, and various national observances which I've traveled to." I said I would like to see the book sometime, and she offered to bring it into the senior center, then reconsidered. "You'll have to come to my house," she said, nervously. Her way of adjusting her life story to the social norms of the senior center was not to tell it at all. Narrators who stay the course in groups at senior centers, however, typically follow the expected scripts.

In the remainder of this chapter, I describe those scripts with reference to studies in autobiographical criticism and illustrate with examples from my interviews. My purpose is to advance toward the argument that, although most older adults write conventional narratives that do not "break script," the writing group serves as a forum for making these scripts visible and comparing their rhetorical effect on others, thus establishing the necessary groundwork for narrative change and personal development.

Scripts for Gender

Contemporary studies in autobiography emphasize the construction of self within a social context. A life story is interesting primarily for the way it reveals—to use feminist critic Sidonie Smith's words—"the way the autobiographer situates herself and her story in relation to cultural ideologies and figures of selfhood." Smith goes on to suggest that "cultural scripts of signification, the figures of verisimilitude or lifelikeness, reflect privileged stories and character types that the prevailing culture, through its discourse, names as 'real' and therefore 'readable.'"[6] In particular, Smith shows how the ideology of gender "has always constituted *a*, if not *the*, fundamental ideological system for interpreting and understanding individual identity and social dynamics."[7] Smith and other feminist critics identify many of the features that have served to represent the female self in autobiography: she is typically self-effacing rather than self-promoting; oriented toward private rather than public life; responsive to others' needs and desires before her own; more likely to foreground relationships and subjective states over accomplishments; and anecdotal in her means of expression. As literary critic Estelle Jelinek notes, women's autobiographies are "not powered by a heroic self-image but driven by a need for self-affirmation"; thus, the self projected in women's writing is "tentative yet proud," a dual construction that often combines apology or defense with expressions of pride.[8] Historically, the self in men's narratives, in contrast, has been assertive and self-confident; oriented toward public life and achievement; concerned with objective states (facts, dates, chronologies) over the expression of feelings; and interested in a unified and logical structure for the narrative. In the apt words of Madeline, the eighty-year-old facilitator of a geriatric center group, "Men are more likely to be expository and to write about external things," while women are more likely to be personal and to write about internal states. Her explanation is that "men are *telling* us about themselves rather than *revealing* themselves." Smith refers to gendered writing styles as "paternal" and "maternal" narratives and offers them as suggestive patterns rather than fixed descriptions. Although both are cultural fictions (gender identities are far more complex than these dualities suggest), the patterns do reflect (and often reify) the expectations that guide many older American's life-story tellings.

In my own study, older people's responses to my request for a brief life review clearly illustrate these gender distinctions. I always begin a life-story interview with an open-ended question: "Tell me something about your life, generally what it's been like up to this point." In phrasing the question this way, I hope to gain an understanding of the respondents' evaluative and interpretive strategies, as well as the content of their narratives. As feminist autobiographical criticism predicts, nearly all the women in my study respond in terms of people and relationships, while the men respond in terms of activities and accomplishments. The following excerpts from my interviews with white women from the geriatric center and the metropolitan Detroit groups illustrate this tendency. Women often respond in terms of relationships with parents and husbands. Jean, sixty-seven, tells me:

> Oh, my gosh. [It's been] very changeable. There have been lots of changes, lots of growth. It's hard to believe I was once the person I started out with. . . . I've grown and matured a lot, and . . . I'm glad about it, but it surprises me, sometimes. For so long I couldn't see any change, and I was so disgusted. And now I see a lot of change. . . . I was a very late bloomer. As I told you before, I was in college at a very early age for all the wrong reasons. To please my dad. And emotionally I wasn't ready. . . . So here I was in college at sixteen, emotionally going on twelve, I guess, so I was very unhappy. And I just concentrated on getting straight As, which I got, and I thought that was so important. And looking back at it, it's so unimportant, you know? But what did I know then? And oh, I don't know. I had a very, very happy first marriage . . . [but] there wasn't any growth whatsoever. My husband was

twenty years older than I, and he never had children, so he wanted a wife who was also a daughter, and that he got, and I got a father and a husband.

Ginny, seventy-nine, starts out her interview with: "Well, it's been good. I never felt that we had any problems at all. My folks were Christian Scientists, and my grandparents on both sides were Christian Scientists. So I was born into this loving atmosphere. And everything was fine. We always had a good—I was supported in what I did, and we were disciplined, of course, but not—I don't know that my father ever spanked me. You know, sometimes we did dumb things like kids do, but . . ."

Catherine, sixty-eight, begins with a reference to her parents ("I feel very blessed that I had a great mother and dad. They had lots of problems. My dad died very young. But umm a really good mother and dad . . .") and then continues by elaborating on the effects her parents and other family members had on her lifelong development. She mentions her mother's working outside the home ("I felt deprived because of that"); her grandmother ("she had an incredible faith in God, and that she passed on to me"); her father's early death to cancer (at nineteen, she took care of him during his illness and was responsible for giving him morphine); herself in relationship to her siblings ("I was the smartest one of the bunch, and then I couldn't go to school because there wasn't enough money"); her relationship with her first husband, who died in his late-sixties ("It was really good. I don't mean perfect, but it was really good"); and her current life with her second husband ("very good in a lot of ways").

The structure of women's responses in terms of where they *begin* their life review varies widely. Some women, like those above, begin with early parental relationships; others focus on turning points that precipitated major changes in relationships and life status, such as marriage, divorce, death, and widowhood. Gilda, aged seventy-three, responds in a way that suggests her life essentially began with marriage:

Well, basically, my life has had a lot of ups and downs. . . . When we knew [Jerry] would be going into the Army, we decided we wanted to get married, and there again, we had another fight [with my mother]: "You promised you wouldn't get married until after the war!" And I said that I didn't want him to leave without being his wife. So, my mother finally consented and we were married. And then he left for the army, and I had a child with him being in the army. And I had to live with my mother because I had no place else to go. So, the whole thing revolved around that. And then he came home, he was sick for quite a while and couldn't go to work. But I had, when I knew he was coming home, I went out and bought a house because I did not want to live with my parents.

Mary, who is sixty-one, on the other hand structures her response around the beginning of the *end* of her marriage:

> Well, I could start with the turning point in my life. I'd been reading Betty Friedan's book, the first one back in 1963, *The Feminine Mystique.* Everything that happened in my life was the ground rule preparing for this book. In 1963, I was a twenty-nine-year-old housewife. I had a seven-year-old son and a little daughter and an alcoholic husband. Actually, the alcoholic diagnosis wasn't defined until a few years later. There wasn't a whole lot of information on alcoholic addiction then, but I knew there was something wrong that I couldn't fix. My life was a mess. Enter Betty Friedan writing about how unhappy, dissatisfied, frustrated, and discontented American housewives were. . . . This book literally took me away from my everyday life, and when I finished reading *The Feminine Mystique,* I knew what I had read. So that would have been '63, and this is '94. So it was over thirty years ago and at that time (it was difficult) to get a divorce from my husband and take care of my kids and make some sort of life for myself.

In reading through all the women's interviews, one gets the impression that their lives have been heavily "peopled"; the important aspects of their stories, in Mary Gergen's words, "depend heavily on their affiliative relationships with others. . . . Their stories highlight the interdependent nature of their involvements and the centrality of emotional well-being to all facets of life."[9] Even when older women tell achievement stories, they usually present them in terms of relationships. Professional writers of women's biographies have found that telling a woman's life never involves a straight success story of linear achievement through individual agency. Rather, women's lives, including professional women's, "are a tightly woven mesh of public and private events," integrating external accomplishments with social happenings, friendships, and family connections.[10]

Cultural scripts for writing the woman's life reinforce these connections. Biographer Linda Wagner-Martin explains that the general reader of women's biographies expects to see the subjects in "approved life roles" that affirm existing values; the biographer is therefore challenged to make the life of the ambitious professional woman "understandable rather than monstrous."[11] Wagner-Martin goes on to say that the difficulty for a professional woman writing her own autobiography is one of "skillfully maintaining a narrative interest, set against a complex of social injunctions about appropriate—and proper—women's lives," especially injunctions about what it means to be a good daughter, wife, and mother.[12]

Many of the women in my study have held jobs, and some have gone to college and established careers; yet none puts her work at the center of her life story. In fact, at least three of the white middle-class women in my study who graduated from college and developed professional careers (teacher, child psychoanalyst, pharmacist) focused exclusively on childhood, family relationships, and personal change in their life stories; they never wrote about their work. When women tell school and career stories, they frame them in terms of complex family relationships and concern for others' feelings, as in the following excerpts from my interviews with Catherine, sixty-eight, Helen, eighty-four, and Charlotte, eighty.

Catherine: We had five children, and I thought it was too many, but [chuckles], that's the way it worked, when you're using rhythm. And I finally decided that God didn't expect people that had five kids to keep on having kids, so I went on the pill for ten years. And right after I did that, when Kitty was about three years old, that was when I went back to school. And I just, I've always felt that was one of the most incredible things. I loved it. And it took me eleven years to get my degree because I just took one class at a time. And I went to night school for a long time because I didn't want to be in with the kids. But I liked it, and I was surprised that I liked it. And I was almost through when Tim had his heart attack and heart surgery and he had to retire. At fifty-four. So I finished my degree, and then I went to work. . . . So then I worked and worked on my master's degree, and I got that. And I was sixty-two. That was in pastoral ministry. It was religion in a sense but a lot of psychology. I had a minor in psychology. And that's been very helpful. It's given me a lot of insights that I might not have had. And, of course, Tim's death was just—[she sighs; there is a pause, then her voice gets very quiet]—But I did survive.

Later in the interview, when I ask her to "tell me about a time in your life when you experienced a great deal of satisfaction or happiness," Catherine describes her college graduation day, again in terms of relationship:

Well, the first thing that comes to my mind is walking across the stage at Saint Scholastica's, where Mercy College had their graduations. Walking across the stage and getting my bachelor's degree. Tremendous, wonderful, wonderful satisfaction in that. Ah [there is a pause]. Well, isn't it funny? That's the thing that stands out. I mean the marriage thing, that's a whole, that's a lifelong thing, a relationship and so on. But if you're talking about an event, that event probably stands out most in my mind. My kids were all there. My mother came. And my mom wasn't very happy about it. I never understood that. I have a picture of myself and her. I have my cap and gown on, and my mother's with me. She doesn't look happy in the picture, and she wasn't happy that day, and I don't know what it was about. It was after my stepfather died.

Catherine goes on to speculate about the nature of her mother's unhappiness, which she now sees in terms of her mother's having "earmarked" her as the family caregiver: "And I couldn't be . . . because Tim was my, the person I needed to take care of. . . . And I needed to work. . . . We didn't have that much money at that time, and had no idea what the future would bring. . . . My older sister ended up being [the caregiver], in a sense, not in her own home, in a nursing home, but I always think my mother felt closer to me maybe because I was there to take care of my dad. I'd never thought about that, you know? I shouldn't feel guilty about not taking care of my mother, should I?" In this story, the pride Catherine feels for her college graduation, a major accomplishment in her life, is complexly intertwined with feelings of loss and guilt related to her husband's heart attack and her mother's stroke.

Helen, a member of the metropolitan Detroit group, also tells the story of her education in terms of family relationships. Her initial response to my request for a life summary is short and succinct: "Well, I always think of it as going in three stages. The part where I was at home till I was twenty-one. And then I got married. Ran away from home—I eloped. And then I went to nursing school when I was forty-eight, and when I was forty-nine, Wally died. And so that's a different section, too. I had a lot of fun, although I would rather have Wally back. But I squandered my money on trips. And so now I'm living from check to check."

Helen has written in more detail about the period of her nursing education in an essay called "A Turning Point," which she submitted to a national contest for writers over sixty. The essay begins:

> One has many turning points in a lifetime, but the one most important to me was my husband encouraging me to enter the newly opened Shapiro School of Practical Nursing at Sinai Hospital. Sinai was a mile from our home in northwest Detroit. Wally, my husband, was sixteen years older than I. He was concerned how I would live if he were to die. A gypsy told his fortune when he was a young man of nineteen in the German army of World War I. Amongst other things, she said that when he was sixty-four years old, he would either be completely paralyzed or die. He was now sixty-three. Through the 27 years we were married, he told me repeatedly what I should do when he left me.
>
> I had never wanted to be a nurse. Nevertheless, I took Wally's advice and applied for enrollment in Shapiro's school. I was accepted to the third class beginning March 17, 1958. I was 48 years old. Three daughters had already left for marriage or careers in different states. Sixteen-year-old Susan would graduate from high school in June, 1959. I was very excited and eager to tackle this new challenge.

In the introduction to the essay, Helen lays out the parameters around her education: she pursued it only at the request of her husband, and she did so after her daughters were grown. After providing some details about nursing school in the essay, she describes her graduation and licensure:

> The night of graduation finally came. It was a cold March 17, 1959. Sinai Hospital had not built their auditorium yet, so we went to Marygrove College. My husband [was there], and two daughters were there with their husbands. My daughter Susan told me recently that she thought I looked years younger that night, as if it were my high school graduation. I started working at Sinai a week later. We were to take our state board examination in June. In August, I finally received my license with a high score. Wally was very happy and made a strange remark: "Now the last thing is done."

Helen completes the story by describing a short trip she and Wally took to New York after her graduation. On the first night, he suffered a stroke, was paralyzed briefly, and died the next afternoon in the hospital. He was sixty-four.

The one woman in my study whom I considered most likely to tell a story of autonomy and single-minded professionalism surprised me. She, too, tells her career story in terms of family connection. Charlotte, eighty, trained first as a nurse during World War II and then became a child psychologist. She has never married and has made her career the center of her life. Yet in the year she has been writing her life stories with the geriatric center group, she has focused exclusively on her early childhood in the English countryside, never mentioning her professional life, even though she had many career-related adventures, including living in Iran as nanny to a family in the oil business. In answer to my request for a short review of her life, Charlotte describes herself as "enormously lucky" to have "been in the right place at the right moment for interesting things" and to be able to pursue her various interests even now:

> *Ruth:* Tell me about how you see your life as being lucky, about those lucky breaks you referred to.
>
> *Charlotte:* Well, I survived two world wars. I was born in one and of course on active service in the second one [pause]. And I have been able to do a lot of the things I wanted to do careerwise. That should be enough.
>
> *Ruth:* What did you want to do careerwise?

With that question, Charlotte launches into an extended narrative about her pursuit of an education "without upsetting father":

> First of all, I wanted to teach. And my father disapproved. He said that he thought teachers were lazy because they had such long holidays. I think that

doesn't sound quite like my father's good common sense. I'm sure he was quite aware that they use their holidays for further study and that sort of thing, and that they well earn them. But his sister was a teacher. And so was his brother-in-law. And though he married my mother, who also was a teacher, there was also in the background that grandma, the headmistress, who was a difficult lady. So I can see where he had some ambivalence about teaching. I also think that he may have been a little envious of my aunt, his sister, because of her education.

She proceeds to tell about her father's lack of formal education (he left school at the age of twelve); that he continued his education on his own and became a head gardener and, later, crop superintendent for a large seaside town; that her mother helped him work out the crop estimates ("She was a whiz at math"); and that he became a weekly columnist for the *Gardener's Chronicle* ("And I mean he could write much better than I can").

Ruth: So what did you do then, when father said, 'Don't be a teacher'?

Charlotte: What I did first of all, actually, was stay home for the best part of a year. . . . To be a companion for my mother. When I first left school, daddy kept me at home with mother. I mean, she died when I was just over sixteen. And then I stayed on keeping house for him, battling with him because when the maid we had left, he thought he should get a really elderly woman to keep an eye on me. And I persuaded him that I needed someone much younger [she laughs]. And I eventually won that one. He did let me have a younger one. And then when he remarried, for eight years I was a nanny. Because— oh, yes, when I wanted to be a teacher, one of the things he said was, it was my job to get married and have grandchildren for him [she laughs again]. So I was a nanny for eight years, and I did that so I could travel abroad. And of course in England in those days if you were a nanny, you needed to do your college training for nanny. And that I did using a legacy I had from my grandmother, which just coincided. And not for schoolmistress, for the other.

As an employed nanny, Charlotte divided her time between Iran and England. Then World War II broke out, and the mother of her two charges, who had had a serious health problem, decided that "looking after her children herself would be her war work, because she wasn't yet strong enough to go into the Women's Voluntary Service or do something like that." This was a positive turn of events for Charlotte, because it "freed me to go and do my nursing training, which I'd always wanted to do, because after my mother died, I said I would never feel so helpless again." However, first she had to find a way to counter her father's resistance:

Daddy fought that, too. Said I wasn't strong enough. And, well, I should add that he won that rather easily. I got accepted for a provincial hospital. He wouldn't let me go to London [where the best schools were], but he did agree I could go to a provincial hospital. And I went to one in Kent that was near where I could go home when I got a day off once a week. But I went and caught diphtheria. That was the second time I'd got it. And they decided that I really needed a long convalescence and I shouldn't take nursing seriously till I'd got much stronger. So instead of going back into hospital, what I did was, I did my nursery nurse's training and looked after children. That meant I could go abroad. That way I got lots of freedom. I didn't have to go home every week [she laughs].

Here, Charlotte explains that she was mostly trying to avoid continued failure "at getting a good relationship" with her stepmother, who "had a terrible time with me" and whom she found "quite difficult." Charlotte continued to pursue the next levels of nurse's training: "Before I finished with the children, I had got accepted to the Prince of Wales Hospital at Plymouth to do my nursing training. Six weeks before I was due to go, guess what happened? The hospital got a direct hit on one of its wards. And they cancelled their intake of student nurses for that time."

This change in events left Charlotte with a dilemma: she was four weeks from call-up age for military service—not enough time to get accepted into another nursing school. Rather than being called up, she volunteered, because "I didn't want to go into the army, the women's army, I wanted to go into the naval nursing service." She knew something about the navy, having worked as nanny for a naval commander in Iran. But the recruiting officer insisted she must have a relative in the navy to volunteer, so "there was nothing for it but to go into air force," where she was "very firm" about getting into the medical division to serve as a nursing orderly.

From her position at sick quarters for the Seventy-fourth Division of the Royal Air Force, Charlotte seized an opportunity to care for the personnel officer, who had been stricken with a nasty bout of flu: "And I made sure that the old boy was really well looked after. I made sure he understood he could ring me any time he liked [she laughs] and then I got up in the night and made him hot tea and all sorts of things. When the officer left sick quarters feeling much better, he expressed his appreciation, saying, "I'm no further away from you than your phone. Anytime there's anything I can do. . . ." Charlotte took that opportunity to request transfer to a hospital, where she could learn more nursing from better-trained personnel. Two weeks later, she got the transfer.

Charlotte's saga of finding her way back to nursing school continues from the hospital at Eastham. After she had been there about six months, the sister of the ward, a member of the Princess Mary Air Force Nursing Service, singled her out:

> She came down the ward to me and said, "What on earth are you doing here, Corporal?" And I said, "Sister, I'm really just finishing the sterilizing, but if there's anything I can do—and she said, "Oh! Phooey to the sterilizing. I'm not talking about the sterilizing. So I said [Charlotte here speaks in a meek, quiet voice], "I don't think I understand." She said, "I want to know what you're doing wasting your time here." And I said, "Well, what is it I haven't done?" She said, "Are you quite dense this morning?" So then she said, "What I mean is why are you wasting your time as a nursing orderly when you should be doing your nursing training?" I said, "Because—" and I told her I had applied, the bomb had dropped on this hospital, I was call-up age and so this is what I did. So she said, "Well, but why don't you do your training now?" And I said, "I can't until I get out of the service. That's why I wanted to come to hospital, because I knew I would learn more when I was working with you people who are trained." She said, "You can get out all right, if you want to." I said, "How?" She said, "If I arrange it for you, will you go?" I said, "Yes!" She said, "I'll talk to Matron tonight." Next thing I heard, the commander, the medical director of our hospital, wanted to see me.

Charlotte met with the review board and got a transfer to the Prince of Wales Training Hospital. She concludes the long story of getting to nursing school by returning to the overriding theme of her father's resistance: "But my father! You can imagine. Here was I, released from the air force to serve a civilian service of greater priority need, going to London . . . when he'd not wanted me to go in peace time. So I did my four years of training. And actually was silver medalist of my year."

Charlotte was twenty-seven at the time of her graduation. She went on for more training in psychological nursing, which led to her subsequent career as a child analyst. An interesting point about Charlotte's career stories are that they are densely populated with family members (primarily her father and step-mother) and others who helped shape her professional life. The persona she adopts in telling these stories is reminiscent of Charlotte Brontë's fictional governess in *Jane Eyre:* she combines girlish innocence and daughterly obedience with dogged determination and a quiet rebelliousness.[13] The emphasis in these stories is on Charlotte's interpersonal conflicts and connections more than her achievements in the physical world, which are quietly mentioned, but never promoted.

The men in my study typically follow the masculine scripts provided by Western culture. There are people in their stories, but "they are relegated to insignificant subplots"; in the conventional "manstory," "emotional ties are mentioned as 'facts,' where necessary, but the author does not try to recreate in the reader emphatic emotional responses," as women writers are likely to do.[14] Excerpts from my interviews with two men from the group at the geriatric center and one from the Jewish center clearly reveal these gender differences.

Robert, sixty-two, is the youngest member in the group, as well as one of the newest members, having joined the same month I began observing. His response to my request for a brief review of his life is structured around a chronology of facts and events, with his father playing an advisory role but not directing his choices: "I was born in Kalamazoo, and I was an only child. And had a good childhood. Went to a good school. Graduated from high school. At that point, I didn't really know what I wanted to do, you know? And my dad suggested, 'It'd be better for you to go to college no matter what you do, even if you don't know.' But I didn't do very well in college at that time."

Having acknowledged his lack of motivation for school, Robert focuses instead on various jobs he held at the time, and what he gained from them:

I had some interesting jobs. I sold tomatoes first. And I got a regular buyer at a supermarket who would take all the tomatoes that I could supply. And twice a day we'd pack 'em up and take 'em down there real early in the morning before school or whatever. . . . We lived in the country at that time. . . . We raised the tomatoes, so I learned all about that. The interesting thing I learned was that the—I had to take the tomatoes back that got squeezed. If there were any where the stem punctured a hole and the tomato wouldn't sell, then I got those back, too. So through that I learned how to pack them better. . . . So that was interesting.

After the tomato business, Robert worked at F. W. Woolworth ("we had dime stores back then"), where he mentions he learned other new skills, as well as something about himself:

I worked in the stock room. And that was a lot of work. On a Saturday, it'd be real busy, work real hard all day. I learned quite a bit about merchandising and getting along with people and one thing and another. And just before I went in the navy, two of us were having a little fun. There was this big bottle of . . . Irresistible, that's the brand name of a perfume. And it was a demo thing to have upstairs, but it was down in the stock room. Big gigantic thing. I was chasing this other guy just for the fun of it, you know, squirting this perfume, which he didn't like. But then he started chasing me with powder. He had a big book or something [he claps his hands], so it could pouf out these big clouds. We were laughing and carrying on and having a great time, and there's all this powder in the air. I said, "All we need now is for Daddy-o to show up." Daddy-o was our pet name for the manager of the store. And just then, he walked right around the corner deliberately, like he'd been standing there for a while. So in a meeting behind closed doors, he suggested that maybe I would learn something if I went into the service.

Robert then briefly describes his time in the navy (a period he has written about in some depth) and mentions a good friend who joined with him and ultimately lived near Robert and his wife in their home port of Norfolk, Virginia. His relationship with both his wife and the friend are cast in terms of the naval narrative and are presented as asides. Neither person is named: "It was somebody I met at college just before I went in the navy. And so when I was twenty-one, I came home and got married, and then my wife graduated from Western [Western Michigan University] early, like in three and a half years or something, and she came and taught school in Norfolk. And then he [the friend] was married and his wife moved down there, too."

Speaking of his college days, Robert emphasizes his success at Western Michigan University: "So I went to school then, when I got out of the navy. I went back to Western and had the bad grades to make up from before. And I wanted to go to engineering school, so I worked. I had already developed good study habits in the navy, and then I became an honor student there, at Western. Which was a lot of fun. And then I just always excelled, was always one of the better students in class."

When Robert transferred to the University of Michigan, however, he did not do so well ("I was lost in a sea of valedictorians"). Rather than internalizing this failure, however, he tells the story of that time with an emphasis on external events: "I'd never had a brother or sister to learn how to compete, although I was on the tennis team in high school and I got a varsity letter there" and "they always had a curve, and, you know, they had to chop somebody off at the bottom." He also mentions a difficult family situation that influenced his school work, but not in terms of others' expectations of him, as "womanstories" are likely to do, but matter-of-factly: "And then we had a lot of family problems going on as well. And uh [pause]—my first in-laws, who I loved very much, they got sick, and we helped them, made a lot of trips over to Grand Rapids, et cetera, et cetera, et cetera. But then they finally both died. And so I was having trouble in school by this time. So I never got my degree, although I did qualify for a pretty good job at the university." Robert does not dwell on the fact that he dropped out of college before graduating, but turns the narrative into a job-success story. The "good job" in pharmacology provided nearly twenty years of full-time employment and led to his current position.

Phil's life stories are even more focused on accomplishment and self-promotion than Robert's. Phil, seventy-five, is in the same writing group as Robert and has been working on his life stories for nearly five years. In response to my request for a brief review of his life, Phil begins this way:

Well, I am quite—what do I want to say—I don't want to use the word *proud*—I think well of myself. Okay. And that was bred in me as a child, I guess, because I'm a Hamilton. So that's it. In fact, I think so well of myself that it's almost egotistical. And have been told so [he laughs]. . . . But I guess, you know, looking back I guess I am. Around in the community, not so much now anymore, but when I was working, and I noticed that I was nearly always called Mr. Hamilton, rather than Phil, by acquaintances. It was always Mr. Hamilton. So I must have appeared egotistical or upper crust or something to other people in the community. So. And well, just recently I was told by someone who said when she first met me, I was the most stand-offish person she'd seen [he laughs]. Until she got to know me [he laughs again] and saw a different Phil entirely.

In the above segment, Phil is constructing a narrative self that acknowledges what others think but does not let it affect him. He later says he thinks his self-pride is a good trait, as well as an inescapable family legacy ("Most of us Hamiltons have the same thing, the same sort of feeling about ourselves").

Phil then relates his sense of self to his career in the air force—a period that he has chronicled extensively in his writings: "I, you know, went into the air force early and was a pilot. A fighter pilot. And now when I look back and think about it and write about it and so on, I wasn't a particularly good pilot, but you couldn't have told me that then [laughing]. I was one of the best. I was right up there." When I ask him about a time in his life when he experienced a good deal of happiness and satisfaction, Phil names the "military time" because "it was structured. I studied. Written rules, regulations, and that sort of stuff. I knew what I could do, and I knew what I couldn't do."

Most interesting in terms of gender issues is the way Phil enters into the story of leaving the air force unexpectedly: "Security is one thing that I said after I left the air force that I was no longer looking for. But now that I'm retired, my house is all paid for, the land's all paid for, I have a good sense of security. I know the community, I know the people around, and so there again, it's more or less structured. I know what I can do, what I can't do, and that's it." In the succeeding segment from our interview, I probe for a description of his feelings about leaving the military:

Ruth: When you left the air force and said you were no longer looking for security, what at that time did you feel you were looking for?

Phil: A living, I guess. I don't know. But I know, see, I was in sixteen years, and then I didn't get promoted to major, so I had to be promoted or get out, and so I had to get out. And before that, I thought that I'd just stay right in the air force until I retire and that was it. And I got quite confident in my superior officer there. And that kind of blasted it. So I decided well, from now on, I'm just gonna look for a good job and not look for security in the job.

Ruth: How did that feel at that time when you weren't promoted?

Phil: Oh. Hmm. It felt very bad.

Ruth: Mmmhmm. Hmm. It must have been a sort of rejection.

Phil: Yeah, it was, because you see, I wasn't a bad officer. I was a good officer. And I was surprised. Everyone else was surprised. And I went to Washington, D.C. and tried to get a review of it, and that year the air force absolutely refused to review any of their promotion procedures or anything. So—although I was told by a fellow captain at the promotion center there that—when I went and asked him, he went out for about forty-five minutes and left me, and then he came back and said, "All I can tell you is do all that you can do to get your case reviewed." That's all he would say. But I can't tell you anymore than that.

Ruth: How frustrating!

Phil: Isn't that awful? Isn't that frustrating? And then couldn't get it reviewed. You know, it was frustrating. So, I feel certain in my self that there was some goof-up during the promotion procedure. Either my name was left off and because it was—because I didn't get promoted, I had to leave. . . . Some procedural thing happened. But I couldn't get it reviewed.

Phil describes his departure from the air force, then, in terms of external situations over which he had no control, rather than in terms of relationships with his superiors: an unknown entity "goofed-up" and left his name off the promotion list, and an anonymous group of officers refused to review procedures that year.

George's interview, on the other hand, is less oriented toward the conventional masculine script and focused more on economic and sociohistorical events. George, seventy-seven, is Jewish and a member of the Jewish senior center group. He structures his response to my request for a brief review of his life in terms of economic hardship:

Well, I went through the depression. I was young during the depression. That was rough. And I guess I had a lot of company. We had nothing. I used to go to school with holes in my shoes. I used to have cardboard in my shoe to cover up the hole. And I had no problem on deciding what to wear to school the next day. You only had one set of clothes. My mother washed my clothes and I'd have them ready for school the next morning. I never went hungry. There were times when I didn't know if I'd have a roof over my head the next day, but I never experienced hunger, for which I am thankful.

George describes his early accomplishments in terms of surviving difficulties through a combination of luck and intelligence, with chance playing a starring role:

> After the depression, things were, well things were really rough. But I wrote civil service exams for the Canadian government, and I guess I was lucky. I passed with very high marks. I got called to Ottawa. And I got a job in the treasury department. I borrowed the money to get there. I didn't have a penny to my name. One aunt left me fifty dollars. Another aunt gave me a present of twenty dollars. And I had to live off—I went there with about seventy dollars in my pocket, and I had to live there for a whole month. Of course, the cost of living was a lot cheaper then. I didn't know a soul in town. I got out of the train station. I looked left. I looked right. I didn't know which way to go. Well, I decided to go left. I ended up living right. . . . I went through the phone book. I wanted to live with people of my own ethnic group, because they would be more able to take care of my needs. So I got a phone book, and I just opened it up, and the first Jewish-sounding name I saw, I called up. I hit it right. A young fellow answered. I told him I had just arrived in town, I didn't know anybody, I was looking for a place to stay and was there anything he could do for me? He said, "Yes, where are you at?" I told him my bags were at the railroad station. He said, "I'll meet you at the railroad station," and it was within walking distance from where I was. He met me at the station, and he took me over to some woman that he knew rented rooms, room and board. It was only a block from his place. And I was there my whole stay in town.

Much of George's subsequent talk constructs the story of a poor kid who makes it to the middle class through hard work. After various jobs as a book-keeper and factory worker, he settled into his job as a meatcutter, from which he retired after thirty years. There are very few people in his narrative who are fully developed characters in terms of names or dialogue. They appear, like the anonymous Jewish man on the telephone, as shadow figures who play a secondary role in the economic or ethnic narrative of his life: family members in Canada whom he supports with his salary from the treasury department; a woman in Ottawa with whom he was "very close" but didn't marry because she was Roman Catholic and he was Jewish ("And at that time, it was taboo to marry between the religions, so I never gave it a thought"); and his wife, to whom he has been married for nearly fifty years. There are two themes running through George's interview: the necessity of supporting himself and others ("But finances, I mean, they shaped my life") and his ethnic identity and the sensitivity it has instilled in him to discrimination of any kind ("I've got a feeling for people, and I hate war, suffering, and I hate discrimination. I hate it terribly").

Linguists analyzing the conversations of ordinary people, composition researchers studying the writing of college students, and literary critics interpreting the autobiographies of published writers, have all found the same gender differences I have described above.[15] In her study of personal experience stories told orally by sixty-eight white Midwesterners, for example, Barbara Johnstone found that men and women have different things to say in their stories and use different discourse strategies. Women's stories take place in the social world and use more personal names; describe background events that involve speech ("we were just talking and visiting"); directly report their own and others' speech more fully; and sometimes express frustration if they are unable to reconstruct a dialogue ("and I said—I wish I could remember what I said"). Men's stories take place in the physical world; provide more details about objects, times, places, and events; and more often refer to people in terms of their roles (a neighbor, a boss) rather than their unique identities. While women employ story plots that reinforce the importance of social interdependence (events happen, and other people help you deal with them), men more often act independently in their stories and employ plots that present fate as being in their own hands (success or failure is a result of one's individual efforts and activities).

Johnstone concludes that these gendered scripts not only *describe* familiar roles for men and women, but also *create* them: "Stories that create familiar roles for men and women reaffirm social bonds between tellers and their audiences, but at the same time, people use stories to socialize one another. As they are reminded what the world *is* like, interlocutors are also reminded of what the world should be like for men and for women. . . . [O]ne of the many reasons a person's talk sounds the way it does is because individuals undergo processes of socialization and enculturation related to language use and gender identity."[16]

Scripts for Race and Ethnicity

The cultural scripts for people of color differ yet again, since ideologies of race, class, and nationality "intersect and confound those of gender."[17] Critics of African-American and diasporan literatures have named the themes of marginality and "otherness" that often structure these life stories and the social consciousness informing them. Indeed, some critics define race and ethnicity as "social construction[s] predicated upon the recognition of difference and signifying the simultaneous distinguishing and positioning of groups vis a vis one another."[18] A significant feature of minority elders' life stories is that race is emphasized over age, gender, and other author-positions.

The few women in my study who identify themselves in terms of ethnicity generally tell relationship stories but orient them around the family's economic status or larger social issues. In response to my life-review question, for example,

Lorraine, seventy, who is Jewish, and Eileen, also seventy, who is Polish, respond in terms of the Great Depression. Both are members of the same metropolitan Detroit group.

Lorraine: I was born in 1925, so the depression was right around the corner, not too many years after that. My childhood was like everybody else's at that time. No one that I knew had anything, really. We were all rather poor. That condition remained with my family 'til the war years. My father was a builder. And he lost everything that he owned during the depression, and then he had to work his way up again. And when the GIs came home—he had already started doing better—and then when the GIs came home, he built a group of 105 what they called GI houses in those days. And that got him on the road to a good recovery financially. . . . So by that time we started doing better. Let's see, the war ended in '45, so in the later 40s that's when things perked up. I was married in 1950. And I had a child in '52 and a child in '54. And we lived in Detroit until we moved into this house, which was about thirty years ago. . . . And we raised and educated our children. I went back to school—I had a bachelor of arts in English literature, which wasn't a very sellable skill in those days. . . . I went back to school when my kids were, maybe two and four or three and five, something like that, and got my teacher's certificate, and it was a long process.

Lorraine goes on to explain how she managed school, childcare, and riding the bus to the university, since she did not drive at the time. She accepted her first teaching job at the age of forty and stayed at the same school until she retired. She notes that "our children married and had children of their own, and we're very doting grandparents. We enjoy that a lot. And really, that's the main thread." She concludes by describing her children and grandchildren: "I think we have two wonderful children. They're both very well educated. . . . We have three female grandchildren. And that's about all. Nothing special."

Eileen, too, offers a narrative oriented around work and family:

Eileen: Fortunately, I haven't had very many hardships. Umm, growing up during the depression, I didn't feel the depression, 'cause my Dad worked all the time. And we didn't have much, but I didn't expect much. I didn't know I didn't have much. I was happy with what I had.

Ruth: What kind of work did he do again?

Eileen: He was a worker, a factory worker. He worked in the wood shop at General Motors. He made things out of wood. So he was very, very good at that. Made cabinets at home and did things for other people. And always came home with little projects that they made at work . . . I had five children. Did not have easy pregnancies, but we don't remember those things after a while. And fortunately, five healthy, normal children. And a supportive husband. Good father, provider. . . . And I had to work hard for my school tuition. I held two jobs most of the time to pay for my tuition. I've always wanted to be a teacher from the day I was little and that's what I became. I had the support of my parents and my sisters. That's it, I guess. And here I am, above ground and kicking.

Agnes, seventy-five, who is Armenian, tells her life story largely in terms of her parents' story (particularly her father's) and her people's story (of either death by or escape from the Turks). She spends the first half of our interview describing the Turkish massacre in Armenia during World War I and its effect on her father. Throughout our interview, she refers back to her family heritage, evidence that she sees her life in a context much larger than her own endeavors:

Ruth: You've talked a lot about your father's life. What has your life been like up to this point?

Agnes: Well, I went to school. I learned most of whatever I can learn. I was slow in learning because of the transportation of going back and forth [from Armenia to America]. I lost three years of my schooling. I was almost eighteen when I did graduate. . . . I wanted to be a cosmetologist, but I didn't like the idea of putting make-up on myself, 'cause I [had] soft, nice, red cheeks and everything at the time. And my dad was against it. My dad was against my hair being cut. Never heard the end of that! But I went to Sunday school when I was in New York, and Norman Vincent Peale was my inspiration for religion. Later on, I found out that I had a background of religion. My father told me I had an aunt that was into religion. And from there, I have my cousin. He's in Boston, Massachusetts. He is a minister now. So there is a religion background in me some way or another.

Like Agnes's story of the Armenian people, the African-American autobiography also leans toward social documentation. The history of the narrator's people and national ideals are as important as (or even more important than) a personal history. As such, the life story inevitably involves either tacit or explicit critique of limiting social conditions, and the narrative self expresses an opposition to, rather than adoption of, those conditions.[19] Feminist critic Elizabeth Fox-Genovese claims that "autobiographies of black women, each of which is necessarily personal and unique, constitute a running commentary on the collective experience of black women in the United States. . . . Their common denominator, which establishes their integrity as a subgenre [of both African-American autobiography and women's autobiography], derives not from the general categories of race or sex, but from the historical experience of being black and female in a specific society at a specific moment and over succeeding generations." [20] This is equally true in the life stories of older African-American writers. In her review of published autobiographies that consider the influences of age, literary critic Barbara Frey Waxman concludes that "in this country, age can only rarely be foregrounded over race as a marginalizing, predominant subject-position." Most often, "writers of color either de-emphasize age or approach aging obliquely as they underscore race." [21] The narrative position of the black woman is thus both public and private, representing a collective social experience while describing an individual one.

The black woman's narrative position exists in tension with the cultural scripts of white bourgeois women as described by Smith and Jelinek. As one example, "much of the autobiographical writing of black women eschews the confessional mode—the examinations of personal motives, the searchings of the soul— that white autobiographers so frequently adopt. Black women's autobiographies seem torn between exhibitionism and secrecy, between self-display and self-concealment," [22] in part because the expected audience—at least for published narratives—has been largely white throughout history.

To the extent that published black autobiographers wrote for other black women, they seem to have written about those who came *before*, for the benefit of those who will come *after*: "Black women's autobiographies abound with evidence of or references to the love that black female autobiographers felt for and felt from their female elders: mothers, aunts, grandmothers. For the most part, those female elders are represented as rural in identification and origin, if not always in current location; immersed in folk communities; deeply religious; and the privileged custodians of the values and, especially, of the highest standards of their people." [23] These scripts for representing mothers reflect the unique concepts of motherhood found in black communities. Several sociologists have identified how very different black and white communities are in their concepts of motherhood. Patricia Hill-Collins explains that Western culture's "cult of true womanhood," which names motherhood as woman's highest calling and assigns the "ideal" woman exclusively to the domestic sphere, is essentially a Eurocentric ideology of *white* motherhood. The beliefs implicit in his ideology—that mothering occurs exclusively within the confines of a nuclear family, that men and women inhabit separate spheres of influence, and that motherhood is linked to economic dependence on men—are not at all characteristic of African-American families. [24]

An Afrocentric ideology of motherhood extends the boundaries of family to include kinfolk and "othermothers" who share responsibility with natural mothers for childrearing; it also integrates women' roles as economic providers into their mothering relationships. Black women have a "more generalized ethic of care" by which they "feel accountable to all the black community's children." [25]

Black women's power and community status come, in large part, from their role as bloodmothers and their contributions as othermothers to community development. In her study of an urban black community, anthropologist Carol Stack concludes that the extended kin network and shared "child keeping" of African-American women is a highly adaptive response to poverty and the contingencies of living in a segregated world.[26] As a result of being reared in extended families, black children are exposed to a range of role models for motherhood, a situation in direct contrast to the isolation of white middle-class mother/daughter relationships.[27] These lived experiences inform older black women's life stories and help explain why they tend to represent their mothers as symbols of strength and survival for both family and community, while white women are more likely to express criticism of, or at least ambivalence toward, their mothers.

Another aspect of the black community that is important to our interpretation of life stories is the role of religion and church. The black church has historically played a major role in the black community, meeting political, educational, physical, and social needs, as well as spiritual ones. Sociologist Sharon Milligan describes the black church as a source of self-help activities and community advancement, as well as "an outlet for creativity and meaningful social positions in a society with increasing social inequities."[28] The cultural and political importance of the black church, coupled with the fact that with advancing age older adults may turn increasingly to religion and spirituality,[29] suggests that religion would figure prominently in African-American life stories. This indeed is the case for all but one of the black women in my study. Most of the African-American life stories mention God, religion, church, belief in an Almighty or holy spirit, and/or prayer as a means of coping and rising above adversity.[30]

In general, then, we would expect the life stories of black and white women to reflect different histories and allegiances. In her introduction to *Skin Deep: Black Women and White Women Write about Race,* Marita Golden explains these differences in a sociopolitical context: "Women are keepers of a community's faith, guardians of its deepest beliefs and lies, harbingers of its most vivid fears in a way that men can never be, in a way that men have traditionally *designated* women to be. And so white women of necessity have been complicit in racism, both institutional and private. Black women have been agitators and warriors against the system white women swore to uphold as passionately as white men."[31] Thus, the struggles to negotiate a speaking position within the life story are different for black and white women. Black feminist critic bell hooks claims that for black women writers "our struggle has not been to emerge from silence into speech but to change the nature and direction of our speech, to make a speech that compels listeners, one that is heard."[32]

If black writers, men or women, choose to write their life stories within white bourgeois scripts, they may appropriate an authorial stance that speaks to a broader audience, but they may simultaneously compromise their racial identity and alienate black readers, censoring themselves from "talking black." In assuming the narrative position of the white writer, they may feel the social imperative to circumscribe both language and self-image—to distort and "make faces"[33] or to speak "with double tongue," like "the trickster of Afro-American folk culture."[34] In her analysis of older black professional women's narratives, for instance, Gwendolyn Etter-Lewis found many examples of what she calls "suppressed discourse" or censored speech. Narrators would modify the impact of statements, omit specific information, negate, hedge, and qualify. Etter-Lewis interprets these features as evidence of social inequities in black women's lives made manifest in their speech.[35] Other feminists posit that such double-voicedness may function as a "defensive-subversive survival tactic."[36] In summary, the life stories of African Americans represent the many tensions of negotiating both race and gender identities.

My study includes interviews with only two middle-class African-American women, both members of the same Detroit metropolitan group, but their stories reveal these tensions. The life review of Cecille, sixty-four, is framed in terms of difficult family relationships and hard economic times:

Cecille: Well, it's been good and bad. We had a rocky childhood with my parents, from the time I can remember. My mother and father didn't really get along. In fact, everybody in my house was afraid of my father, 'cause you never knew where he was going to be temperwise. It wasn't that he drank or anything, it was just that—I remember my mother calling him a liar once, and he slapped her. So, they were back and forth when I was a kid, and by the time I was ten, my mother left my father. . . . But then it was the depression and it was very difficult for her. See, my mother had not worked, not at any consistent job while we were small. So then you had to go through that, of her not being in the home and various people taking care of us and just, well, we never had much to start out with, but then things were really bad.

The undertone of this story, which is made more explicit later in the interview, is the difficulty blacks have had finding and keeping good jobs in a white-dominated society. At one point, Cecille notes that her career choices were severely limited as a black woman. Even though she showed aptitude in marketing and design and had an artistic flair, she chose to pursue nursing. In the following excerpt, she talks about school counselors' advice, based on her tests of aptitude and interests:

They said to me, "Whatever you do, don't go into nursing." But the kinds of things they were suggesting to me, like buyer in a department store, in the early-6os and late-5os, nobody—that wasn't feasible. I mean, they didn't even have black saleswomen in the big department stores then. And they talked about interior design. Well [she sighs], you know [then she chuckles]. I had to see whether I could make a living, my thing was to make a living at whatever I did. And that might have been short-sighted, because somewhere in the late-60s, early-70s, these things opened up, probably because everybody was trying to have a token black person in these positions. But I had to be concerned with making a living. So I made the choices I made.

Selma, sixty-nine, tells an even more explicit story of race relations. In response to my request for a life summary, she starts in the present and moves backward, first telling me a detailed story about a trip she recently took with "two white girls I used to work with." The point of the story is to illustrate Selma's efforts to "cross the gulf that exists" between blacks and whites whenever possible. The story includes an incident of unconscious racism on the part of their host at a bed-and-breakfast in northern Michigan:

When we got there, there were two rooms. We knew in advance. This woman had three bedrooms all together, but one was already rented to a honeymoon couple who had been there before, and they wanted the same room. The other two rooms, one had a double bed, the other one had twin beds. Now, it's interesting, as we walked in, of course this woman [the host] had no idea that I was black or anything. But, as we walked in, she assumed that I was going to be in the double bedroom, which has just one bed, and the other two girls would be in the twin-bed. Well, on the way there, Michelle had said to me, "The last time you had the separate bedroom, do you mind this time if I take the separate bedroom, and you share the twin with Nancy?" So I said, "That's fine with me." . . . So now when we walk in, this woman immediately starts addressing me to this room with the one bed it in. I didn't say anything, I listened to her talk and everything. Then she told them about their bedroom. I wondered if they noticed it, but as soon as she was out of sight, they said, "Well, now, did you notice that, Selma? She just assumed that you were gonna be in that separate room." I said, "I know." They said, "We just wondered if you noticed that." I said, "I wondered if you noticed it." You know, we had a big laugh over it. But anyway, when it was all over . . . we really enjoyed ourselves and she was hospitable and lovely in every way. And I went out of my way to compliment her on everything. . . . Now, I singled her out to focus on her, to let her know that I'm a decent person, and you've met a positive black person—all these things were in the back of my mind, but even if that incident about the bedroom hadn't happened, I still would have done those things to her because I appreciate her effort and whatnot and everything that she'd done. . . . So before it was over, we hugged and so forth. So I try with every encounter I make, when possible, to cross that gulf that exists.

Most everything Selma writes reflects the experience of blacks trying to negotiate the white world. She casts her family's history in terms of the larger history of the black race living and working in white America. One of her essays directly articulates her sense that family history is part of black history and that the two inform one another. In one meeting of the writing group, she reads a life story she has written based on notes she took from a conversation she overheard between her cousin Fonza, who was about eighty, and her mother, who was close to one hundred. She tells the group, "This cousin and my mom . . . the two of them would talk about old times, and I would just be sitting there. And I'd get my scrap paper out, and I'd just copy what they were saying. . . . I started asking some questions, and I wrote this story." She begins the story with reference to the passing of her older sister: "Since my sister Viola's death, it seems to me my mind reflects more on the family tree than on my own life. Today I want to tell the story my cousin Alphonso told me." She proceeds with the story of the great Lake Okeechobee flood in 1928 Florida, told from the perspective of Fonza. He and several other Bahamian men had been at work "cutting sugar cane for a white man to clear the land for a sugar mill" before the rains came. They had finished the job earlier but were told to "come back in two weeks" for their pay. Fonza and his friend had to hitch a ride from Miami back to Belle Glade and then "sat on a stump all day waiting for this man to return and bring their earned money." The white man never showed up, and they were caught in the rains. They went to an uncle's migrant shack in a Lake Okeechobee area called Chosen, looking for shelter, food, and companionship as they decided what to do next.

> Uncle Earnest was cooking a pot of beans and corn, and he invited us to eat. On the other side of the shack, which was like a duplex, were several other young men drinking and playing cards. And we could hear everything because the walls were thin. The rain grew heavier and heavier. Uncle Earnest said, "This rain reminds me of a hurricane." By this time night had fallen. We decided to step outside and go next door to join the other fellas in the card game. As we stepped outside our door, the whole house collapsed, and we were swept away with the fast current. We did not know that Lake Okeechobee was overflowing. There was no electricity or radio to warn us. Later, I'm told, some Seminole Indians who lived in the area had come through warning the people, but I don't know that this was so. The water was knee-deep. My friend and I held hands and tried to walk or swim our way to some high ground. There was total darkness, logs and debris everywhere. After a

long time, the water getting deeper and swifter, my friend asked, "Are your legs cramping?" I said, "No," and he let go of my hand and slipped away with the current and debris. At that moment, a bright light seemed to shine out of nowhere onto a nearby tree that had overturned. I swam with the tide and reached it through the nighttime darkness. I survived that night sharing the tree with many snakes escaping the high water. My friend drowned, along with eleven various cousins and friends who were workers in the area. In all, thousands of people, white and black, lost their lives. Uncle Earnest was found alive several days later, more than a mile into the woods.

After reading this story aloud, Selma tells the group that last year she visited Lake Okeechobee for the first time. She discovered that the Chosen area is about ninety miles from Miami and that "in those days . . . it used to take almost twenty-four hours to get there because they didn't really have paved roads, and the cars were in poor condition." She saw the sugar mill and visited a museum that describes life in the area before and after the flood: "They had a scale model of the city and the lake and who owned which farm and all, the store and so forth. They have a list of names of those who died. When I inquired of my eleven relatives, they were only included in the 'hundreds of Negro workers' who drowned. They only had the whites listed by name. No one really knew the blacks' names there, then or now. Only those of us who loved them."

The visit was a moving experience for Selma, having grown up hearing the story of the eleven relatives and friends who drowned. She informs the group that family members who spoke of the event "just told the story, and they went right onto something else. They didn't dwell on anything." Selma's retelling in the context of her own life story—and in the context of a writing group that is mostly white—is a way for her to send a message that speaks to issues much larger than the recording of a family history. Selma sees her own life story as a vehicle for teaching about—and learning to overcome—limiting race relations in the United States.

Scripts for Class

As the scenarios I described at the beginning of this chapter suggest, scripts for race and gender overlap and intersect in complicated ways with scripts for socioeconomic class. Political economists are only beginning to study the effects of social stratification among older adults. We do know that all older women are at economic risk (they make up 63 percent of the elderly poor), but black women are especially vulnerable because of their rates of widowhood, as well as limited opportunities for jobs throughout the life course. Black and working-class women in the labor force "earn less money on which retirement benefits are calculated and are also more likely to retire for health reasons than white women and women of higher social classes."[37] These economic situations obviously influence the structure of women's life stories, a fact suggested by Amanda Barusch's interview study of sixty-two low-income women, most of whom were in their seventies. Barusch found that poverty was not a central aspect of these women's self-concept, despite objective criteria to the contrary (many lived below the poverty level, and several were homelessness). Rather, women living in poverty compared themselves to others less fortunate and constructed relatively *positive* life stories, reflecting their resistance to the labels "old" and "poor" and their strategies for maintaining a positive self-image. More than two-thirds referred to themselves as "lucky" and "blessed," especially in comparison with peers in their immediate environment who were less fortunate. Barusch concludes that these self-interpretations are highly adaptive; they are, in fact, "stunning examples of the resiliency that is an essential component of successful aging under adverse circumstances."[38]

The cultural scripts available for telling about oneself in terms of economic status, as well as the material conditions of living in poverty, clearly affect women's life stories. Certain ways of telling are more likely to be used by low-income and working-class narrators than middle-class narrators. Sociolinguist Charlotte Linde found in her analysis of job narratives that working-class speakers are more likely to explain their circumstances in terms of fate or destiny. She posits one reason for this difference from the perspective of middle-class values: "Maintaining the proper balance of causality seems particularly important as an issue for middle-class speakers, who have had some degree of opportunity for professional or class movement and for whom, therefore, fate or determinism on one hand and randomness on the other represent undesirable ways to understand one's professional position, since either would detract from the individual's personal achievement."[39] In fact, middle-class speakers, particularly those born after World War II, generally *assume* that professional choices are dictated by personal abilities and psychological health rather than differentiation in social status. Working-class speakers, on the other hand, commonly represent themselves as subject to external limits imposed by social class, race, and ethnicity.

The initial reference point for all the working-class black women in my study is socioeconomic, as is evident in my interviews with women from the urban Detroit centers. Ella, seventy, is an example:

Ella: My life has been . . . how could I put it? Like the weather, would be more of the description of it. Because it kept changing so many different ways. Because when I was a little child growing up, I knew I had it rough. And I always wanted to do the things that I had seen other people do. Like I saw people on the highways going down—because we were so near the highway—and saw people going down the highway in these nice-looking cars. I have always wanted to do that. I have always wanted fine clothes like I have seen other people wearing. I wanted to go to school. I wanted to graduate from school. I wanted to be a nurse. Some of these things came true. But some of 'em didn't, because after I growed up, I left home, which my mother sent me away from home because my sister here was sick, and she wanted somebody to come and stay with her. And I was the one that had to come. . . . And I left home, and a couple of years after that I got married. And I was married for quite a while before we got the car. But I did get the car. I did get nice clothes. I did have plenty in my house to eat at all times. And that part of everything worked out for me.

The following narrative, told by an eighty-year-old African-American woman at the West Side Center, focuses on the socioeconomic limitations black women faced when looking for work in 1940s Detroit:

During the war, I was working for this boarding house, and I was looking for something better, because I didn't want to do the housework. And there was an ad in the paper. They just began to hire blacks. It was always all whites. And so I called. And at that time, they only wanted light girls to work there, because they were going from the whites to the blacks. And of course the white girls, they were going to the factories, you know? They were hiring them. And so I got the job. She asked me what color I was. I told her about the color of Cab Calloway. Cab Calloway—he's a hidee-hidee-ho [she chuckles]. So [more chuckles]. So I got the job. I went down and applied and got the job. And I worked there. . . . In fact, I guess they didn't even mind to put ads in the paper that said, "Must be white." And this was when people my color got the chance to get certain jobs even in the hotels, was when the factories opened up and all the white people went to the factories, because they were better-paying jobs. Then they had to depend on my color to take these [waitressing and housekeeping] jobs. Because I remember the housekeeper telling us when I quit there that she had so many good white girls that worked there, and they just quit, and now we [blacks] got a chance to get these jobs and talk about we should be proud to have them. But when I got ready to quit, and I told her, she asked me if I would reconsider, because I know I'd done a good job. I always done a good job at whatever I started.

More often than not, a lifetime of work and hardship is made easier through spiritual guidance, as in the stories of Florence, seventy-five, Annie, seventy-seven, and Letta, sixty, from the East Side Center:

Florence: Well, I've had a good life. I've accomplished quite a bit through the help of the Lord. I worked all my life. I never made a lot of money, but I've always had a job. So I'm thankful for that. I'm on my—let's see one, two, three, four—I'm on my fourth house now. So I was able to always—I never wanted my children to be raised up in a house where they had to move, and so I always tried to buy a home. That was my first priority in life. I rode a bus and all that, I never thought about buying a car, but I always wanted a home to raise my children up in. . . . And so my children have always had a home and clothing and everything. They didn't know about the depression and everything. I said sometimes it makes 'em lazy now because they never knew hard times.

Annie: Really and truly, since I've had to work for myself all my life I've always tried to save or whatever. As my mother would always say, "A rainy day's coming. Don't ever get rid of everything. You've got to never let nobody know everything you've got." Otherwise, I mean, I did start getting disability because I got down in my back. And . . . I just took care of myself, and I didn't ever bother my husband about taking care of me. I always do the best I can. I'd always tried to make the best of everything I had. . . . And along the way, I can say I've been well blessed, too. I've been well blessed. So I get enjoyment really out of going to church and singing in the choir. Things like that. I still haven't had to beg nobody. I'm doing pretty good. . . . Taking care of myself, and still haven't had to go to a nursing home or whatever. . . . I always say, things may not come where you want 'em, but it always on time. And with my Social Security and my pension, why I do pretty good. I do pretty good. And so, I'm still trying to hold up and keep on moving.

Letta: How can I explain it? At first, I thought it was pretty difficult being a single parent, raising six children by myself. . . . It was difficult at first, and I thought I couldn't do it. But the Lord blessed. And there was a time when I thought I was doing it all myself. I thought well, I can do it and I'm doing it myself, but I didn't realize that God was helping me all the time, 'cause without him, we can't do nothing. So, when was it?—January 24, 1982, the Lord came into my life and right away I got saved, sanctified, and filled with the Holy Ghost, and it made me understand a lot of things that I didn't understand as my kids were small. But I reflected back to see how God was moving in my life. And I had comfort then in knowing that he was helping me out, that there was nothing impossible for me to do as long as I relied on him. And even when I didn't, he loved me enough to see me through the difficult times. So, I don't know if that answers your question or not, but that's the way I feel about it.

These women's writings and group talk reflect the all-encompassing influences of socioeconomic status, especially in relationship to the black experience, and the uses of religion and spirituality to cope with the exigencies of daily life.

Final Observations

The purpose of this chapter has been to illustrate the various cultural influences on the ways older people tell their life stories, and, in the process, to demonstrate the social construction of the self. Studies in autobiographical criticism indicate that the stories I have excerpted here are more generally representative of life stories told by most American men and women. My conclusion that gender differences hold across the life course in terms of life-story telling raises interesting issues for developmental psychologists. If, as psychologist David Gutmann has argued, a "cross-over" occurs in later life between the genders, why is this not apparent in the structuring of older men's and women's life stories? Gutmann posits that, after the "parental imperative" of midlife passes, men become more nurturing and internal, while women become more assertive and external in their orientation; a sort of reversal in masculine and feminine roles occurs, which Gutman posits as both normal and necessary to continued development for both genders.[40] If this is indeed the case, we would expect life-story patterns to reflect these shifts in emphasis, yet this has not happened. Obviously, changes in cultural scripts lag far behind those that take place in individual lives. We need to learn much more about the ways that race, class, and ethnicity interact with age and gender in constructing life stories, as well as the connections between individual change, social change, and narrative scripting.

We know that standard scripts represent conventional values and beliefs and tend to reify race, class, and gender differences. But we also know that these scripts exert varied effects on the storyteller: the paternal script empowers, while the maternal script silences certain aspects of identity (personal ambition, for example) and valorizes others (nurturance and self-sacrifice). If a male writer chooses to assume the textual position of the female self, he risks the loss of power and authority associated with the male script. Similarly, if a woman writer chooses the textual position of a male speaker, she appropriates the authority that comes with his position but mutes that part of her that articulates and affirms her difference as woman. On the other hand, if a woman writes from the maternal position, she risks not being read or taken seriously beyond the private sphere of family and friends, since the general public (along with most literary critics) still expects the assertiveness and self-promotion of the paternal script. Published women's autobiographies reflect the tensions that arise from trying to negotiate these two positions simultaneously.[41] Along these same lines, religious and survival stories can inspire and empower the narrators who tell them, as well as those to whom the stories are directed—usually friends and family members who are well-acquainted with hard times. The implicit lesson is always one of hope and sustenance: I survived, and you can too.

The very least that should happen in writing groups is a raising of consciousness through which older writers become aware of the patterns underlying their stories and learn to use them more deliberately to empower themselves and others. This kind of narrative awareness seems a basic prerequisite for the "spiritual eldering" that Rabbi Schacter-Shalomi and Ronald Miller describe in their call for increased generativity among older adults.[42] Minority elders are generally aware of the potential force of story—especially the survival story. White middle-class elders, particularly women, are more likely to dismiss the significance of their life story with a shrug: "I lived an average life. There's nothing special about me."

But the life story always has value in the telling. One drizzly November day during the course of this study, I went to speak at a senior health fair on "Women's Journals." The fair was held at a small church in a poverty-worn neighborhood on Detroit's north side. There I met a woman who works in the Detroit public schools. She told me about an eleven-year-old girl who got pregnant three times last year. Her father is missing from the home, and her mother is emotionally absent. The girl speaks regularly of suicide and told the woman, "I've got no one to love me. At least a baby would love me." The woman began to cry. "Don't worry," said the girl. "I can take it." "But *I can't*," said the older woman. Since then, the woman has been trying to think of some way to intervene. She believes that sharing life stories might be the way. Elders, especially those who have come through hard times, could provide the kind of hope that troubled youth need, just by showing up and talking about why they have *wanted* to live, all these years, and how they have been able to do it.

Ella

THIS EXCERPT from Ella's life story is based on an interview at the East Side Senior Center in Detroit.

Many people know that I was not raised, as the old people used to say, "on the flower beds of ease." That mean you didn't raise up easy. You came up in a hard way. And it's something that you should never forget. That's the way I feel about it. I have talked to my daughter Vicki about the hard life, and she said, "Well how did you all make it?" By the grace of God. Really and truly that is how we made it, by the grace of God.

I am going to write more about my childhood and how things were, like how we had to pick blackberries to make supper, because we had no food in the house. We had flour. But like rice and grits and meat and vegetables and stuff like that, we didn't have at the time. So we'd go out and pick blackberries and take those berries and stew them down and eat them for dinner or supper. Or we would go fishing. Catch fish and go back home and cook the fish for your dinner, so you could have something to eat. Until the weekend come, Friday, you'd get paid. And Saturday you'd go to the market and buy your groceries. Things like that is what I want to leave for her, so if she should happen to get into something like that, she can sit back and say, "Well, that's the way my mother was raised. And I'm no different. If she could make it the hard way, then I can too." That's why I want to do it.

Nowadays, life is better, because I have learned not to wish for things that I see other people have. And I have learned to know that those are things you're going to leave here on this earth. You're not taking any of those with you. And I have turned closer to God now than what I had been before. Thanks to one of the men that met me up here at the senior center. Because—I don't know—my mind just wasn't functioning right. It was just like, "Hey, your husband is gone. Your daughter is grown. Now what are you going to do? You have nothing to do. You have nothing relevant to you in no kind of way. So, just forget it." And I was in the hospital, out of the hospital, in the hospital every year for two weeks, until I met him. And we started talking. And he just looked at me one day and said, "There's something on your mind, and you should get it off." I said, "How? There's no one to talk to." He said, "I'm here. And I will be here for you. If you feel like talking, you call me." I turned and asked him, I said, "Will you really be there for me?" He said, "Don't you bother about that, you just call on me." And I started calling him. And he started calling me. And he called and asked me could he come over to the house, and I started letting him come to my house. And we sat down and talked. And he really helped me a whole lot because he made me talk about myself, and things that was bothering me. Now I feel free of it. I don't go in the hospital now like I used to. I think since I met him I've been in the hospital twice, and that was just overnight. They had me on observation. They kept me overnight and the next day they said, "Go home. You can do anything you want to do. You're all right." And that's just the way that I have been going, ever since.

Here lately, I've been feeling more like myself all the time. And one of the reasons is because I have gotten closer to God than what I had been. And with being closer to him, I'm more at ease now. My mind isn't wandering away like it used to do. My mind used to be just like the ocean, rolling away. But now, it's not like that. This came about because of the light that I saw. Me and my daughter both was in the living room, and we just saw the light as it came down in the yard. And I thought it was a helicopter. But when we went to the door, there was no helicopter. There was no police car. There was nothin' but just that light. It just brightened, kept brightening itself, and it just brightened up and then it went back up. Just like that, it was gone. I felt then that God was trying to tell me something. My daughter turned and said to me, "What was that?" I said, "It was just a angel, God just sent a angel down to protect us, that's all." I felt more satisfied than I had felt before, and it has stayed with me.

And that's not the only time that I've saw a light. Another time I was sick. The doctors had me in bed. My daughter was in high school at the time. And the lady that used to take her to school sometimes along with her daughter—we used to go to this lady's house, and she would have a prayer meeting. One day, she just sent word by Vicki and asked me did I mind if she come to my house and prayed with me. Not *for* me, but *with* me. And I told Vicki to tell her to come on. And she came to the house that next day. She came in my bedroom and she stood by the side of my bed and she told me, "Now I'm not going to pray *for* you." She said, "I'm going to pray *with* you." She caught my hand, and we prayed *together*. And after the prayer was over, she told me goodbye and left.

That next day around twelve in the day, I was laying there in the bed, and I just said, "Oh, Lord," I say, "When are you going to let me get up out of this bed? Because I'm tired of it." Like that. And all of a sudden, a light just came right from the corner of my bedroom. It came straight across my bed and come down—did you hear that sound when I hit myself just then? Well, that's just the way it sounded, right in my chest. And my bed just started going like this, shakin'. And I said, "Oh, Lord," I said, "What in the world is happening to me?" And the bed stopped. I got up, put my clothes on, washed my face and hands in the bathroom, and I went in the kitchen and started cooking dinner. My daughter came in from school and she heard me in the kitchen, and she dropped her books on the table and come running to the kitchen. She says, "Mama, you're not supposed to be in here." I said, "Well, I am not supposed to be nowhere else, baby, but here in the kitchen."

I called that lady after she got off of work that evening. She said, "Don't tell me, I know." I said, "You know what?" She said, "I know when the light came down on you, 'cause I was sitting at my desk. It was about twelve, or a little after, and I saw it." I said, "Lord, have mercy!" A couple of days after that, I went to the store. My neighbor said, "You're not supposed to be carrying them packages." I said, "Who else supposed to be carrying them but me?" I said, "I'm okay, I'm fine."

And that is when I started turning myself around and going back to God. But I didn't go fully. Because I was still saying in my mind—I would never say it to nobody else but I would just say it to myself—"I wish I could meet somebody that I could take up time with. I wish I could meet a man that could come around, maybe even get married again." And I had just about give up going to church, because I didn't like the Catholic church. I didn't like the spiritualist churches. The Baptist church was too far from me, which I didn't like them either. The Methodist church, I would have had to catch two different buses to go to that church. And I said, "Well, I'm not gonna get out there on that street by myself to go catch no bus like that. Somebody liable to rob me or hit me in the head or something." I thought, "I'll just stay home," and we wouldn't go.

Well, one Sunday morning, I got up, put my clothes on. I said, "I am going to church somewhere today." I got out on my front porch and I looked down at the Catholic church, which was down there by me, and I said "No, I'm not going there." I turned and went the opposite way. And when I got down at the corner of the street that I live on, I stopped. Because I was waiting for the cars to go by so I could cross the street. I was gonna go in the church across the street. And a voice came to me and said, "Keep walking." I looked back behind me, and I said, "Wait a minute!" But I walked on down the street. I didn't see nobody. I said, "Now, that's just somebody behind them bushes out there on the street, so I'm gonna keep on walking." I got down to the next corner and there was a church down on that corner. The voice said again, "Keep walking." And I said, "Well now, I'm going to see whoever this is behind me." I said, "I'm going to see them, they just got to kill me out here, because I'm going to see who it is." I turned around on the street and I looked all around and there was nobody. And it talked to me three times, it told me to keep walking. And then I got down to the corner, and there was a sign up on the church down there which had been a Baptist church. But they had moved out of it. And I said, "Oh, well, here's a

Baptist church here." And when I got down there, the voice stopped. It didn't say nothing more to me. So I turned the corner, I went on into church. But when I got in there, it wasn't a Baptist church. It was a Lutheran. And I went on into church and after the services were over, people began to come to me. The minister came up and shook hands with me and welcomed me to the church and all. And they invited me to come back. And I have been going to that church ever since. I became a member of that church.

I do believe there is life after death. I do believe that. But I say, with death, I've always said, "So shall you live, so shall you die." And that is the way that I have lived. If you live a good life, you will die a good death. And you will return. To me, a good death is when you don't have to suffer. You just slip away. And when people can see your spirit—well, I call it your spirit, I guess it is your spirit—they can see you in different places, that's a good death.

I have seen people myself, like when my brother-in-law died. He had belonged to the Masons. And they had a—oh, what do you call it—a motorcycle club. And he went down to Cobo Hall one Sunday for this program. He rode his motorcycle downtown that Sunday to watch the rest of them and got in an accident. When they got him to Receiving Hospital he was dead. He died just instantly. And I have seen him since then. As a matter of fact, I saw his death, before he had died, I saw him. And his wife did, too. But we didn't know when it was going to be. Because she was telling me about a figure that she saw, a man that she saw at the head of her couch. And it walked away and went right towards her bedroom. And then I was telling her about the one that I saw came in through my front door and stopped right in the dining room and went into the kitchen. And she said, "I wonder, what is that?" And I told her, I said, "Somebody is leaving us, and it's not going to be long before they go." It wasn't but two weeks after that when he died. So that's why I tell you there is life after death. I do believe.

My feeling is, whenever God get ready for me, he'll just take me on. But I'm hoping and trusting in him that he don't let me suffer. Make me go to bed and not wake up when he gets ready to take me home. The oldest age that I can imagine myself would be about eighty. I might not reach that age, and then I might go past that age. But that's about the oldest that I can see myself.

My plan for the future is just to keep living my life the way I am now. To keep on trying to live a good life, trying to live a Christian life, and trying not to hurt nobody. And try to help my daughter all I can with the things that she wants to do. That's all the plans that I have.

FOUR   Memory and Truth

O VERHEARD AT A senior center:

"Did you hear the one about the hereafter? An old guy goes down to his basement and says, 'What am I here after?'"

That joke got a big laugh at the senior center. Most people experience memory loss in later life, and it helps to be able to see the funny side of it. In this chapter I discuss memory from a social constructionist standpoint and examine the various ways memory comes up as a topic of conversation around life-story telling. Any exploration of memory necessarily raises questions of "truth" (what is it and how we recognize it) and the relative value of factual verification. I have found that, in the process of writing and sharing life stories with their peers, most older writers come to see moral or narrative truth as more important than factual or historical truth. This shift in perspective is significant developmentally because it extends the range of possible interpretations for one's life; with this extension comes increased potential for personal change and growth.

Social Theories of Memory

Conventional wisdom holds that memories are a private stash of fixed truths, stored in the brain and easily retrieved when the memory is working properly. Current social-constructionist research calls this treasure-chest metaphor into question, suggesting that memory is naturally (indeed, necessarily) less fixed and far more communal than we have previously thought. The autobiographical memory (remembrances of personally experienced events that are relevant to one's sense of self and life history) is best seen as a process that "originates from social interaction and serves to initiate and sustain social bonding"; an event is valuable and memorable, then, primarily because of the feelings of social connection it generates.[1] Our memories are better seen as processes of becoming, rather than permanent states of being. We are continuously deciding, evaluating, assessing, recalling, repressing, creating, and altering the stimuli of daily life. The memory is a hub of social transactions, always situated in a rhetorical context, involving particular speakers and listeners. In the words of social psychologist Kenneth Gergen, "what can be said about one's past and how it can be made intelligible are fashioned by the rhetorical conventions of the time.

'Personal memories' are not thus distinctly personal. Instead, they exist in a state of intertextuality, borrowing and bending and replying to the cultural conventions of writing about the personal past."[2] Even the *meaning* of a personal memory is determined by its social functions—the way it helps us fit in with others, maintain a sense of self distinct from other selves, sustain family ties, and create new relationships.

What does this constructionist concept of memory mean in terms of how we tell and write life stories? Most importantly, it means that other people greatly affect what we remember and that memories are structured in conjunction with narrative conventions for the *telling* of them. In short, we remember what others teach us to remember, and we report on these memories using the scripts that family and culture provide for us. Psychologists have found, for example, that children's personal narratives told after the age of two (when children have an awareness of the mental state of remembering) are strongly influenced by cues that parents give for organizing "memory talk." Through questioning, clarifying, correcting, and providing examples in their own life-story telling, parents model for children the kinds of memories that are "reportable" and convey the extent to which talking about memories is valued. Some studies suggest that young children whose parents regularly assist in reactivating their memories by expressing interest and eliciting talk are more likely to have longer and more detailed autobiographical memories than children whose parents do not engage in memory talk. Parents who regularly ask their children to "tell me about your day" and who express genuine interest in hearing a child's elaborate accounts, may in fact be extending their children's autobiographical memories. This activity is not merely a technical one of "exercising" the memory, but, more significantly, a process of social and emotional development. Children learn that personal experiences and their feelings about them *matter* and that telling memories is a valued part of relationship building.

Parents also help construct the form by which their children's memories are reported. Psychologists D. Edwards and D. Middleton have determined that one way children learn to tell about family events is by going through family photographs. Parents prod their children to give descriptions and narratives and then correct, supplement, or affirm their accounts.[3] In effect, through talk and questioning, parents are tutoring their children in "what this event means" and "how we talk about our family history." The research of psychologist Robin Fivush further confirms this familial aspect of memory. In her study of parent-child interactions, she finds that mothers prompt different memory reports from their sons and daughters, eliciting more facts and details from boys and more elaborate emotional content from girls.[4] Early memory conversations between parents and children contribute to the emergence of a child's self-concept ("I am the smart one in the family" or "I was always shy, even as a baby"). Memories that are congruent with a child's developing self-concept are likely to become part of the autobiographical memory, while those that are unrelated are more likely to be altered or forgotten, at least until the self-concept changes. In summarizing social constructionist studies of memory, Kenneth Gergen concludes that the past is "molded from conversations" and that remembering our former selves and our family histories "is not so much a matter of consulting mental images as it is engaging in a sanctioned form of telling."[5]

Of course, adult memories are social constructions as well. Across the life course we are continually influenced by memory cues from friends, family, co-workers, and associates who elicit particular memories and expect to hear them told in particular ways. A cultural commonplace is the request from grandchildren to "tell me what it was like when you were little." If not specifically prodded as such, the adult memory apparently has a preference for later time periods. Contrary to popular opinion, older adults (approximately seventy years old) do not live in the past any more than middle-aged adults; in fact, nearly 30 percent of their reported memories are from the relatively recent past. Even more interesting is the pattern of reported memories from the distant past. Several studies, summarized by cognitive psychologist Joseph Fitzgerald, have determined the existence of a "reminiscence bump" in the trajectory of the adult memory, with a majority of memories clustered around the ages of fifteen to twenty-five and more than half of an older adult's vivid memories occurring before the age of thirty. In tests of younger adults ranging in age from thirty-one to forty-six, psychologists have found the same peak of memories. Fitzgerald hypothesizes that adults find the events during this period particularly memorable because they center on self-definition and identity formation; during this time period, most people establish organizing themes that provide a framework for interpreting later life experiences.[6] Memories from these formative years may also be elicited and rehearsed more often in everyday conversation and are therefore more readily accessed in tests of memory.

Another factor influencing older-adult memory and life-story telling is the degree to which narrators assimilate or accommodate to memories that do not fit their self-concept. Psychologists Susan Whitbourne and Charles Powers propose that, in order to maintain a positive sense of identity, people telling their life stories either deny events that are inconsistent with their sense of self (assimilation), or they report the events, particularly those with high negative content, and perhaps change the self-concept as a result of them (accommodation).[7] Whitbourne and Powers suggest that these cognitive processes are associated with personality traits, but they are also associated with particular age cohorts. In my observations of older adults in writing groups, I have found that assimilation through denial is the preferred strategy for most writers, but that some gradually alter this approach over time when they see their peers using accommodation strategies.

"Truth" in the Life Story

If we accept that memories are in large part social constructions created through conversation and narrative convention, we must also problematize the nature of "truth." In our interpretations of life stories, we need to consider both historical truth and narrative truth. As defined by psychologist Donald Spence, historical truth involves concrete objects and events; a memory is historically true if it can be factually verified. Narrative truth involves the connections *between* events, which are not verifiable because they are based on values, interpretations, and emotions. A memory has narrative truth when it captures an experience to the satisfaction of those telling and listening to it. Narrators who focus on historical truth see themselves as "archivists," guarding original records and trying to keep them pristine, while those who focus on narrative truth are "mythmakers," creating a story "that speaks to the heart as well as the mind" and "seeks to know the truth and generate conviction about the self." [8]

The Personal Narratives Group, a collaborative network of scholars and critics in women's studies, makes a similar distinction in their discussion of truth in women's autobiographical writing and oral history. Members of the group have found that "when talking about their lives, people sometimes forget a lot, exaggerate, become confused, and get things wrong. Yet they *are* revealing truths. These truths don't reveal the past 'as it actually was,' aspiring to a standard of objectivity. They give us instead the truths of our experiences." [9] These are the truths of personal history, perception, and interpretation that carry emotional weight and social meaning. Another way to distinguish between historical and narrative truth is to consider the difference between recollection (a striving for historical truth) and what anthropologist Barbara Myerhoff calls "re-membering" (the pursuit of narrative truth). Re-membering entails a re-thinking of our past in order to create a "tidy edited tale" through which "completeness is sacrificed for moral and aesthetic purposes. Here history may approach art and ritual." [10]

Originally, Spence proposed the narrative/historical truth distinction as an argument against the conventional belief that psychoanalysis is a kind of archeological dig into a client's memory to "restore" to consciousness what has been repressed or forgotten. That belief rests on the assumption that a memory has a single meaning and that historical accuracy is possible in fitting memories together to establish clear causal relationships. In this view, it is theoretically possible for a person to say unequivocally "how things were" in the past and to report them objectively in the present. Challenging this conception of memory, Spence asserts that life is essentially a chaotic flux of events that have no meaning in and of themselves; rather, meaning is *assigned* retrospectively to events in the process of fitting them together into a *story* of life, made clear and coherent for the telling. Those who listen to this story have a hand in its formation by ascribing meanings to what is being said. The meaning of a memory, then, is far more complex than a simple resurrection of events.

Spence's primary contribution to our understanding of life story is his emphasis on the importance of language and interpretation to memory making. While Freud believed that language could accurately map our thoughts and mental images, Spence acknowledges the limitations of language and the fact that much of what is seen in the mind, including an early memory or a dream, cannot be adequately captured in words. In the very act of telling about them, we distort our mental images, filling in the missing parts with words and making a memory seem more, or less, significant, depending on our purpose for telling about it. Again, a memory is not so much recovered intact as created through language in the process of social interaction.

The interesting thing about "languaging" a memory is that the verbal form takes on a life of its own and eventually supplants the visual imagery. A memory becomes "true" simply because it was stated, a procedure that Spence describes this way: a narrator interprets a visual image in the form of words and tells a memory to herself or someone else; once stated, the verbal interpretation becomes partially true; as it is repeated and elaborated upon, the interpretation becomes familiar; with familiarity comes plausibility, and the interpretation becomes completely true.[11] The narrator gradually becomes convinced of the veracity of her own memory through the repeated telling of it. Professional writers are intuitively familiar with this process. In describing the process of writing her autobiography *An American Childhood*, Annie Dillard explains the dominating influence of language on memory: "Memory is insubstantial. Things keep replacing it. . . . If you describe a dream, you'll notice that at the end of the verbal description you've lost the dream but gained a verbal description."[12]

Narrative psychologists who study the interactions of social context and memory argue that it is virtually impossible to preserve historical truth in telling life stories. This is because, in addition to the language factor, there are at least four different selves vying for attention in the autobiographical memory: *the historical self* that participated in an actual event; the *perceived self* that experienced the event in a particular way; the *remembering self* that later recalls the event for a particular reason; and the *remembered self* that is constructed at the time of recall.[13] Even when a narrator strives for accuracy, a memory may not be historically correct because of the perceptual differences among the autobiographical selves, all of which are subject to the influence of implanted memories (suggested experiences that are accepted as "real"); false memories (those that are verifiably wrong but *seem* right to the narrator); and blended memories (multiple events combined into the memory of a single event). Given these influences, Ulric Neisser concludes that "autobiographical memory is best taken with a grain of salt. The self that is remembered today is not the historical self of yesterday, but only a reconstructed version. A different version—a new remembered self—may be reconstructed tomorrow." [14]

The influence of the remembering self on life-story telling is profound, for it speaks from its present perspective on behalf of its current moods and interests. In the words of Anthony Paul Kerby in *Narrative and the Self*, "[T]he meaning of the past is not something fixed and final but is something continually refigured and updated in the present." [15] A good example of "updating" a memory as a result of articulating it through narrative was provided by Emily, eighty, in our interview. Emily tells me she began to think about a childhood experience differently after reading a life story aloud to her writing group:

> I was telling the story of when I broke my leg. I dashed out of the house, and I dashed across the driveway and . . . [fell down]. But I knew that thrust and that dash must have come from something. I must have quarreled with my mother, because that would frequently happen, and I've always thought that something of the sort, something propelled me out of the house. But after I read it, I said, "You know, maybe I was to go for a walk with my mother, my father, his two sisters—my two aunts—but for some reason my mother wasn't coming. Maybe the whole thing was that she was jealous of my father's attention to his sisters, maybe it wasn't about me at all, but I would have caught her in a negative mood." And I said, "That's the way I think now, and I'm writing about how I was then." So Madeline [the group facilitator, another eighty-year-old, as we saw in an earlier chapter] says, "It helps to put in perspectives now," so she encouraged me to put that in, which I did. And now I'm trying to deliver more of that.

In the process of writing and telling a life story, Emily comes to see it differently. She decides that it is all right—maybe even preferable—to allow her older remembering self to offer new explanations for an event that the historical self, the perceived self, and the remembered self never had. Perhaps most importantly, in shifting the cause of the accident from a conflict between her mother and herself to a conflict between her mother and her aunts, Emily resolves longtime feelings of discord between her mother and herself. The new explanation serves as a kind of emotional repairing.

The influence of the remembering self on memory construction may also explain why so many older adults' life stories have religious or spiritual overtones. Of the thirty older writers I interviewed at length, all but four made direct reference to God, religion, or spirituality in our discussions, either as a consistent theme throughout the life or as a theme emerging in later years. Although life stories told at any age are in some sense morality tales (informed by beliefs about what a person *should* be and do), religious or spiritual narratives—especially those told in secular settings—are more likely to be generated by older adults.

Support for this generalization is provided by gerontological studies that suggest that belief in God or some other universal force becomes more prominent as we age.[16] One Gallup poll determined that nine out of every ten older Americans say religion is important in their lives, and nearly three-fourths say that it is *very* important.[17] Ethnic and minority elders, in particular, indicate high involvement in religion.[18] Clinical psychologists often describe this turn toward spirituality in later life as a means of coping with the unknowns of aging, death, and dying, while life-span developmental psychologists tend to see it as evidence of further growth toward personal integrity in the final stage of life.

It is also the case that narrators may not even strive for historical accuracy in recalling the past. Some people vary their accounts more freely from one context to another, bias their stories in self-serving ways, and consciously create different versions of the same event. An incident I observed involving a former member of a writing group and his brother neatly illustrates these variances within a family. During a dinner party, Les, seventy-eight, was telling boyhood stories about himself and Paul, eighty-three, who sat next to him. Les and Paul were the only people at the table who had actually experienced the events being recounted. Except for Les's wife, everyone present was much younger and therefore unable and unlikely to call into question the veracity of Les's accounts.

One of Les's stories began something like this: "Paul wasn't spoiled, not him! He was stuck out there on the farm with grandma and his own pony" (group laughter). "He worked at the golf course as a ranger and rode that pony up and down, scouting for undesirables and kicking them off the course. I used to visit him over there once in a while, and we'd chase balls and sell them back to the golfers. We made quite a bit of money that way." Les's story presents Paul as the favored son in the family and the two of them together as enterprising youths who engage in an essentially harmless and profitable, albeit unethical, activity that is justifiable, given the economic constraints of the depression.

In a private conversation later, Paul told me that he has heard his brother tell the story about the golf course many times and in many ways, and "it's always wrong." Paul informed me that, in the first place, he no longer had the pony by the time he was working at the golf course, and even if he had, he would not have ridden it on the turf. "I loved that course, and I would never have done anything to damage it," he said. "And they wouldn't have *let* me, anyway." In the second place, Paul never sold balls back to the golfers; "As ranger, it was my job to see that kids stayed off the course so that *wouldn't happen*, and I took my job very seriously." So why didn't you correct Les? I asked. Paul's response addressed myriad family relations and long-standing feelings. The two brothers had the same father but different mothers, and Paul admits to a prejudice against Les's mother that he is still cautious about transferring to Les. Then there is Les's storytelling style; he's well-known for his "gift of gab" and would probably continue to tell the story however he wanted to anyway, even if Paul challenged it. In the end, Paul prefers to keep the family peace; maintaining conviviality during a social occasion is more important to him than policing the truth. Besides, says Paul, "There's no harm in it. It's a loose-change version of the truth." It is not clear to Paul whether Les knowingly alters historical fact in the service of a story, or whether he actually believes that the version he told at the dinner party is historically accurate. Whatever the case, Paul sticks to his version of the truth but keeps it to himself.

A Preference for Narrative Truths

There are life-story tellers, too, who deliberately create fictions, actively seeking narrative truths *instead of* historical truths. An example of this kind of storyteller is Samuel, a member of the Jewish senior center group. Samuel, now ninety-two, began writing in his eighties as a member of another group at a Jewish community center. Everything he writes is a fictionalized version of the "truth." Samuel takes events from his life, changes names and places, adds little details to flesh out the plot, and calls it "short story fiction." There are many elements in these stories, however, that are consistent with Samuel's self-presentation when speaking with others face-to-face: they display a wry sense of humor and an inquiring and skeptical narrator, and they offer information and a moral lesson. Through his "fiction," Samuel writes about a wide array of topics, including childhood days of poverty in New York City; time spent in an orphanage and foster care; various activities—some of them illegal—engaged in during his years as a seaman; and romance and sexuality among senior citizens. He has submitted some of these stories for publication to a local newspaper for senior citizens and has acquired a reputation around the senior center for being a "good writer." During one of the group meetings, Samuel reads a story he wrote five years ago, which he prefaces by saying, "It's fiction, but it's based on a true story which still haunts me." This is Samuel's story, summarized:

A widowed mother can no longer care for her nine children, and three are sent to an orphan asylum somewhere in New York City. But there's no room for them there, so they are "farmed out" to a "professional foster parent" who requires that all the children, but especially the older boy, work very hard. The foster mother has taken the children solely for profit, not out of compassion. She treats her own children much better than the foster children: her own eat first, and if there is any left, the orphans eat. If there is no food left, the orphans are given bread and tea, "with the scent of pot roast lingering in the air." One time, the older boy and the foster mother's girl are in the garden together. The girl sneezes, and the boy yawns simultaneously, an occurrence the foster mother uses to point out how "industrious" the girl is and how "lazy" the boy is. This declaration "cuts into the boy like a knife," for he has been doing all the garden work. Finally, a day comes when the boy reaches the breaking point. The cat on the farm has had kittens, and the foster mother tells the boy to take them to the woods and leave them. He recoils from this "evil deed," protesting, "But *you* killed them last time by flushing them down the toilet! Why make *me* do it?" The woman persists. The boy pleads with the neighbors to take the kittens. They decline, saying the kittens are too young to survive without their mother. This makes the boy even more angry. Still, his fear is stronger, and he obeys the foster mother by taking the kittens to the woods. He starts to leave them but is stricken by their mewing. He finally kills them so they will not suffer. This deed "haunts him all is life," but he does get revenge. When the investigators come from the orphanage, the boy disobeys the foster mother and tells them the truth, including the fact that he sleeps on a fold-out cot in the pantry. At the end of the story, the three children are taken back to the orphanage.

The group is moved by the reading, and Rose asks if it is a *true* story. "Yes, it's based on truth," Samuel says. "I was twelve at the time." Three weeks later in a group session, we do some impromptu writing on the topic of a "vivid memory," and Samuel again writes the story of the kittens. He repeats the same events, but this time assumes a nonfictional stance toward the narrative. He adds the date (1916), writes in the first person, and provides more detail. He describes the foster mother as a "mercenary, exploitive woman who abused me and my brother and sister by demeaning us verbally and physically," and reveals the method of killing: "I tried to walk away. They cried so pitifully that I went back and angrily stomped them to death." Albert concludes the reading by telling the group, "This is the memory that revisits me and leaves me very disturbed. . . . This sticks in my mind of me killing those kittens in the woods, stays with me forever. It's an albatross around my neck." Telling this story multiple times is therapeutic for Samuel, and fictionalizing it allows him to deal verbally with memories that are profoundly disturbing to his self-concept. We could say that Samuel is engaging in a creative and sophisticated form of assimilation.

Strangely enough, fictionalizing our life stories may be one of the best ways to get at the narrative truth about ourselves, a point made by novelist Phillip Roth, who ironically constructs his autobiography, *The Facts*, as a book of fiction with a self-reflective narrator who questions the very possibility of knowing and telling the truth about himself. In a more clinical vein, psychologists Michael Ross and Roger Buehler hypothesize that writing about ourselves in the third person induces a degree of detachment, putting us in a better position to analyze and understand disturbing episodes from our past. Ultimately, a distanced stance helps us to separate from our emotions in order to put negative incidents behind us.[19]

Samuel is often hard to pin down in terms of the historical facts of his life, even in person. In my interview with him after the writing group is over, he spends a lot of time talking about the stories he has written and brought with him, rather than the actual events of his life. Writing and publishing these stories has been a major accomplishment for Samuel, who immigrated to the United States as a boy who spoke only Yiddish and left school at fifteen. Samuel has come to create a new identity for himself around the stories he has written. He even tells stories about his stories—how he came to write them and the kind of public reception they have had. Samuel's response to my interview questions in terms of his autobiographical *writing* is another example of how language comes to supplant lived experience, and narrative truth takes precedence over historical truth in the telling of a life.[20] Indeed, through writing fiction, Samuel has dramatically increased the range of autobiographical topics he is willing to discuss and has broadened his strategies for making sense of life in ways that also please and inform his peers.

It is likely that a preference for narrative truth over historical truth is an aspect of our culture and class. There are more examples of what I call "historical fact talk" among white middle-class writers in my study than among working-class writers in the urban groups. There are several possible explanations for this difference, one of which is the suspicion with which ethnic and minority cultures often view the historical "documentation" of white, mainstream society. In her essay on "Genealogy as Autobiographical Pedigree," Julia Watson, a scholar of women's studies, reminds us that the pursuit of genealogy itself is a class-based activity that assumes a traceable (white middle-class) past. As such, it erases lives that do not leave conventional tracks in the form of birth certificates, marriage licenses, and deeds, including the lives of various ethnic groups and immigrants, the poor, mentally ill, and homeless.[21] Because authoritative documents erase many forms of cultural difference, and because historical truth is elusive, minority narrators may be more likely to value narrative truths.

This preference is poignantly illustrated by novelist Connie May Fowler in a *New York Times* essay in which she describes the experience of tracing her family history. Fowler explains that, in her original search for knowledge about her grandmother, she consulted official records in government archives. But her grandmother did not have a birth certificate because the government did not keep detailed records on American Indians. When she found her grandmother's death certificate, she discovered that it was incomplete and a "lie" as well: her grandmother, a Cherokee, was listed as "white." This "historical fact" had been supplied by the woman's son, for reasons unknown. Through the search for her own past, Fowler came to distinguish between "European facts" and "Indian facts." She finally decided that "when the official chronicles are composed of dashes and distortions and you still hunger for the truth," the best thing to do is to return to oral history. Fowler concludes with an elegant call for narrative truth: "[T]he greatest measure of truth exists [in] the stories shared between mother and child, sister and brother, passed around the table like a platter of hot biscuits and gravy and consumed with hungry fervor." [22]

Variations in Family Remembering

Given the different orientations toward truth, we can expect that the narrative reconstructions of family members will differ. One narrator's life story may be "true" to her perception and sense of self ("Dad was always busy with local politics and had no time for us kids"), while a sibling's re-membering may be equally "true" ("Dad was a civic leader and a great role model to us all"). Spence, after all, observes that narrative interpretations are persuasive "not because of their evidential value but because of their rhetorical appeal: conviction emerges because the fit is good, not because we have necessarily made contact with the past." [23] While individual life stories do entail historical truths, they are held together by narrative truths, which can change depending on when, where, why, and to whom the story is told.

Most older people recognize that family members construct the past differently. This realization provides an occasion for checking their own memories and either altering them or adhering to them. I have found that older writers are likely to change verifiable facts and background details in their own life stories as a result of talking to siblings, but they are much less likely to change memories related to their self-concept or emotional states. Emily, a member of the group at the geriatric center, tells me during our interview that she checks up on "factual details" with her brother because "he remembers more precisely than I do, and it gives us something to talk about." He also remembers different things, which has been useful to Emily when writing about her father's experience in World War I: "My brother knew just where he was stationed, the little village of Aprana, near the Marne, and how they could hear the guns in the Battle of the Marne; all that was in vivid memory. I'd heard it, too, but what I remembered was the hair ribbons. My mother stuck the hair ribbons in his baggage so he'd have some little gifts for the little girls, and I have no idea what the comparable gift for the boys was."

At the time of our interview, Emily is writing about a childhood experience and is planning to call her brother to ask him, "When we turned the horseshoe crab over on its back, was it able to get back and flip itself over again?" Emily's act of verifying the facts for her own life story represents something more than a desire for historical accuracy; as revealed in the quote above, it also gives her and her brother, who lives in another state, something to talk about over the phone and helps them connect emotionally as family members. But Emily relies on her own memory for the subjective details of that day at the beach—how she felt about her parents at the time, her excitement over the horseshoe crab, and her own reasons for remembering that long-ago day *now*.

In a similar situation, Margaret, the group facilitator mentioned earlier who also writes her own life stories occasionally and shares them with her groups, tells me during our interview that she, too, calls her brother for verification of the facts. In one of her stories, Margaret lists all the places she has ever lived, prompted by a daughter's erroneous assumption that she had once lived in Cleveland. She mentions calling her brother, who is nine and one-half years younger, to find out why the family had moved so often in the early years: "Unfortunately, he didn't know either, but he did remind me that we lived in four places rather than three in Toledo." Margaret considers the accuracy of these details "very important" because the list is "probably an outline of my life." Like Emily, however, Margaret relies on her own memory to develop the personal story around these facts of geography. Indeed, it is the re-creation of emotional states and the writer's interpretations of them that distinguish one family member's life story from another's.

When family members are not available for consultation on aspects of the life story, other sources are sometimes consulted. Charlotte, a history buff, regularly reads books and talks to friends in the process of reconstructing her childhood in England. In one group session, she reads a long piece about an early trip to York in which she describes favorite sections of the city that include gates, stairs, and stone effigies. At the conclusion of her reading, several members comment on the amazing amount of detail in the writing, to which Charlotte replies, "Well, thank you, but I feel it—I still want it to be polished up quite a lot more. And I also want to find out a few more facts." Charlotte is not yet sure "how many of the gates had stairs going inside, up the inside, and how many had the stairs *inside* the city, but going *outside* the gate." For this reason, she concludes that "I really need to go back to York myself or else get a much more efficient guidebook than I've been able to come across." An only child who has no family to pass these stories along to, Charlotte sees herself as writing a broader cultural history of an English girlhood and would like to publish her stories eventually. Given this rhetorical purpose, getting the facts right is especially important to her.

Much of the life story, though, cannot be factually verified, and these aspects are not generally altered when they differ from the accounts of other family members. Group members recognize that family members have their own take on family "reality" and their own reasons for selecting and telling memories. One writer (Phyllis) once told me a story about the "terrible mistake" she had made in giving the family photographs to an older sister for safekeeping. The sister sorted through the collection and threw away or altered the photographs that "weren't good," including the one picture that Phyllis considered most important. It was taken on a day when all the siblings had been picking wildflowers together and happened upon a rattlesnake, which their father promptly killed. The older sister did not think it was a "good picture" of anyone but Phyllis, the youngest child, so she cut everyone out and left Phyllis standing alone, holding the wildflowers. Phyllis considered the gesture destructive and thoughtless, for she most wanted a remembrance of the family *together*. The example speaks to the different ways in which the two sisters think about memories and the recording of family history. For the older sister, pictures are kept and memories shared on the basis of how they make people look. For Phyllis, pictures are kept because of the personal stories behind them ("the time Dad killed the rattlesnake") and the feelings they evoke ("the time we were all together picking wildflowers"). Phyllis discovered that family members' understandings of "family history" and the role of the family album can differ dramatically.

Joanne Leonard, professor of art and women's studies at the University of Michigan, evocatively illustrates this point. Through slide presentations, she demonstrates how family albums, like written and spoken life stories, are socially constructed and influenced by beliefs about how a family *should* look. Leonard gives public lectures on the connections between photography, narrative, and autobiography, juxtaposing her own artwork and family photos to describe how visual representations of the family reflect time, place, and class expectations. She observes that the family album serves a highly normative role in concealing socially unacceptable images—poverty, divorce, alcoholism, disability, illness, depression, child abuse, and the burdens of caregiving. Usually compiled by mothers, family albums are designed (consciously or unconsciously) to present motherhood and the family in the best possible light, as well as to protect people's feelings. The purpose of an album is not to relay objective "truths" about family history but to construct a "happy family." Interestingly, the very existence of an album may affect the structure of each family member's autobiographical memory. When recalling her own childhood, Leonard admits to remembering the visual images in the family album more vividly than the actual experiences they represent.

Examples from my interviews and observations confirm that older adults are quite aware of the variations on "truth" among family members. Cecille, a member in the metropolitan Detroit group who has never had children, says she is writing her life story for her twelve nieces and nephews so they will get a different version of the family history:

> Some of my nieces have expressed an interest in reading it, because everybody has their own idea about things, which is why I would never have my mother come to the [writing group]. Because she would argue with me, and her visions are colored by her experiences and I think by how she wants to

appear to us. And so I write from my perspective, not from hers, nor do I always take what she says as gospel, you know [she laughs]. If I don't believe it was that way, I write it my way. And so I think that the kids have been hearing from my mother a long time things, and then their parents will say, "Well, that's what she says, but it wasn't that way. This is the way it was." So I think because I don't have children, they want to hear how I feel it was, because they feel that their parents, [too], may shade it a little.

From Cecille's perspective, her own life story functions as an alternative (even corrective) version of the family history as told by her mother. In my interview with Eileen, another group member, we discuss the differences between her personal memories and her sister's memories and the effect these differences might have on her own life-story telling:

Eileen: And I'm thinking, my sister Martha, who's seven years older than I— I think she resented me a lot because she was next to take care of the little [sister]. And I imagine if she were to write something, it would be a lot different, you know? And all of my sisters would be a lot different, from their perspective. But I can see that she probably resented me a lot because she had to be there to see that I wasn't getting lost or in trouble or whatever, as I was little.

Ruth: That seems to be a concern, at least initially, for a lot of people in writing groups. "Well, am I getting the truth? Is that the way it really was?" Well, it's always a partial truth, because it's from your perspective with your blinders on and all of your hurts and resentments.

Eileen: Yeah, because I've talked to my sister about a couple of these things that I've written about, my aunt and uncle's relationship and my parents and stuff. And she said, "Oh, no, no, it wasn't like that, it was like this." You know? [she laughs].

Ruth: And what's your reaction to that? When you hear it?

Eileen: Well, it could have been. It could have been. You know?

Ruth: Does it make you want to change your story?

Eileen: No.

Ruth: That wasn't the way it was for you?

Eileen: Yeah. Yeah.

Another incident with Paul, eighty-three, and his family revealed to me how strong and enduring family influences are on the way events are remembered and fashioned into life stories. I was visiting Paul one day when he received in the mail a written version of the family history from his half-sister Frances, who is in her early seventies. (Paul's father Warren had three children—Paul, Blaine, and Gertrude—with his wife Elizabeth, who died in the flu epidemic of 1918; Warren later married Carrie, who also had three children, and the two of them had three children together—Les, Frances, and Jack). Since Paul now has trouble focusing his eyes for any length of time, I read aloud to him much of the document Frances had sent, which included old photos of Warren and Carrie and all their children, family trees for Warren and Carrie's sides of the family, narrative segments about Frances's childhood and early adult years, and two short segments on Les and Paul.

Some of the siblings are barely mentioned in Frances's narrative, reflecting her lack of knowledge about their lives, as well as the fact that most are now dead. Most revealing, though, is her representation of the blended families—a description with which Paul often disagreed. In one section, Frances mentions that everyone would have gotten along better if Elizabeth's mother—the grandmother with whom Paul had lived for a time—had not "interfered." Hearing this, Paul launched into an impassioned explanation of how hard his grandmother had tried *not* to interfere and how she never did, except to support Paul in his desire to live with her on the farm. Earlier, in writing his own life stories, Paul had told how his grandmother had promised his mother on her deathbed that she would take care of Paul, the youngest of the three children and a boy of four at the time of Elizabeth's death. Paul and his grandmother developed a strong bond and lived together off and on until she died, when Paul was in his early twenties. Sixty years later, Paul still speaks adoringly of his grandmother, tells many stories about her love for him, and attributes to her his lifelong appreciation and respect for women of all ages. Of Frances's comment about his grandmother, Paul claims, "She didn't even know my grandmother. That isn't even Frances talking—that's something *Carrie* would say about my grandmother. I never got along very well with Carrie; she felt threatened by my grandmother, and she didn't like me because of it." Paul's comment suggests that Frances's negative opinion of his grandmother was formed by her *mother's* opinion, and that Frances has carried her mother's prejudice throughout her own life, reinforcing it and passing it along to others through the telling of her life stories.

There are other segments of "the family history" that Paul would tell differently, including the story of Warren's divorce from Carrie. In her narrative, Frances sides with her mother and bitterly names the influence of "another woman"; in a counterresponse to this narrative, Paul sides with his father and celebrates his late-life escape from a controlling, demanding wife. What Paul remembers is how *happy* his father was after the divorce; what Frances remembers is how *unhappy* she was the day he left (her wedding day, of all times) and how her father essentially abandoned his children thereafter.

Paul and Frances's different versions of the divorce raise compelling issues related to the interpretation of "truth" in life stories: first, although neither Paul nor Frances's stories are strictly true historically (they know very few of the "facts" surrounding the breakup of Warren and Carrie's marriage), both versions carry strong narrative or personal truth; secondly, it is the narrative truths that most distinguish Paul and Frances as unique individuals in a family that they experienced quite differently. Although some of the historical facts also bear witness to the differences between Frances and Paul (they had different mothers, different grandmothers, were born to different age cohorts, lived in different locations as children), their narrative truths are what they rely on in old age to articulate not just the *fact* of their lives but the distinct *meaning* of their lives. It is, after all, the particular interpretations and emotional responses that a person passes along to successive generations that make an individual life both understandable and memorable. For this reason, neither Paul nor Frances would consider altering his or her version of the "truth" to assimilate the other's. Indeed, Paul's overall reaction to Frances's text that day was a renewed desire to write more of his own version of the family history.

The fact that narrators do not alter their own life stories in the face of conflicting family "truths" is explained by a number of psychological theories. In their article on "creative remembering," Michael Ross and Roger Buehler summarize research indicating that most people have more confidence in their own memories than others' memories, insisting that their accounts are more vivid, plausible, and accurate. Ross and Buehler offer a psychological motivation for this preference: If individuals cannot have faith in their own memories, they may feel they have lost touch with their life histories and, even more, an enduring sense of self.[24] There are surely other explanations as well, not the least of which are power dynamics in the family, as suggested by Eileen's example, and the perceived authority, credibility, and motivation underlying various family members' accounts, as suggested in the example of Paul and Frances.

Fear of Forgetting

While in pursuit of narrative truths, older adults are surely writing their life stories as a hedge against future memory loss. Although they do not always articulate their motives in just this way, my interviews suggest that older adults write their life stories in order to document a strong sense of self in the face of an unknown future. The specter of Alzheimer's disease looms large among members of writing groups, even though the disease is not nearly as prevalent as most people think. The incidence for all types of dementias is estimated to be only 2 percent among people in their late sixties and 6 percent for people in their late seventies, increasing to 22 percent for people in their late eighties.[25] Yet most people experience some measure of memory loss, as well as considerable fear of memory loss, which psychologist John Kotre interprets as "the fear of losing the self that is supported by the autobiographical memory system."[26]

Loss of memory is a socially stigmatized age-identifier. In a culture that puts a high premium on memory and "cognitive status," people with severe memory loss become nonentities. Older writers' concerns about memory loss were apparent in more than one group conversation I observed. During a session of her Detroit metropolitan group, Eileen brought in a *New York Times Magazine* article by Linda Wolfe called "Runaway Memory," explaining that it was "relevant to our concerns here." She asked the facilitator, Margaret, to read it aloud. The article describes how Wolfe's mother, now ninety and living in a nursing home, spent time in her seventies writing about her memories of the pogrom in Russia and life as a poor immigrant in America. When finished, the mother tried to get the memoirs published but was not able to do so, so she put the stories aside. Eventually, her health began to fail, and she became senile. At the end of the article, the woman's son goes to the nursing home to tell his mother that her memories will be published after all: they have been selected for inclusion in an exhibit at the Ellis Island Immigration Museum. But the woman cannot remember writing the stories, even when the son reads them aloud to her: "She had always loved stories. But she had no idea that they were *her* stories, that she was listening to the ragged memories of her own life." As Margaret read the last lines of this article, her voice faltered. She stopped, apologized, and composed herself before going on. "This speaks to me," she explained to the group. "I know what you mean," said Eileen. "That's why I asked *you* to read it." Wolfe's last paragraph best articulates the feelings of the group: "I have been emotionally under the weather ever since this happened. I have felt over and over again, and with sharper and sharper intensity, the fear of aging that haunts all of us, the dread of Alzheimer's and incapacitation, and the bitter recognition that memory is not something to be counted on as giving solace in one's later years." The group's emotional response to this reading points to a profound fear of losing, not just memory, but identity itself.

Given the prevalence of this fear, a writing group provides interpretive frames for thinking about memory and accepting memory loss. In the following excerpt from another of Margaret's groups, members discuss variability in memory. The conversation occurs after the group has debated whether it is possible to have memories before the age of two:

Arlene: But, you know . . . I have very little memory. I have like spotty memories. I don't have a very continuous memory.

Margaret: I'm with you. I'm with you.

Arlene: And you know what? I think that there is something—one of these days I will find out what happened, because there seems to be a blank with a lot of my childhood. And there's something about a basement. And I have not, I've thought about it a lot. But I have not been able to pin down exactly what it is about that basement that I'm afraid of, and why I can't remember things. If I had to write a childhood experience, which I'm going to do, it's very spotty. And I could probably do it in two pages, because I do not have very much memory. And I'm curious as to why. Was my childhood so dull that I just turned off the memory?

Margaret, as several voices reply: —I know, because I have periods of my life also that, I don't know, it was just such a blank time through it. I guess I— maybe we would—who knows what would happen if we went to a psycho-analyst? But I'm not going! [group laughter].

Arlene: Well, some people can just go into detail about what happened when they were children, like you did [to Charles]. That experience is very vivid.

Charles: Well, that was when I was small. . . . Now, I can remember that almost like yesterday. But some things that happened a few weeks ago, or a year, I don't remember.

Arlene: Uh-huh.

Charles: I can't remember things like that. So I don't, you know—yeah, I wonder about that sometimes. I guess it's getting old.

Gilda: We all have that, we don't remember. I mean that's part of aging, I guess.

The conversation serves the social function of assuring Arelene that she is not alone in her inability to remember and that gaps in memory are a normal part of aging. Margaret's comment raises the possibility that Arlene's memory loss may be psychological, rather than age-related, and she normalizes that possibility, too, using *we* to include everyone in the category of people who might have repressed memories. She adds a note of levity to the discussion by alluding to the fact that people of their generational cohort do not usually seek the help of a therapist to understand such things, and this is quite all right!

Narrative Possibilities

An eighty-year-old writing-group facilitator paused in her conversation with me once and said, as if suddenly struck by the insight, "Isn't it surprising that you can get to be eighty years old, or seventy years old, and not know who you are?" She had been telling me that life-story writing, above all, is an exploration of identity, that autobiographical writing inevitably leads to self-examination. As Edmund Sherman found in his study of oral-reminiscence groups, "to the extent that we are reconstructing our pasts and ourselves through reminiscence in the life review, we are 'becoming' someone in the process—someone who is a little different from the one we took for granted in the past or perhaps a very different person from one we ever imagined in the past." [27] Many of the older adults in Sherman's study became aware of key choices they had made only when they talked among their peers about various periods in their lives: "It is as though they did not know the selves they were when they made those decisions, but now they are embarked upon a kind of self-discovery in the life-review process of old age. This is certainly a form of becoming, of becoming aware of who you are, have been, and will continue to be to some extent into the future." [28]

Sherman focuses on the ontological self, whereas I, in my analyses, shift the focus to narrative representations of the self. My claim is that writing and sharing life stories in groups is valuable from a developmental perspective because it makes public our interpretive strategies, and seeing and hearing others' life stories broadens the scope of interpretive possibility for our own lives. As anthropologist Barbara Myerhoff found in her research on Jewish elders, telling life stories provides the opportunity to become visible to one's self and therefore enhances reflexive consciousness, both of which are essential for continued development in late life. [29]

Because of the creative and constructive nature of remembering, rhetorician Janine Rider sees memory as a generative force—a muse—in the interpretive process of writing the life story, for "remembering leads to inspiration and to understanding. Life makes sense not when we live it but when we remember it." [30] Along these same lines, narrative psychologist Mark Freeman describes autobiography as a method of "rewriting the self." He proposes that telling the story of a life is an engagement in a process of figuring anew one's past and one's self through interpretation. For Freeman and other scholars, rewriting the self is a natural and desirable means of making sense of who and what we are becoming. Continued development actually *depends* on such revisionist narratives. Rather than a steady, evolution-like movement forward, as traditional theories of stage development would have it, adult development is more likely a narrative creation "contingent on the backward gaze of recollection." [31] As such, life-story telling carries an infinite potential for transformation and growth—at least for as long as we can remember.

Selma

FOR OUR SECOND interview, Selma selects the following life story to read aloud and discuss with me. Her reading is interspersed with occasional commentary, and she offers some prefatory remarks: "I think my kids will want to know these things that I write. Even though they may not be interested right now, I think they will be. And again, this particular story I was going to read to you today—I thought this may in some way help us as a nation. Now, you know, certainly I don't expect the nation to read this, but on the Fourth of July weekend, this past weekend, I decided to read you this one. We were sitting in the yard, my husband's son's wife, who would be my stepdaughter-in-law, and my own daughter-in-law, and my daughter. Now, two of them have their master's degrees, and the other is a senior at the University of Michigan. The three men were talking in our screen house, but the three women were out here in the yard. The conversation I could hear back and forth was basically the same thing, we were all talking about jobs. What's happening on the job, and dealing with people on the job, and affirmative action, and discrimination. You know, all that's going on in Washington now. While they were talking, I thought, "Oh, I know which one of my pieces I'll share with Ruth." And that's the one of my first job. I thought, yeah, because here it is fifty years later, and our kids are still having the same problems I had then. I thought maybe sharing my story would be appropriate in this context somewhere.

Being a Nurse at Jackson Memorial Hospital, 1946–1947

In August of 1946, I was thrilled to have completed three years of nurse's training. I had attended Mercy Hospital and School for Nurses, 5000 Woodland Avenue, Philadelphia, Pennsylvania, since September of 1943. World War II had just ended in 1946. The boys were returning from overseas, and life for me then could not have been brighter.

Returning home to Miami, as usual I looked to my older sister Idella, for direction. She usually made all the family decisions, and this was no exception. Idella was eleven years older than I and was also a registered nurse. She was working at the city hospital, Jackson Memorial, and I joined the staff there.

The only other hospital in the city for black nurses was a small private one called Christian Hospital. It was little more than a house really. It was born out of segregation. Here was a place black doctors could take their patients. These were usually middle-class blacks who did not want to be cast in the open charity wards at the city hospital. Many of them had no desire to be treated by white physicians, who had a reputation for caring little for blacks and often using them as guinea pigs. Nearly all of the black nurses at Jackson had been there for years. Idella was amongst the youngest and more recently employed. She seemed to be held in high esteem. Being younger she probably was more knowledgeable of recent trends in nursing.

The hospital had just added a new wing or done some renovations which moved the white patients to the new area, vacating what appeared to have been their charity wing. It was on two levels. Black patients were moved now into this area that had just been vacated by these whites, before I applied. This was a vast improvement over the old colored ward—as we were called colored people back then—and black people were very happy about this. Now we had one whole level for medical patients and one whole level for surgical patients. Also there were rooms with four or six beds, when before we had one long room for all men and one long room for all women regardless of their illness. The only privacy was a curtain between the beds. Children had also been at one end of the female room in cribs. Now we had a pediatric ward, which was a change. Tubercular patients had been at one end of this open room as well—and I'm talking blacks now; the whites had a whole building for tubercular patients. Now, with this new [arrangement], the tubercular patients were separate. We even had a cafeteria to eat our lunches.

As I recall—and my sister says I don't recall correctly—the white nurses were paid by check, and the black nurses were paid with cash. There were no black doctors on the staff. Black nurses took care of only black patients. White nurses were addressed as Miss or Mrs. Whoever. Black nurses were addressed as Nurse Whoever. Because I had been trained to address myself as Miss Hastings—Hastings is my maiden name—in my Philadelphia school, I found this demeaning, and I refused to call myself Nurse, and I called myself and all other nurses Miss or Mrs. This made the black nurses very uncomfortable. And somehow I did not fit in. My sister was unable to persuade me that it did not really matter that I was being called Nurse as opposed to Miss or Mrs. Whenever anyone referred to me as Nurse Hastings, and they—black and white—all did, I answered. When I answered the phone *myself,* I would say Colored 1 or Colored 2, as the wards were identified, and I would follow that up with "Miss Hastings." This so annoyed the white nurses that I was continually called in to the office about this. Near the end of my first year there, one supervisor decided—and all supervisors were white—she'd had enough of my disobedience and confronted me in the hall, insisting that I follow protocol immediately. I asked her why she felt that I owed her more respect than I was willing to give myself. "Because it is the law," was her answer. I gave my thirty days' notice in writing and left this job. In other words, they could shove it.

By then, I had heard that the Veterans Administration had opened a hospital using one of the hotels on Miami Beach to be used for returning veterans of World War II. This is now 1947. Because the United States government had financed the last two-thirds of my education, called the Cadet Nurses, to prepare the nation for the care of the wounded returning vets, I applied there for a job. (I don't know whether I should explain that the Army took over most nursing schools during World War II. They wanted to be sure all nurses were able to complete their training. Because of finances, they wanted to be sure they had enough nurses for these vets when they came home.) If the Veterans Administration hired me, this would be breaking new ground for black nurses, and I would have been thrilled. I remember making a flawless appearance in *uniform* for my interview. My manners were impeccable, and I knew my performance as a nurse was excellent. At the interview my credentials were reviewed sympathetically. Then I was told, "We really would like to hire you, but we are hiring whites only. We are so sorry." Somehow I believed this nurse to be sincere. I thanked her, went home, and applied to the University of Chicago's Lying-In Hospital in Illinois. I was immediately accepted, and I started working there October of 1947, leaving a tearful mother in Miami and a sister, Idella, with mixed emotions.

(When I started to write this, it was my intent to write about nursing, but you see the social aspect took over, fifty years later.) Sometime after this, I remember Idella telling me that this practice had been dropped and all nurses were now called Miss or Mrs. This might seem a small thing to some, but it digs deep into the hearts and minds of a people to conform to a second-classmanship. I don't know when things changed for the black physicians, but I do know that this [earlier] thinking is alive and well in the hearts of many whites today. Black people see this clearly like iridescent light in the dark. Many young people, black and white, are speaking up, but not nearly enough. I believe the current United States president [1996] is sincere in his desire to be fair, but I am very worried that our country is headed back to state's rights, which leaves blacks particularly at the mercy of many hearts of many years ago. (I don't know if that makes sense.) I doubt that another world war can blot *this* stain from our nation's hearts.

One recommendation I would make is that our United States history be taught as it really happened, including the views of blacks and native Americans. Few, seeing history as it was, could remain unchanged, I believe. Some reading I would recommend for students in our schools would be *Up from Slavery* by Booker T. Washington and some of Frederick Douglass's writings, Mary MacLeod Bethune, Langston Hughes, Cab Calloway, and some of the older black people today who could really share with them the facts of life.

FIVE   Group Effects on
              Writing the Life

BY NOW it should be evident that constructing the life story is a highly social process—that the "individual self" of the story is a communal self, "a construct largely community generated and community maintained."[1] By telling our life stories in the presence of others and responding to their stories, we create new meanings that foster change: "We engage our cohorts in an exchange of values, and through them, we accommodate, assimilate that which unsettles and un-nerves."[2] This chapter and the next will visit several writing-group sessions to observe exactly how group dynamics influence storytelling and personal growth.

As we saw in chapter 3, local environment has a hand in shaping the life story. Certain narrative tellings are appropriate in certain environments: narratives about spiritual conversion are conventionally told in religious settings, not at a government office while applying for a driver's license. Equally affected by the local environment are the ways in which people interpret narratives. In his research on support groups, sociologist Jay Gubrium shows that, in meetings of the Alzheimer's Association, stories of a family member's forgetfulness are framed in terms of the early symptoms of Alzheimer's, while the same stories told around the family dinner table may be construed more normatively as "get-ting on in years."[3] The center for senior citizens is a unique social environment in its own right, with specific rules for behavior and self-representation. Most of these rules are tacit, but members recognize them immediately when they are broken: getting into a fistfight or even a loud verbal match with another senior citizen, for example, is against the social code.

Writing groups are social environments within the environment of the senior center; they are discourse communities operating on rules that determine the content and form of what can be told and written. The fact that writing groups are persuasive communities is well-recognized among rhetoricians and creative writers who study writing-group behavior.[4] Indeed, a common complaint among literary scholars is that creative-writing groups foster "an atmosphere of group-think," "an unspoken consensus on politics and aesthetics," and a predictable, conformist prose.[5] We would expect writing groups among older adults to func-tion similarly, in this case as a community of peers who negotiate and model for one another how best to write about the personal past. Those unwilling to adhere to group norms will either self-select out of the group or be subtly eased out by members themselves. Thus, the group functions as a microcosm of the larger society of older adults, limiting and extending narrative possibilities. What is most relevant in terms of adult development is how members resist or accommodate these norms while maintaining individual integrity and acceptability within the group. The writing group mirrors the central challenge we all face across the life course: how to remain unique individuals while sustaining our group identities.

Group Norms

There are at least two norms that typically operate in all writing groups, in and out of senior centers, and a third that assures the smooth functioning of a senior-center group in particular. All writing groups, in order to proceed without undue conflict, function on the basis of collaboration and consensus. Two norms are clear: (1) members are to demonstrate an interest in each others' writing and a willingness to listen, and (2) members are to support and encourage each other, creating an environment of confidentiality and trust. Although these norms are consistent across writing groups of all ages, they may be negotiated differently in senior centers, depending on the facilitator. A third norm applies in particular to groups of older writers: members are not to pry, probe, or criticize the writer or the writing in any way. These three norms may or may not be stated outright by facilitators, but they are implicit in every group meeting.

The facilitators of senior groups I interviewed all focused on the importance of creating a "listening" environment that fosters comfortable interaction and a genuine interest in other people's writing. Madeline, eighty, who is a retired English professor, suggested that a major difference between college-student writers and older-adult writers is a certain "recognition of age" and what it brings: perspective, a willingness to talk about the past, and an ability to listen without criticizing or feeling compelled to advise. A primary reason older adults, particularly women, join writing groups is to be listened to and heard on their own terms.

Many group members articulate this desire in their interviews. Phyllis, a member of the group at the geriatric center, explains her need for an accepting audience and her reason for participating in my study: "I just need all of these outlets—the writing, the interviewing, the new outlets—to vent, just to talk, and to be listened to, and to be validated. And I find more and more people who *do* listen and then don't necessarily have a comment, but they just listen. I have a nice poem someplace about listening: 'Listen to me. I don't expect you to have an opinion. Just listen. Just listen to me.'" Catherine, who is in the same group with Phyllis, responds similarly: "What you go to a writing group for—I went to write, to have somebody listen to my writing, to listen to other people's writing and see what they were doing and how helpful that could be for me." Sheila, a member of another group, says the main advantage of group membership is "that you have an audience for it. I guess that's what writing is mostly about." These women have found it difficult to find respectful listeners in their daily lives outside the groups; most people, especially younger family members, are always pressing upon them unsolicited opinions and advice. What older writers really want is friendship, community, acceptance. Writing groups become support groups; they provide a forum for meeting with people who have similar interests and who join together for the sole purpose of assisting each other in telling stories about themselves. Group assistance is nondirective and takes the form of listening politely, commenting with interest, asking benign questions of clarification, and accepting whatever is written.

Listening and accepting is necessary for the realization of the second norm— participation in developing a supportive and encouraging environment for the reception of each other's life stories. In my interviews with group facilitators, all mention the importance of fostering a "safe" and "comfortable" and environment. Some do it subtly, while others make it a point to be as overtly encouraging as possible. Margaret, who as mentioned earlier is seventy-eight and has had training and considerable experience as a facilitator of many kinds of groups, including women's support groups, explicitly promotes members. She speaks to them positively about their character and personality ("You're really inspiring"; "You're very important to this group. I'd love to see you come back"); identifies with their writing ("You know, I lived through the times, and I mean, you've touched me very much"); and serves as cheerleader for the group as a whole ("Aren't we great?! This has been a wonderful group!") Margaret has become personal friends with several of her group members and often socializes with them outside the meetings. And she supports each person's unique way of presenting a life story:

> *Gilda:* I'm not gonna give it to [my kids] until it's all done and maybe not until I'm gone.
>
> *Margaret:* You'll do exactly what makes you comfortable.

Margaret's approach sends the message that there is no right or wrong way to write and that everyone's life is inherently interesting.

Other facilitators, particularly those who identify themselves more as writers, find gentle ways to suggest improvements while simultaneously supporting each writer. Madeline, the retired English professor, asks questions that reflect a genuine interest ("Is there a sequel to that story? Did your father ever understand

that you had been telling the truth?") and that prompt more detailed development ("What are you going to say about the contacts with the police in those
days?") or a smoother way of phrasing something ("I'm wondering, is there any
way of maybe just a little transition that connects them? Anybody have an idea
about that?") Despite the fact that she taught college writing for years and has
published her own work, Madeline is careful not to set herself apart from the
others or to present herself as an "expert" on writing. She believes in creating a
collaborative workshop where everyone has equal voice and authority. Both she
and Margaret take it for granted that they will be readily accepted as members
of their own groups. Madeline acknowledges that her feeling of "belonging" to
her own writing group is one of the differences between teaching college students
and facilitating a group at a geriatric center:

> For one thing, I'm one of them. There's essentially no age difference, al-
> though there may be fifteen years or twenty. For another, no assignments. . . .
> I believe very strongly that if you want to write, you have to find what you
> want to write about. It means that people flounder for a little while. . . . I
> think also it makes them feel comfortable to know that they can write about
> anything they want to, so I say, "Write about what's important to you." And
> the other thing is that I pay no attention to grammar or even to sentence
> structure. . . . I think the important thing for them is to get their ideas down
> and to develop them, and to find out why they're writing about what they're
> writing about: What's the significance of this? Why should anybody be inter-
> ested? Why were you interested? Why is it interesting enough for you to tell
> us? Although I don't think I've ever put it in those words for them. But you
> take away all of the critical paraphernalia that turns people off. And after all,
> these people are seventy or eighty years old! They should write the way they
> want to write.

One mark of the peer status of Margaret and Madeline is the way they acknowledge age and its importance. Margaret is ever conscious of the limitations,
as well as the potentials, in growing old. She frequently expresses concern about
room temperature, light, and the physical comfort of group members, checking
periodically to assure that they have enough light to read and can hear when
others are speaking. (Margaret herself wears a hearing aid and often asks for
repetition.) She engages in much validation talk around age. In one session,
while reading aloud the life story written by Celia, a family friend who has since
died, Margaret comes upon a section that is unclearly written. She acknowledges
the confusion, then immediately repairs any damage her comment may have
caused to the writer's status: She reads: "His name was Nathan. We used to get
together several times a week, sometimes go out for a walk and sometimes for
ice cream or to a restaurant. He had several friends, and we used to get together

and meet. This continued about a year until he had to go in the army. He went away, and I was left with his friends"—Margaret breaks off and comments on what she has just read: "Now, this sounds as though he went away to the army, but you'll see that that's not what happened. But she's—when I'm over ninety, I hope that I can do as well." A group member, Betty, affirms the thought: "Oh, yes, I hope I can too."

Younger group facilitators share much the same philosophy as Margaret and Madeline but feel they must deliberately create an environment in which they are accepted members, given generational differences in values and beliefs. Lee, a fifty-year-old social worker who has taken some creative-writing workshops, has a slightly different facilitating style than Madeline, but she still follows a support-group model. Each week she brings members exercises from writing books and offers a thought-provoking topic for those who wish to pursue it. ("As we journey through life, we cannot help learning more about ourselves. Do any moments of self-enlightenment stand out in your mind? A gradual learning, a special project you undertook just for the purpose, an unwelcome mirroring of yourself from someone else? A welcome mirroring?") Lee's goal for such topics is to encourage in-depth reflection and analysis, but she is careful to let participants know they need not pursue a topic that makes them uncomfortable, and she never probes for details beyond what members willingly offer. Her comments on group members' writings serve her primary purpose of validating and encouraging: "Yeah, it was realistic. I wouldn't say you were bad at dialogue"; "Some of the descriptions you used were really interesting"; "That really brought it to life."

Lee has decided not to write along with the group, although she would like to. This is partly because she knows her writing would distinguish her as a member of another generation. She says, "There were things I wasn't comfortable sharing with them," including stories of "old boyfriends and sex and things like that—sex without being married—or things I thought might offend them." It is not that she is patronizing or attempting to "protect" group members from beliefs they may disagree with, but that she makes group harmony a priority over difference, especially when she herself is the source of difference. Lee discovered earlier in the year that there were tacit boundaries in the group around sex talk. In one session, Mary, sixty-two, and the youngest group member, read a story about "learning how to make love" as a young girl. The older sister of Mary's best friend got on top of her sister to demonstrate and began poking her with a finger. Meanwhile, the younger girl described to Mary exactly how it felt to be underneath. At the end of this reading, group members responded politely, and Mary replied that she might write about another episode. When she did not bring any more sexual stories to the group, Lee asked her about it, and Mary indicated that she "just didn't feel comfortable" reading them at the geriatric center. She had, however, written about two more episodes and read them aloud to another writing group to which she belonged—one in which members ranged widely in age and where she was one of the oldest writers. Lee concluded from their conversation that writing about sex in anything other than vague and romantic terms can cause discomfort in a group at a senior center.

Avoidance of sex talk occurs in most older writing groups. In my interview with Robert, a member of Madeline's group, he says he does not plan to cover "the X-rated parts."

Ruth: Why is that?

Robert: I wouldn't mind writing about it probably, but it just, you know, might be offensive to some. It's probably not in good taste to include that. And I'm not sure how my kids would react to that. I know my son would be interested in it. And the one daughter on my [second] wife's side, she'd like to know about my love life and stuff like that.

Ruth: So that's what you consider X-rated? Your love life?

Robert: Yeah. Yeah. I probably wouldn't want to share that with the group necessarily.

Ruth: Do you think you'll ever write about that for yourself?

Robert: Yeah, I probably should. Before I started, I asked all the children what they'd want. I still have those things in my—I don't know, a lot of people don't talk about their sex life at all, and in that regard, it'd be good to write about it. Maybe put it in a sealed package and [say to the kids], "Here, when I've lost all my mental faculties [he chuckles], open this and enjoy reading it.

The uncomfortable response to expressions of sexuality in Lee's and Madeline's groups is understandable, given that they consist predominantly of middle-class white women between the ages of sixty-five and eighty who were socialized to avoid explicit sex talk. Most grew up ambivalent about expressing their sexuality privately, much less publicly. Many of the women I interviewed emphasized that "some things you just don't talk about," and "sex is nobody's business but your own." They were typically reluctant to speak of earlier behaviors (like sexual liaisons in and out of marriage) that they are "not proud of" and therefore do not want their children to know about. The life story, for most women of this generation, is a morality tale that enforces their beliefs about the right way to conduct one's self in the world. Women, especially, seem to feel the weight of this responsibility in presenting themselves to children and grandchildren, although Mary is an exception who offers the group an alternative script.

Elaine, thirty-four—the youngest facilitator I observed—made efforts similar to Lee's in adopting a "noncontroversial" persona in order to avoid dissention. At the time of our interview, Lee was completing a dissertation in English education and studying the ways writing works as a form of "healing." Of her work as group facilitator at the geriatric center, she says, "My role is to help people tell the stories that they need and want to tell. . . . I try to cultivate a group that can serve that function for each other. The group takes on a life of its own, if I've done it well. People are providing the care and support for each other." Although Elaine is an avid writer and sometimes writes her own life stories along with the group, she is careful not to address sensitive subjects or to draw attention to her personal politics. When I ask about her group persona, she describes it this way: "I think I have sort of a young writing voice. And that is how I choose to write a lot of times. In fact, as a facilitator, a lot of the exercises I suggest have the older people going back to a child—writing a book for a child, a story for a child—in the first-person voice, the present tense. You know, 'I am ten years old.' So I don't know, maybe that's something that I like to do that I impose on them." As a result of taking on this voice in her own writing, as well as the fact that Elaine looks much younger than her years, group members tend to respond to her as a young girl: "When I write something, I think the older people think it's sort of charming. And they're looking at me more the way they would look at a grandchild or a child."

Elaine makes good use of the child persona to establish group harmony and provide what she calls "compassionate support." At the end of our interview, when I ask her what she least likes about working with older people, Elaine offers an extended example that reveals the tensions between normative and non-normative behaviors in writing groups:

Elaine: There was a woman in the latest writing group—I'd given them an exercise to write about a photograph. And to direct the writing to the person in the photograph, so the first line would be something like, "In this picture you are—" and then take it from there. And that day we were meeting in this woman's house—I'll call her Sylvia—and she seemed real nervous. She was kind of jumping up and fixing the shades. And people were reading, and it was an interesting reading that day—people were talking about different family members. When she read her piece, she didn't want to show—you had to bring the photograph in—and she said, "I'm going to show the photograph at the end." And the piece was called "The Mother of the Bride." And it was talking about how they never thought this daughter was going to get married, she was always such a tomboy, and here she was, she even had grown her nails out for her wedding day. It turns out it was a lesbian wedding. And her daughter—it was her stepdaughter—had asked her to give her away. Sylvia was totally choked with emotion, and I could tell it was extremely cathartic for her to read it. And for me, 'cause I'm gay—I've never come out to a group of older people because I feel like I'm going to be judged. And for me, I was just kinda stunned. I'm like [Elaine says this enthusiastically], "Oh, what a nice story!" [she laughs]. And the people [in Elaine's writing group] had a funny reaction—especially the men were very funny. When she passed the photograph around with those two women in bridal gowns, they went like [Elaine speaks in a controlled, polite manner], "Oh, look at that." [she laughs]. They were all polite. And I thought that was an incredibly brave thing [for Sylvia to have done], because I know there are parents in these groups who have adult children who are gay, or grandchildren, and I think a lot of them feel really ashamed and don't want to talk about it.

Ruth: So was that a moment of struggle in you? [Did you wonder] "Should I say something?"

Elaine: Yeah, yeah. Yeah. What I decided to do is—I think she may have suspected that I was gay—and she kind of like gave an avenue if I wanted to say something, but I didn't. I thought I'd write her a note, because she also had sent me an article after the group was over. Because I want her to know how much that meant to me, even though I didn't quite have the courage to address it at the moment.

Elaine's story richly illustrates the workings of group norms and generational difference, as well as the potential for narrative change in writing groups. Writer Sylvia takes a risk and chronicles the public display of her daughter's sexual orientation. She is clearly nervous about how her peers will receive this story, which draws its surprise value from the act of breaking the standard script for marriage tales. Both Sylvia and Elaine are relieved to find that the group accepts the story and the storyteller. Elaine, however, who is a member of the daughter's generation and a lesbian herself, does not feel that the group will accept *her* if she tells her own unconventional tale and therefore remains silent. She chooses to reveal her sexual identity privately to Sylvia only after the writing group has stopped meeting. Elaine's example raises interesting issues about *who* is allowed (or who perceives that she is allowed) to tell narratives that "break script" and how age and cohort influences might make a difference in how these stories are told and received.

Elaine has been estranged from her parents and says the senior groups help her understand the generational conflicts in her own family. She tells another story about a woman in a group she facilitated at the Jewish community center who wrote a letter to a daughter who had totally cut off communication with her.

The daughter was in her thirties, and it was a tremendously painful thing for the mother. You could tell it was the biggest pain she had. It was just lodged there in her heart. And so she started crying a little bit when she read the letter. And in me it touched something, because I was having a really hard time with my family. As a matter of fact, I wasn't talking to my mother. I had a decision then; I didn't know if I wanted to bring so much of my life into the group. I decided not to, although I did talk to this woman in private about my issue with my mother. And that was nice, because it kind of made a bond between us. And we talked about it many times in the next two years.

For these reasons, although she feels she cannot be open about all aspects of her life, Elaine "gets something back" from the older writers in her groups: "I've just learned so much, mainly about patience. The stories they tell are astounding to me, the trials that people have been through. . . . Sometimes when I listen to their stories, I kind of, I don't know, I guess it's sort of selfish, but I try to draw strength from what they've done." Obviously, group facilitators, as well as participants, find role models and interpretive strategies in writing groups that can lead to their own development.

A supportive group environment naturally fosters confidentiality and trust among members. Writing-group participants often describe themselves as "intimate strangers"; group members know more about them than their family and close friends. It usually takes a few months, but eventually writers begin to tell stories that they have never told before. This was the case for Arlene, a member of Margaret's group. As a preface to reading "Long-time Secret," Arlene tells the others:

> It's interesting that all of this came out because I started *not* to write this, but I ended up doing it because I think it brings a closure to a part of my life that nobody, including my husband or my sister or my mother, knows about. And even if you remember in the piece I did about [my best friend], I said a line that in all that talking I never told her the secret. . . . All this is preliminary to say that this was very difficult to write. I was hesitant about writing it. But it's a basic part of the way I am as an adult. And perhaps you can see some relationship to it. And I appreciate this group because it's given me the freedom to write this, and this is a part of me that most other people do not know.

Facilitator Margaret responds in kind, supporting what Arlene is about to confess, while asserting her own feelings of pride at creating an environment in which Arlene feels she can speak so freely: "And I appreciate the fact that there's a place like this for people—that I've established a place and the aura for people to be able to say things like you're just saying. That makes me feel very good."

Arlene begins the story of the secret by telling about her strict religious upbringing in an evangelistic home, where "religion and church dominated my life and formed the core of my character." Her uncle, with whom she, her sister, and her mother lived, was working to build a denomination in an eastern city, and the family home was a base for many evangelists passing through. Arlene "was trained to be gracious to strangers and always to show them hospitality and obedience." She writes:

Because of our living arrangements I had a second bedroom in a hall. Unfortunately, a few of the ministers who came took the opportunity to fondle me, as I pretended to be asleep. I was caught in the most unsolvable dilemma anyone could be in. I was caught between the commandment, "Thou shall obey any adult, especially a preacher" and "Thou let no man put his hand upon you until you are married." I can't say how often this occurred or how far it went. I can say that it is a mental situation which should not be in young children.

Even more devastating, [in later years] I found myself in another city being subjected to the same thing by another minister. This time, it was the assistant pastor of the small church my parents joined and my father's best friend. In addition, his daughter was my best friend. It started when my parents were out of town. I remained home because of school and work. I escaped by pretending there was someone at the door. From then on, it was a constant battle to keep myself from being anywhere within arm's reach of him when there was no one around. I had to stop going over to my friend's house because I never knew if he'd be home. The end result was to be convinced by him that I had started it, and of course if I revealed it to anyone, they wouldn't believe that an elder in the church and my father's best friend would be capable of such actions. Even when our paths no longer crossed, it left me with a feeling of unworthiness and a less than acceptable mind.

Under reflection, I realized how pervasive this experience was. I couldn't seem to trust anyone. I never spoke about myself among friends because that secret might come out. Yet at the same time, I was attracted to any male who spoke to me, even if only briefly. This uncomfortable feeling about things of a personal nature even carried over into my marriage. I carried this secret for forty years. Then in the middle of a health challenge, when I was in the hospital, a friend brought me a talking book, *I Know Why the Caged Bird Sings*. The young girl's experience brought mine back to me, and I had to deal with it again. But at the same time, someone else brought me a tape from a service that was going on at my church. At the time, I was unable to see, and I could only listen to the radio and tapes. By God's providence, the minister spoke on the bent-over woman, and the phrase "It was not your fault" jumped out at me. Alone in the middle of the night, that forty-year burden was removed from my mind. I was able to see that I was a victim and not an instigator. The relief lasts even now.

The one thing I am grateful for is that my experience did not make me leave God, in spite of the failure of his servants. I still have a personal relationship with God, and I know that he did not charge me for the sins of others. I am able to speak more freely about other things that have happened in my life and to be sensitive to situations where abuse might possibly occur. I'm also able to discuss with young girls the importance of speaking out about these situations the first time it happens. While not comfortable enough to reveal the details of my own experience, I can say to others caught in situations beyond their control at times, "It was not your fault, and God loves you still."

The group responds to this story by confirming its importance and supporting Arlene's interpretation. Margaret repeats with interest, "And this is the first time you've written that?" Gilda follows with a compliment: "It's excellent writing." Arlene replies, "It's a relief to have it written down, whether anybody ever reads it." Margaret turns to me and marks the significance of this moment, thereby enhancing the value of Arlene's narrative: "That's a very important—I think that goes very deep, a very important part of the research that I hope is being done. I think that would be a section of it, about women speaking out. . . . It seems to me that could be a very strong part of this research." Arlene confirms that I am planning to refer to her by pseudonym and then explains why she is telling this story now, as the tape recorder is running:

> *Arlene:* And I also kind of reread my diary that I used to keep, and this— without saying this was the cause—I could see how that [experience of abuse] affected my life, even in my twenties before I got married. And sometimes I wonder how many other people that we don't know have a "secret" or something that they have never been able to share with anybody.
>
> *Margaret:* It's so pervasive, it's frightening.
>
> *Arlene:* And [to believe] that it doesn't happen in the church, and the way we were raised, like I said, "Thou shall obey any adult, especially preachers," I don't know about other churches, but there is a compelling sense of obedience to the ministers. . . . It's very difficult for a person in a position of authority and religion joined together to be rebuffed or be turned off by a youngster.

One of the reasons Arlene has not told this story before is because she has not had the proper forum. The nonjudgmental (and perhaps secular) environment of the writing group makes certain narrative constructions possible for her that previously seemed impossible in the context of her family, friendships, and church circles. Here she can show church elders to be abusive, deceitful, and manipulative, and she can find ways to verify her own faith (still an essential part of her identity) despite the humiliation she suffered at the hands of "God's servants." In Arlene's case, writing-group norms extend, rather than limit, the possibilities for her personal narratives.

The writing group's measured response to Arlene's story of the secret also illustrates the operation of a third group norm that is more specific to writing groups among older adults: members are never to probe or criticize. Arlene's narrative is very vague as to what kinds of abuse occurred or how long she endured it, and she does not specify exactly how the abuse affected her subsequent relationships. She also distances herself emotionally from the traumatic incidents in her childhood, shifting to the third person when describing her reaction ("It is a mental situation which should not be in young children"). Yet the group does not ask for these details or question Arlene's hazy representation of the past; they accept whatever story she offers and support her particular way of telling it. This is very different from the way a group of professional writers or would-be professionals respond to one another. They are more likely to encourage narrators to recreate the past with as much physical detail and emotional revelation as possible, moving toward some personal reckoning, no matter how painful, in the narrative itself.

There are many incidents from writing groups in which members do not ask for details or clarification about difficult periods in each other's past. A member in one group mentioned in passing that two family members committed suicide. Group members *tsked* politely but did not ask her to elaborate. Members in other groups have referred to rapes both experienced and observed, time spent in mental institutions, untimely deaths of loved ones, periods of debilitating illness, and other traumatic events. Fellow group members respect the gaps and silences in these narratives, following the unspoken rule not to pry into sensitive matters.

Interestingly, however, group members do not always agree on what constitutes "prying," and this must be negotiated in each setting. In my interview with Charlotte, eighty, who is a member of an all-white group at a geriatric center, she reminded me that these kinds of tacit understandings are cultural, as well as cohort-related:

Charlotte: There's a certain curiosity rather than a critical—I mean, I tried not to show it, and I hope I didn't, but I used to get at times very irked by questions that were probing about "and what else?" and so on and so forth. My British reticence sort of reared up, and I wanted to say, "I told you all I'm willing to tell you. All I want is for you to critique and criticize as much as you like the way in which I've presented it so that I can present it better.

Ruth: I see. And not what I've presented?

Charlotte: Huh?

Ruth: You weren't interested in the critique of what you presented but how you presented what you chose to present?

Charlotte: Yes, and I didn't mind what, too. But I objected to the intrusive questions about more than I had written.

Ruth: And you see those questions as coming from where?

Charlotte: The group, not from [the facilitator].

Ruth: Yeah, from the group, but the group's desire just to know more about you as a person, or why do you think—

Charlotte: I put it down to American curiosity, which is something that is very difficult for an Englishwoman of my generation to deal with. It took me years to get used to it. I can tell you a very funny story. Once—it was when I was in New Orleans the first time. Tulane University has various houses they've bought up around the uptown campus, which they let out to faculty. Usually, they're big enough for several apartments in them. I had a small apartment in one of those houses, upstairs with a married couple, recently married. She was from the arts department, he was from engineering. And then the other ground floor, alongside of me, was a young psychiatry resident who was actually in child psychiatry, so we were pretty friendly.

We were asked to a housewarming upstairs for the newly married couple. But my friend was on call that night, so I went up alone. I was standing in the bay window talking to a couple from the law school whom I'd met briefly at some other function, and the wife of the chairman of engineering bore down towards me, like a frigate in foresail, and in a booming voice that stilled the rest of the room—it wasn't such a large room—said, "My dear, when we were introduced, I didn't catch what your husband does." I was appalled! I was not wearing a dress ring, let alone an engagement ring or a wedding ring. She couldn't have mistaken the fact that I was unmarried! I was absolutely floored at the rudeness of the woman. And I flung up my hands and said, "I'm a spinster!" And she looked taken aback. I had no idea at that time that in polite society, as I was promptly told, you don't refer to yourself as a spinster in America. It's perfectly legal and perfectly correct. And so I [she chuckles] sort of thought, if the woman must know everything, I said, "And as a matter of fact, my department's child psychiatry." Dead hush. My young hostess rushed over and put her arm around me as if I was in need of support, and I was just livid! She said, "Come in the kitchen, dear, and help me make some more chocolate." Ugh! That's what I mean by—you know, we would never, never, never in an English [gathering] say, "I didn't catch what your husband did" or "I didn't catch what your wife does." You might say, "Is your husband in the same field as you?" Or put out a gentle thing that you could just say "no" or "yes," and if you wanted to say "yes," you could elaborate and say exactly what he was doing. But if you didn't, it was all right. It would be dropped at that point.

Ruth: Hmm. Have you gotten used to that American curiosity?

Charlotte: Well, I find myself in trouble with it in the group. But I have managed, I think, not to say anything so outrageous.

The norm to avoid probing and criticizing distinguishes writing groups for seniors from those that operate in universities or among professional writers and whose primary goal is to improve writing. In contrast to senior-center groups, these groups usually operate in a critical mode; members take it upon themselves to look for problems in each other's work and to suggest rhetorical approaches for solving them. The focus is always on probing and changing *the text*. My interviews with group facilitators Elaine, Lee, and Madeline helped me see this distinction. They informed me that, at the senior center, people's *feelings* come first, and the quality of the life story *as text* takes a distant second place. Elaine most wants the writers in her group "to have a positive feeling about writing," and "to feel that they can write what they need to write," while Lee sees her role in terms of making sure that "everybody's included. Everyone gets a chance to express themselves." Her desire is to facilitate a group that is completely "egalitarian." Madeline sees her senior writing group as a community of intermingling voices that she likens to a group of madrigal singers: "There's a wonderful ensemble feeling that comes out of [madrigal singing] which is emotional. It's bigger than the individual components of the group. Something else comes out of it. And I think that's the pleasure that comes out of this [writing] group. It's partly social, and it's partly personal, but it's partly intellectual. All those things come together at once."

In most academic and professional writing groups, the creation of good writing (as defined by the group) comes first, while establishing and maintaining positive feelings is secondary. Writers are expected to separate themselves and their feelings from their writing and not to take criticism "personally." As a consequence of these goals, personal writings created for professional writing groups are more "reader-based," while those created in groups at senior centers are "writer-based." Reader-based texts are written for an audience that is *expected* to be critical and demanding, whereas writer-based texts are written for the writer's personal benefit and for the interest of generous, like-minded readers.[6] Rhetorician and creative writer Peter Elbow describes these different orientations as "two ways of being in the world of texts." The writer-based author gets satisfaction merely from discovering meanings through words; sees writing as an important and creative part of life; and identifies with readers, assuming they will be accepting and interested. The reader-based author sees writing as an intellectual and personal struggle through which she proves her own worth *linguistically:* she wrestles with complex issues of self and text; confronts hard questions; and reflects upon the struggle of writing itself, imagining and identifying with skeptical, distrustful readers who will challenge everything she says, even when describing her own life.[7]

The ways facilitators and group members respond to life stories are determined by these two stances. As we have seen, senior groups (that is, writer-based groups) accept all life stories uncritically and support and encourage writers in whatever they create. From this stance, the life and the life story are emotionally linked; to critique the story would be to critique the life and the person who lived it. Groups of professional writers (that is, reader-based writers) separate the life from the text and hold the text as superior. The life story is considered distinct from the event or the person who experienced it; it is a rhetorical transformation of the event and the person into something entirely new. Events and personas are textual. In fact, "the event *becomes* the telling. There is no return to the event except 'virtually.' The event is overtaken, mediated by language."[8] From this stance, professional writing group members respond to life stories, not so much in terms of the writers' feelings, but in terms of the writers' language. Here, for example, is rhetorician Judith Summerfield listing the features that English professors usually comment upon in their students' autobiographies: "The choices of noun and pronoun, the implications of such choices, and the possible effects on the reader; . . . the position the narrator takes toward the subject, where the 'I' stands in relation to the event, as a participant or spectator, how much the 'I' knows at the beginning of the text, how much the 'I' knows at the end; . . . the ways the narrator can effect changes of circumstances and consciousness within the text; or . . . the ways the narrator might evaluate the events represented."[9] Multiple subject positions are attended to in this kind of response: the writer (a physical person) is questioned on word choice and its implications; the narrator (a persona who fashions the text) is questioned on her positionality and her relationship to the I character; and the I in the text is challenged in terms of what she can actually know and tell about a life, as well as her relationship to the narrator. Contemporary literary critics (always reader-based) evaluate personal writings in terms of the awareness and sophistication with which these positions are negotiated.

The larger issue here is the possibility for growth: how do the two rhetorical stances, writer-based and reader-based, constrict and enhance narrative possibility, self-understanding, and adult development? Most older writers in my study do not recognize the differences between writer-based and reader-based narratives and are therefore surprised when "outsiders" do not receive their life stories as enthusiastically as their writing group. While they may begin by writing for their families, in the process some develop bigger goals and aspire to publish their memoirs. Phil, a member of Madeline's group, was initially motivated by the desire to write about his experiences as a World War II pilot. Over time, however, he developed an interest in publishing these writings and signed up for a more professionally oriented workshop conducted by Elderhostel. What he learned there was discouraging: commercial publishers are bored by the personal recollections of an unknown senior citizen, and the only way for most people to get their work into print is to publish it themselves. Phil gave up his dream of publishing and returned home, content with the process of writing for his peers at the local senior center. Writing for publication would require, among other things, developing a critical stance toward his life *as text*. Given that most older writers in groups at senior center are really seeking validation of their *lives*, few assume this stance. Those seeking additional narrative possibilities must join other groups, as Mary did, in order to tell stories that do not meet the writer-based norms of the senior center.

Noncompliance with Group Norms

In their book *Guiding Autobiography Groups for Older Adults*, James Birren and Donna Deutchman suggest that norms of the kind just described are essential to successful group functioning and should therefore be actively cultivated by facilitators, preferably by "screening" potential group members. They also recommend a few additional rules: be willing to complete and share all writing assignments; commit to attend all meetings, if possible; and maintain confidentiality. Birren and Deutchman base their advice largely on their experiences guiding mixed-age summer writing groups at a California university.

My experience with senior-center groups, particularly those in urban settings, suggests that such a carefully controlled method of group development is highly optimistic, extremely difficult to realize, and probably class-based. As a facilitator in urban settings, I had little control over who attended the writing group meetings or how often. Since the urban center directors were constantly called upon to prove the popularity of their services in order to maintain funding, staff tried to sign up as many people as possible for all center activities, including the writing groups. Once groups were formed on paper, actual membership was highly unpredictable from week to week, given the complications of daily life (late buses, bad weather, health problems, family emergencies) and competition from other center activities scheduled at the same time, especially those for which free transportation was provided. Once, before Christmas, I went to my writing group on the east side of Detroit to find nobody there; the center staff had failed to tell me they had scheduled a shopping trip to a local discount mall, and most of my group members were on the bus. It was also very difficult for me to say "no" to any new member, especially when attendance of the "regulars" was sporadic. The boundaries of my urban writing groups were shifting and fluid. People came and went as they pleased. They arrived late and left early to catch a ride or run errands (getting to the bank before it closed usually took precedence over staying until the end of the group session). Some wanted to sit in but not write. My role was to keep the group going and work with whoever came on any given day. In actuality, the city writing groups more often achieved normative behavior through direct conflict between members or self-selection in and out of the group.

Most people who were noncomplying in terms of group norms self-selected out of the group. An example is a man named Larson who came to the first meeting of a downtown Detroit group and decided for himself that he did not fit in. During the first fifteen minutes, Larson, a man in his late sixties, broke most of the rules: Coming in late, he sat down and immediately exchanged harsh words with John, another group member. He talked loudly about his past while others were trying to write. On that day, I was offering writing prompts in the way of general questions, which group members were to answer on paper. One of my questions was, "What was life like for you as a child?" to which Larson responded loudly: "Oh, Jesus. What you're doing is excellent, taking us step-by-step, but I come from what they call a dysfunctional family. I had no childhood. It was stolen from me. My father couldn't keep a job. I remember nightmares: running around the streets of New York nude, with just an undershirt." After writing a few lines, Larson put his pencil down: "I got a book in me, but it doesn't fit with your parameters," he said, and he left the table. In subsequent weeks, Larson sat at a nearby table in the community room where we met, outside the circle but close enough to hear what was going on. Although he had an urgent, even obsessive need to tell his life stories (Larson often cornered people at the center to repeat the story of how he had been victimized by the legal system and lost over $100,000), he did not "fit" into the Write-Your-Lifestory Group. At one point, I tried to work individually with him, but the experience was unsettling for both of us. Larson became anxious and hostile while recalling his abusive father, and we stopped the interview. I later spoke to the social worker at the center, who told me she was aware of Larson's problems and had been working to get him into therapy.

Group members who do not comply, but do not leave on their own, become a source of discussion and concern to the other members. In my interview with Lorraine, who has been participating in various writing groups for nearly five years, I asked, "Have there been any groups in which certain members didn't fit in, or the feelings were not so pleasant [as you just described]?"

Lorraine: Yeah, we once had a woman who—she had never married, and she lived, I believe with a sister. She had a negative view of everything that ever happened to her, every experience. And she had a negative comment about everybody else's experiences. She was just a sour person. And I was very happy when she didn't reenroll for the next time. I don't remember her name. I barely remember what she looked like. But she was not pleasant. And that is unusual, because everybody, I don't know, puts on his best face when he comes, or she.

Ruth: I'm surprised the group didn't have an effect on her.

Lorraine: No, it never buoyed up her spirits. She was just a negative, sour person. And you never heard her laugh or enjoy anything about her own life. She was very bitter about the way she had spent her life. She was a retired teacher, and I remember thinking while she was reading, "Am I glad I never had to be in her class, and I sure feel sorry for the kids who did."

Ruth: That's really kind of a tragic story there.

Lorraine: Yeah. Yeah, it really was.

Ruth: Did she have any awareness that she was this kind of person?

Lorraine: I don't know. I really don't think so. Although how she could not have is hard to understand. But I don't know, she didn't seem to think that— although she heard other people's writings and her own—she didn't seem to understand the difference.

Ruth: Hmm.

Lorraine: Because everybody has bitter experiences and unhappy ones. Some people write about them, and some don't. But they're not unique, and she wasn't singled out to get the one worst life in the whole world. But she seemed to give that impression, that she felt that way, that she was dealt a bad deal and was very unhappy about it.

Lorraine's description of the ill-suited member suggests a reason why writing groups resist those who are critical of their own lives and the lives of others: such a person is seen to lack the mature perspective expected of older adults. Members believe that writers must get beyond their individual troubles, as well as their need to air grievances, in order to place their lives in a larger frame. Group facilitator Margaret calls this "maturity":

Margaret: Anyone who is not really mature doesn't last in the class. It's mature people.

Ruth: What do you mean by mature?

Margaret: There are people who are over sixty or seventy or eighty who never have matured, and they are very demanding, and they lean on people. They are easily offended. The opposite of that are people who have grown up, and I feel that most of the time, people I have in my groups are grown up.

The Effect of Groups on Story Construction

As Lorraine's comment suggests, group norms affect the content of life stories and the way they are structured, as well as the ways writing-group members interact. The writing produced for life-story groups in senior centers has a distinct tone and a calculated effect: overall, it is positive; it does not dwell on the negative, and when negative sentiments are expressed, they are usually overcome by the end of the story or at least interpreted by a narrator speaking from the wisdom of hindsight; and they offer hope and resolution. Sometimes the writing is sentimental, to which facilitators and members react variously. Some groups like it; others do not. Lee says that her group tends to "pretty things up," and she makes no effort to change this. Margaret, on the other hand, does not appreciate rosy-hued versions of history, personal or otherwise, and she lets her groups know it. For one meeting, she brings a magazine directed to senior citizens and initiates a discussion about it, in the process creating an ethos about what constitutes "good" versus "uninteresting" writing about the past.

The following conversation occurs after Arlene has told about the sexual abuse in her childhood and Gilda has just read about her husband's Aunt Ann and Uncle Al, who were associated with Al Capone's gang.

Margaret: It's interesting. And what I love is how different people's stories are. After all these years that I've been doing this class. I mean, it's. . . . Remember we talked a week or so ago about—Ruth, you said something about magazines . . . something came up about magazines. And I said I don't particularly like the magazines that are put out for senior adults.

Arlene: Mmmhmm. I remember that.

Margaret: Do you remember what I said? I don't remember exactly.

Arlene: You said that they were dull.

Gilda: Yeah, to read. I remember that.

Margaret: Did I? Yes. Well, this is one that somebody sent me, for instance. It's called *Good Old Days* [reading from the cover]: "Featuring stories of the happy days gone by." I mean, right away that sounds, yee-ahhhh [she rolls her eyes]. I mean, what happy days went by? Now this is [looking at the table of contents], as I say, September of '94, so it's very recent. And it's got "The Old Country School," "Smoked Out of the Old Outhouse," "Walking to School," "A Surprise at the Box Supper," all that kind of stuff. Departments: "Looking Back," "From the Mailbox," "Good Old Days in the Kitchen," et cetera. Most of us who've worked and have some education and—this isn't the kind of thing that—somehow, we're not interested in it.

Arlene: Mmmm.

Margaret (speaking to me): So I just thought, if you'd like to have this . . .

Ruth: I'd like to look at it. Mmmhmm.

Margaret: Sure. I don't know, you know what, I didn't even look to see how it happens to be published. Look and see, I have no idea who sponsors that. I had it in my car all this time. That's why I never really got to looking at it.

We determine that the magazine is published by an organization called the House of White Birches in Indiana. Looking at the publication information, I tell the group that the editors will accept manuscripts if anyone wants to submit something.

Gilda: I don't think they'd want to hear about madams and Al Capone's gang [group laughter].

Ruth: Oh, really? Your stories are a little too risqué for them? [laughter].

Gilda: Oh, yeah, [my uncle Al] would love to tell.

Arlene: But they wouldn't be dull [laughter].

Gilda: They wouldn't be dull. I'll have to put it in—he told us the story about the guy he saw dumped in the river.

Arlene: Ohhh [several say, Mmmm].

Margaret: What? That they dumped in the river?

Gilda: Yeah, they dumped—he didn't do it, but it was somebody from the gang. Shot the guy and dumped him in the river. And I guess that's when he decided it was time for him to leave.

At this point, I offer a comment about nostalgia and stereotypes of older people, referring to a play I have recently seen at a local playhouse that directs its productions to senior citizens. Margaret had attended the same performance on the previous Saturday and had commented to me that some of the dialogue seemed overly nostalgic:

Ruth: The whole concept of nostalgia among older people is an interesting one. I think there's a sort of general stereotype that people over sixty-five are just interested in a highly romanticized version of the past. But I think your comment last Saturday, Margaret, at the play about how those weren't necessarily better, kinder days in the '40s and '50s, because there was a war going on—and a lot of times, the past that we reconstruct from memory is not often the past, or the reality, that most people lived.

Margaret: I was a little shocked at her presentation. [She explains to the group:] There's a community theater here in the old church, and they put on this "WSRO," it's an old radio show.

Gilda: Oh, yeah, they do that some [other place].

Margaret: Yeah, they put on the old radio show, and in the presentation at the beginning, the announcer said something about this goes back to the—she mentioned the '40s, and I still think that they should correct that. I don't want to bother people about it, but she said these were kinder, gentler—what?

Ruth: I think she said, "kinder, gentler days."

Margaret: Gentler days.

Gilda: In the '40s? Those were one of the worst, it was World War II and everything.

Helen: Oh, I—[she makes an expression of disagreement].

Margaret: Yeah, that kind of upset me a little bit, because I felt that they were not with it, that was not the reality at all. And I don't want to get—I know who has written [the play], and I know who I could talk to, but I decided I'm not gonna disturb—to leave it alone. It's not something that is affecting the world. They just happened to say it there at the play and okay, let it be.

Ruth: It was a good show. It was a lot of fun. . . . It was worth going to. It was fun.

Margaret: And, but you know, you could be very pragmatic about things. They were not kinder days. And right after that came the McCarthy days. And when you talk about what was kinder, gentler times, they were not necessarily so. Look at your story! [to Arlene].

Arlene: Right. Mmmhmm. Right.

Margaret: You know?

Gilda: Well, during wartime, it was not kinder and gentler times.

Margaret: That was for sure in the '40s. Of course, [in the '50s] the war was over, but we were hearing about all the horrors.

The talk around *The Good Old Days* functions to support what members of the group have already written (through reference to Gilda's and Arlene's stories), while calling into question nonmembers' nostalgic renditions of the past. At the same time, group members are guided into thinking about the nature of "uninteresting writing" (romanticized, glorified) and, by comparison, "interesting writing" (realistic, socially in tune).

Margaret's response to *The Good Old Days* also informs group members that some types of autobiographical writings are negatively marked for age and should therefore be avoided. Stories of a charming yesteryear, as suggested in titles like "The Old Country School," are probably naive and overly sentimental, and Margaret links them to writers who have not been educated and have not circulated much in the world. There are other types of age-marked stories, however, that Margaret considers appropriate and even desirable. These include stories in which an older narrator is providing information about daily life in the past, is explaining social differences between the past and the present, or is offering a seasoned perspective on a current issue or problem. Many such stories are told in Margaret's group, and they are always received enthusiastically. In the session in which she reads the narrative of Celia, the family friend, Margaret's voice waivers with emotion during the last paragraph. The group responds positively to the reading, and Margaret explains why she considers this story important—and, by extension, everyone else's life story:

Charles: That's quite a story.

Margaret: But look what she did.

Betty: That's wonderfully precise, isn't it?

Margaret: Didn't she write—I mean, better than nothing for the kids, the descendants to have. I mean, it does give you a picture of where she came from and what it was [like]. I remember her husband was, I'm not sure, he had something to do with construction. And I remember a big old house in Rochester they bought. It was fascinating, with big fireplaces and all. And other things about them. They had their cottage, and everybody used to gather there, you know? So of course in reading it, I can picture [their lives]. And even at that, her descendants wouldn't have a picture of it, but there's a story there. They know where they came from. And you're all doing the same thing. You're all doing exactly the same thing. And I think that's wonderful—

Betty: Yes, I really admire the way she did that, put it all together—

Margaret: Yeah, it's, you know, it lets you know your own relatives. If you're talking with any of yours, tell them that they can do this kind of thing [too]. They don't have to write all the details.

Betty: How did she start this out? I don't know—

Margaret: She says [reading], "I don't know what the reason is for my wanting to write and whom it would interest, but one sits alone too long—" [Margaret inserts a comment:] She was by herself then. [She resumes reading:] "—long, there comes out of one's mind the life of one's childhood and what children from poor parents go through." And so forth.

Betty: And then she ended it, "Your grandmother . . ."

Margaret: Yeah, it was like she was writing a letter. She ended up [reading:] "Stay well and happy. Your mother, sister, grandmother, and great-grandmother, Celia." Of course, you see, I'm picturing—she was a beautiful lady. She was a lovely person. And so, actually, you know, I relate to it more than anybody else can. That's why I'm asking you how it impacts you. Does it have impact?

Charles: Uh-huh.

Ruth: The general impression I'm getting is that this person is a real survivor. Tenacious and persistent and strong. And quite a role model.

Margaret: Yeah. Yeah, she was. Everyone loved Celia.

Arlene: I feel I can just almost see her sitting on that bench.

Margaret: Yeah. Anyway, that's that.

Here, group members affirm the value of Celia's life story in terms of its content and impact. Margaret asserts its value as family history, in addition to its emotional value. She also gauges the effect of the story on outsiders who did not know Celia. The group responds in particular to the style of writing and the fact that Celia was able to condense more than ninety years of living into seven handwritten pages. Margaret's selection of this story as an example to the group illustrates the kind of narrative persona she most appreciates in older people's writing: one who expresses a strong ego and acknowledges the importance of her own life without being showy or self-aggrandizing.

One particular genre that is highly valued in writing groups for older people is grandparenting stories. These stories feature an elder narrator who offers a wise response to a difficult situation, shows a willingness to continue learning about herself and others, is self-reflective, and can interact meaningfully with younger generations. Lorraine, a longtime member of Margaret's group, tells many such stories. In our interview, she recounts a recent family gathering in which she assumed the role of an "old serene" grandparent:

I think raising children is one area where I see it differently now than I did [when I was younger]. Now I'm not harassed by them [she chuckles], and I'm not overly busy because of them, and I have now all the patience in the world and all the time in the world. And when I have that serenity now, and I look back on how hectic life was then, I see it very differently. Sometimes I wonder why I felt that my life was so hectic. It really wasn't, but I felt then like it was. . . .

We had an incident the other night. We took our children and grandchildren and my brother and mother and my closest friend to dinner at Mountain Jack's to celebrate my [seventieth] birthday. We had one long table. And my youngest granddaughter, Alise, who is getting close to nine, is a very special child, very interesting and unusual, and she does things in her own way. Anyway, she looked at the menu, and she couldn't see anything that appealed to her. My daughter [her mother] was sitting across from her, and my daughter and her husband are divorced, so she's in full charge. So my daughter asked the waiter for a children's menu. Alise looked at that and—my granddaughter's very stubborn—she said, "There's nothing here that I like, nothing here that I want." So my daughter was getting kind of peeved [Lorraine laughs]. She said, "Well, you have your choice. You have two menus. You either order something from one of those menus, or you can have bread and water [she laughs]. My granddaughter said, "Well, no, I want something like everybody else is having." So my daughter said, "There's the menu. Everybody else is having something from the menu."

Well, they could not—my daughter was getting really upset. After they finished their discussion, my granddaughter was pouting, and she still hadn't made any choice. And I walked over. I had overheard this. And later I said to my husband, "I should have asked my daughter's permission before I did this, but I didn't think to do it." I walked over to the child, and I went over the menu with her, and my eyes happened to hit on the appetizers. I don't know—they hadn't thought of that. And there were baked potato skins on the appetizers. I said, "Does that appeal to you?" "Yes." So we hit on something, and she was very, very pleased. And I was pleased because my daughter, as I walked by, said, "Thank you, Mom." Because I had the time and the patience. You know, I don't contend with this all the time, and it's very different as a grandparent with a child; your own child, you contend with it all the time, it drives you crazy. . . .

So, that was one of the differences between being a young parent and being an old, serene grandparent. The perspective is very different.

In this story, the "serene grandparent" can appreciate the "special" and "unusual" child that the harried parent finds so difficult. Lorraine gets pleasure out of telling this story, smiling at several points in the narrative. Part of its appeal rests in Lorraine's ability to take an ordinary event and create an inspiring parable about the value of age. She also presents herself as a reflective person, discussing the incident with her husband and acknowledging that she may have overstepped her boundaries as mother *and* grandmother, thus indicating a respect for generational difference.

Phyllis, a member of Lee's group, also tells many grandparenting stories. In our interview, she informs me that she has learned much through life experience, as well as recent counseling at the geriatric center, and she uses this knowledge regularly in communicating with her grandchildren. Prior to telling me the following story, Phyllis had revealed her own concerns about weight and described her negative body image:

> I heard my thirteen-year-old granddaughter, Lindsey, saying to me the other day, "Well, Grammie, on Friday I'm going to start a diet." Now, Lindsey is not even one hundred pounds yet. And, oh, the signals went off in my head: "Oh, my goodness, she's going to be obsessive about her weight, and she's going to be anorexic or bulemic." And that's where, Ruth, this is a good example of how I've learned not to begin to spout pronouncements. You know, "Lindsey, how can you talk like that? Look at your body!" I'm not to give out unwanted, unneeded advice . . . or to think that it's my place to tell her what to do and how to do it. And so I just listened to her, and I'm so glad I did, because she said, "You know, Grammie, I think I'm addicted to sugar." And I said, "Oh, I think I agree with you, Lindsey, because all the Halloween candy that your mom bought for Monday night is all gone. It was in that bottom drawer, where has it gone?" She said, "I know, Laura Beth and I eat it when we come home from school." So she said, "Friday, I'm going on a diet." And I said, "What kind of a diet?" See, I've learned to listen. I've learned to ask the needed questions. . . . And she wasn't thinking anything that I was thinking anyway. She said, "It's only going to be candy, Grammie. I'm not going to eat sugar anymore." So all my concerns that I almost laid on her were not true at all.

These are the kinds of stories that writing group members support and promote. In contrast to the typical narrator of stories like those found in *The Good Old Days* (an older person who is looking back wistfully on "better days"), the narrator in these stories is grappling with present-day concerns in the service of building and maintaining relationships. By turning their daily lives into language, ordering the language into story, and sharing the story with others, these narrators validate their existence *now* and demonstrate (to themselves and others) that age really can be interpreted positively and that older adults still have an important place in the world.

Diversity and Normative Behaviors

Norms for writing and responding to life stories obviously function to create coherence and collaboration within groups. They apply to all members and, if followed, help to minimize conflict. Following these norms is particularly important in senior-center groups that are diverse in terms of race, ethnicity, and gender (significant class differences are unlikely, given the social stratification of most senior centers). Members who are insensitive to difference may cause group dissention, thereby disturbing the atmosphere of unconditional support. In my interview with Margaret, who facilitates racially mixed groups in metropolitan Detroit, she mentions that she once had to "ease out" a group member whose writing was racially insensitive:

> I eased somebody out of my class once because I think I've always had some, one or two, African Americans in the group, and this [white] woman wrote a piece about walking out of her apartment, and these four young black people were coming around and how she got frightened and some other things. She was expressing herself, yes, but this was not the place to write that. I think there should be sensitivity. . . . I was brought up to respect people and the way my parents treated people, and, I don't know, it just came automatically to me, and [I've always] had great intolerance, a tremendous intolerance for people who made snide remarks about other nationalities. I look wherever I can to be involved in groups that stress diversity. . . . Because the worse and worse our society gets, we have to learn to get together. I know it's not easy. I know it's not, but it sure is pretty heavy when people in my class. . . . I really don't like to be with bigoted people.

Such issues didn't usually arise in the more homogenous groups that I observed at the geriatric center, where members were exclusively white and middle-class. The metropolitan and urban groups, however, provided both the opportunity and the challenge for group members to articulate and negotiate social differences in both life and life story. Gilda, a Jewish woman in an ethnically mixed group, commented in her interview that the people she has met through her writing group are "very different" from her friends and the people she grew up with: "They're from different walks of life. . . . Like the older lady, which she has so many stories to tell about Germany and everything. I mean, she had a lot of different things happen in her life than my friends do."

In a similar vein, Cecille, Lorraine, and Selma—all members of a Detroit metropolitan group—suggested in their interviews that diversity is what makes attending worthwhile. Cecille, an African American and a native Detroiter, says she is intrigued by both differences and similarities:

> There have been some very interesting people there, and I learned some things that I did not know simply because they were relating their experiences. For instance, the guy that used to teach at [a local university] who has the degenerative nerve disease? He was from Vienna. Jewish. And had left Vienna in 1939 and gone to Shanghai to escape the Nazis. And that was quite interesting, because I had not known that there was a Jewish settlement in Shanghai, but what do I know about Shanghai? . . . And a lot of the people in the group . . . are around the same age, so when they talk about things that have happened to them, or the way things used to be, particularly those who grew up in Detroit, now that is quite interesting to me because I've always been interested in how things were. . . . But even when they come from different parts of the country, it's interesting to hear how they grew up, how they got to be where they are, and how they feel about things.

Lorraine, who is Jewish, points to the writing of Selma, an African American, and the writing of a woman who lived overseas in her response to my question, "What do you most like about being part of the writing group?"

> *Lorraine:* Listening to other people's stories. They're fascinating. I find every one of them interesting. Some more and some less, of course. But everyone has value and interest to me. And some I find very exciting. Selma's particularly. I love her writing. Everything she writes is worth listening to.
>
> *Ruth:* What is it you respond to in her work?
>
> *Lorraine:* I don't know. Her personality. Her character. Her experiences, of course, and the way she saw them. Just everything about her. I find her to be an exceptionally delightful and charming and interesting and sweet and good person.
>
> *Ruth:* This is a topic that's interesting to me: What makes an ordinary life interesting?
>
> *Lorraine:* Well, I think part of it is shared experience. And part of it is exotic experience. Part is what you don't know, and part is what you do know. We at one time had a woman who had lived in Laos. Her husband was a pilot during the Vietnam War. And she raised a large family and lived over there, and some of her experience was very exotic and very different from mine. And some of the experiences that I've heard are very much like mine. And I relate to both of those kinds of experiences. I find them both interesting.

Lorraine goes on to say that an ordinary event takes on special value by the way it is told and interpreted. By way of example, she retells one of Selma's stories:

> The very first time that I remember Selma reading, she started out by saying her son wanted to go three blocks down the street—he was a little boy—to play with someone, and she said, "No, I'm not comfortable with that." She didn't want to let him go. And he said, "But Mama, you let me cross our street." And she said, "Yes, I do." And he said, "How is our street different from the other streets that I have to cross?" And that made her stop and think. And so she let him go, and very soon after that she took the children on a long trip. I don't remember where she lived at the time and what her destination was, but she put them in the car, and she went on a long trip, because she said, "If you can cross one street, you can cross any street." And that shows you the perspective that she had. . . . Now, somebody else might have just said, "I put the kids in the car, and I went." I think that's the crux of it, that's what makes writing so interesting: What she understands from [an experience] and lets us understand from it.

In my interview with Selma, who grew up in Florida but whose ancestors came from the Bahamas, she too, comments on what she has learned from the diversity in her writing group.

> *Selma:* I really enjoy hearing the others and what they have to say. Some I find more interesting than others, but all of them are interesting.

> *Ruth:* What kinds of things are you particularly interested in from the others?

> *Selma:* I guess just what they're talking about, what their life was like. See, because having grown up in a segregated society where I was, I had no contact with white people when I was growing up, except to brush past them maybe in the dime store. I mean, we didn't even sit next to them on the bus to have a conversation with them. So to have nothing to do with white people, all you're doing is looking but having no interaction with them, it's really eye-opening to me to hear them talk about their lives when they were children. . . . It helps me to see, because . . . they take me in their homes.

She focuses in particular on Eileen's description of life in Detroit as the child of Polish immigrants:

> Just listening to her talk about her early life and her father's struggles, having immigrated here, and his building the basement beneath his house, I learned a lot about how much a person can do to help themselves to get ahead to meet the needs of life and the struggles that they had. I learned, too, by

comparison that they had some real struggles. When I say "they," I mean the members in the group, and since most of them are white, that's who I'm talking about now. Of course, I learned some things from the other blacks, but you see, a lot of what the blacks might be saying, I already know that from my own experience. From the white standpoint, it was kind of an eye-opener to me. It made me realize life has not always been easy for them, either.

Selma would like for the group to make those differences a point of discussion. Although group norms foster harmony, politeness, and acceptance of the status quo, Selma asserts, passionately, that good can come from direct challenges, too, especially to people's unexamined attitudes about race:

> I would like to know how they feel about the racial things I write. I don't get any feedback on that, except maybe "Mmmm" or "Ohhh." I'd like them to be honest and tell me how they really feel: How did you behave during that period of time toward blacks? And has your attitude changed any since then, or do you still think like that? I understand how [racist] thinking could be inbred. But what are you doing about it now? Do you think any differently? Are you making any effort to look at your past and examine what's been fed into you and see, is that appropriate? Or should I make allowances for the others or try to understand why they are like they are? I don't know. I think that's important, not just for me as an individual but for our country. Because I don't think a person or a country can reach its potential as long as it's holding somebody down. . . . All that energy needs to be used to help each to reach his potential. I never thought about it before, but now that you've asked me, that's exactly what I would like to see. I'd like to hear them tell me their feelings about race when they were young. What their parents said to them and fed to them to cause them to feel and behave as they did or do. And have they thought about that? And what are they teaching their children now? Or did they teach their children? And what changes, if any, have they made?

Selma's questions resonate far beyond the functioning of her local writing group; she is, in fact, suggesting that all groups of older adults interrogate their "commonality" and make their diversity the basis of self-examination. She believes that older adults need to explore the changes, or lack thereof, in their attitudes toward others, consider where these attitudes came from, and examine their continued effects on future generations. Selma is arguing for adult development through narrative *challenge*.

Selma raises a crucial issue for writing groups of older people nationwide. In their book *Guiding Autobiography Groups for Older Adults*, Birren and Deutchman argue that "from the viewpoint of human development, there is little of greater importance to each of us than gaining a perspective on your own life story, to find, clarify, and deepen meaning in the accumulated experience of a lifetime." [10] Yet Birren and Deutchman emphasize personal reflection and *individual* development within a group context without considering how the local setting of the senior center or the larger cultural milieu shape and are shaped by narratives of the self. This lack of sensitivity to social context has historically been a blind spot in developmental psychology. Gerontologists need more encompassing theories of aging that help explain how actual interactions among diverse people spur individual development. Such theorizing might well begin with close studies of older adults who are negotiating life's meaning in groups of their peers.

Jean

JEAN SELECTED a letter to read aloud during our interview, not because she thinks it is her best work ("In fact, I don't know whether it's even particularly good") but because it was so cathartic to write. The letter exemplifies the kind of emotional honesty Jean considers so important in writing her life stories. Occasionally, she turns from her reading to speak to me.

Dear Dad:

Although you have been gone for over twenty-seven years, I'm writing this letter because when you were on earth, we somehow were unable to communicate on any but a superficial level. I never had the chance to really even know you, nor you me, besides the fact I was your daughter for forty years before you died. I tried in so many ways to talk to you, to get you to really look at me and love me. I desperately wanted you to be proud of me, but I couldn't succeed.

In so many ways, we were alike. I shared your love of the theater, the symphony, opera, books, and nature. I was happy when people told me I looked like you. You were a handsome man. My compulsive, perfectionistic, organized personality was just like yours. Why were we unable to reach out to one another? There remain unanswered questions, such as why did you not want a daughter? And did you really cry all night when I was born? It haunts me that these questions will never be answered. Personality-wise, I'm sometimes more like you than Mom. We were both bright, sensitive, idealistic, introspective, and enjoyed solitude and our daydreams. We were creative, though your choice of media was a paint brush and mine a pen. We were highly imaginative and disliked mediocrity. You used to say that any person who is imperfect should be eliminated by a firing squad. Being human, none of us are perfect, nor will we ever be.

But I couldn't share any of my deepest thoughts and feelings with you. I'm sure you wanted to be loved, but due to extreme shyness and fear of rejection, you would never risk reaching out to anyone, even your own children. You only felt secure with Mom. She made a mistake by not allowing you to share in our upbringing. I recall her telling you, "Frank, you attend to business, and I'll take care of the children my way." Dad, kids need both parents. I grew up feeling I was ugly, dumb, and incapable of doing anything. I longed—[Jean turns to me: "I can't believe after all these years this still bothers me. That I would feel—I'm not reading this, I'm reacting, as tears come to my eyes. OK, where was I?"] I longed for you to hold me, tell me I had something positive, and that you loved me. As a child, you gave me bonds for Christmas and my birthday. This was a paper with numbers on it and was meaningless for a little girl who wanted a doll or stuffed animal you had picked out just for her. I grew up wishing I was poor because I didn't realize one could have both love and money.

I got involved with Richard in Detroit because he was poor, placed me on a pedestal, and treated me like his princess. But I quickly discovered he was not what I was searching for either. He was uneducated, and I couldn't reach upwards and go with him. Dad, I wish you were here now, even for a little while, so we could have a second chance to talk, get to know each other, and I could tell you how very much you have influenced my entire life, both positively and negatively.

As a young woman, I was afraid to be alone with you. I never understood why. Did it have something to do with a fear that perhaps we loved each other too much and were terrified we might get too close? Thank you for not abusing me in any physical way. I think you got involved with Jenny, my roommate in nursing school, because you really loved me. But she was not your daughter, so you could show your love to her in a way that you never showed it to me. This insight came after years of therapy. Did you disapprove of psychiatrists because the truth can often be too difficult to even look at, much less talk about? We are both basically private individuals, so exposing our thoughts and feelings is too risky.

Dad, you were a self-made man and a very successful businessman. Why am I still afraid of success? Maybe because it's the other side of failure. I grew up feeling I could never be as smart as you, so I got attention by being sick and purposely failing in several areas. . . . I couldn't be the prettiest child, so I was determined to be the fattest and most unattractive. Do you realize, not once in my entire life did you ever tell me I was pretty, although some photographs show I was? Did you hate and resent me so much for being born that you would barely acknowledge my existence?

Daddy, you burned your hand one evening in scalding water by accident in Florida shortly before you died. Louise and I were visiting. You refused to allow me to help, though I'm a nurse and kept telling you to put your hand under cold water. You were in pain and screamed that I hated you and wished you were dead. Many times, I admit this was true. You made me feel so inferior to you, I couldn't bear to be near you. But underneath the anger was a great deal of love and respect. [she cries, then says: "Sorry. This isn't even the sad part."]

You were a very honest man [pause]. I was much closer to Mom, but growing up, you were the one I trusted to be honest. Mom said and did all the right things to compensate for what you weren't able to give me. Both you and Mom had tempers. Yours was much more erratic. Unfortunately, I inherited a temper also, although I hid it even from myself at times, choosing to eat down my feelings or acting out my hostility in more subtle and destructive ways. Playing the dating game for me was extremely stressful and unrewarding. For much too long, I didn't know who or what I really was. And so I tried to be whatever I felt anyone wanted me to be, and of course I failed because I had failed myself.

The world was so frightening I wanted to remain a female Peter Pan and never grow up. This in part is what happened, and I had to be dragged into the world of adults by psychiatrists, screaming and fighting and rebelling much of the way. The grown-up world has its flaws, but it isn't nearly as awesome, frightening, or unpleasant as I was led to believe it was. And although I'm a human being with many faults and imperfections, I am basically sane, someone you might love and respect and even not be ashamed to acknowledge as your daughter. [Umm, boy!] I had to fight hard to get this far from the completely dependent child I was with no solid identity. I have far to go, but God isn't finished with me yet. Hopefully, I will have time to continue to grow until someday I will join you, and we will be reunited.

Daddy, I've been scared of you, I've hated you, and I've wished you'd go away. Now, I wish you were back so I could tell you how much I've grown to love you. You were the product of an unhappy childhood. I lacked the insight and compassion to realize where you were coming from. I know now, and Dad, I'm proud and glad you were my father. I forgive you for not being able to reach out and give me the love I needed. I believe in your heart you felt it, at least at times, but just couldn't show it. Please forgive me for being a far cry from all you longed for me to be. Mom, relatives, and friends love me. If I was a bad person, I'd never be blessed with my wonderful friends. Thanks to therapy, I can now love myself, too. I lack your self-discipline in part, Dad, but I can now pick up the pieces and start each day anew.

Goodbye, Dad. You will always be alive in my memory, thoughts, prayers, and heart.

—Your loving daughter

SIX

Gender and Emotion

A THEME IN contemporary fiction is the reluctance of older adults to discuss the more troubling aspects of their lives. The narrator in Carol Sheilds's fictional biography of Daisy Goodwill Flett, an eighty-two-year-old woman looking back on her life, allows that "there are chapters in every life which are seldom read, and certainly not aloud." This is especially true for women of Daisy's generation, who were socialized to offer an "edited hybrid version" of their life stories "without apology" and "without equivocation." A blend of distortion and omission, these are often the only stories older women allow themselves to tell.[1]

Similarly, in Doris Lessing's *The Diary of a Good Neighbour*, the middle-aged narrator, Janna, comes to accept her older friends' romanticized versions of the past, realizing that they function socially as "good stories" and psychologically as forms of face-saving and self-preservation: "I know very well that what I hear from Eliza about her life is not all the truth, probably nothing like it; and I commend her, as I would the writer of a tale well-told." Another of Janna's older friends, Annie, aggressively edits her life stories in order to sustain a pristine version of an earlier self, creating and perpetuating a narrative persona that suits what she thinks she *ought* to be: "a timorous, refined, refraining persona, one from whom all unpleasant facts must be kept." The working-class older women in Lessing's novel, now disabled and homebound, need to "pretty up" their histories, for "it would be intolerable to have the long heavy *weight* of truth there, all grim and painful."[2]

The need to construct an emotionally tolerable past occurs for fictional men, too. Harry Weinberg, the elder-narrator in Leslea Newman's short story "A Letter to Harvey Milk," reflects on the anxiety that his young writing teacher, a woman, at the Jewish senior center is causing him. She encourages the group to discuss events, relationships, and emotions that they have long concealed. But Harry's idea of telling personal history is to focus on the positive and to block out negative memories: "Believe me, life in the shtetl is nothing worth knowing about," he says. "Hunger and more hunger. Better off we're here in America, the past is past." For Harry, early memories are too painful to recall, much less write about. After one group session, Harry chronicles the unsettling effects of remembering without censure: "I got myself upstairs and took myself a pill, I could feel my pressure was going up. All this talk about the past—Fannie, Harvey, Frieda, my mother, my father—what good does it do? This teacher and her crazy ideas. Did I ever ask my mother, my father, what their childhood was like? What nonsense. Better I shouldn't know." [3]

The dynamics of some senior writing groups may promote the desire to put a happy face on the past. In her short story "The Happy Memories Club," Lee Smith describes a fictional writing group at the Marshwood Total Retirement Community, where group members are deeply shaken by the rough-and-ready reminiscences of protagonist Alice Sculley. Alice is unlike her peers in attitude and temperament and has already garnered their disapproval (and jealousy) by carrying on openly with Dr. Solomon, the most eligible bachelor in the community. In her writing, Alice is bold and unflinching: she tells of her father's suicide, her mother's mental illness, her younger sister's escape with a "fast-talking furniture salesman," and her own teenage affair with a local boy that ended in pregnancy and public disgrace. Alice reveals that, as a single mother, she once looked at her screaming, red-faced love baby and "had an awful urge to throw him out the window." Group members are astounded, stricken, outraged. One woman bursts into tears. "Alice! Now just look what you've done!" says the blue-haired group facilitator. The others want to hear only about the "good" times—Alice's long marriage to a pharmacist, her children and grandchildren, love in the old refrains. But Alice persists in the service of narrative and personal change, admonishing her peers and the reader as well: "Of course I loved Harold Scully. Of course I love my grandchildren. I love Solomon, too. I love them all. Miss Elena is like my sons, too terrified to admit to herself how many people we can love, how various we are. She does not want to hear it anymore than they do, any more than you do. You all want us to *never change, never change.*" [4]

In their provocative ways, novelists and creative writers encourage us to ponder the many social and psychological reasons why older people fashion their life stories in the ways they do. They show us the emotional conflict in reminiscence and raise the issue of intergenerational response—how narrators concern themselves with the reactions of others (especially children and grandchildren) but also with the impact of the narrative on themselves. Academic research confirms the existence of cohort differences in the expression of feelings. Large-scale psychological studies have determined that older adults in general report fewer negative emotions than young and middle-aged adults; they conclude that this is evidence of highly adaptive coping strategies. Older adults are better able to regulate their emotions, making more choices in terms of "contextual appropriateness"—where, when, and to what degree to express emotions—even in their personal writing.[5] My own study puts a human face on these findings. More than one writing-group member has reminded me that her generation, unlike mine, neither "dwells on the negative" nor "airs its dirty laundry in public." Once in a meeting of the Jewish center group I facilitated, I met with some resistance while attempting to get members to list things they had never done. I initiated the exercise by reading aloud an excerpt from Carol Shields's *Stone Diaries* that detailed some of the things Daisy Goodwill Flett had never experienced at the end of her life (skiing, jalepeno peppers, religious ecstasy, body massage, outraged condemnation, and so on).[6] "But it's all so *negative!*" Samuel, ninety-two, protested. "I'd rather tell the things I *have* done!" For him, the purpose of life-story writing was to celebrate accomplishments. Samuel did not see my exercise as a heuristic for expanded thinking; it was instead a potentially depressing display of "never dids but probably should haves."

Graceful and compelling as they are, the fictional accounts of older adults' resistance to "emotion talk" are also in some ways overdrawn—too ready and obvious—and perhaps a bit unfair. There are always exceptions to the norm—real people like the fictional Alice Sculley who offer counternarratives to the more traditional feel-good stories. Within writing groups, older adults employ a wide range of strategies for dealing with strong emotions, and a writer's willingness to experiment with these strategies usually develops over time. As they become more experienced in writing about themselves and see how other group members express feelings (or do not express them), most older writers begin to adopt new ways of displaying emotion. Woman-dominated writing groups broaden the narrative possibilities for older men, in particular, by gently encouraging them to "tell us more" and "tell us how you felt." This gender dynamic is rarely considered in gerontological studies of reminiscence, life review, or auto/biography, nor is the fact that expression of feelings is largely a social construction and is therefore likely to change through interaction with others. We will see in this chapter exactly how older adults develop their ability to express themselves emotionally in life-story groups, maneuvering around, through, and beyond four different narrative strategies: avoidance, self-censoring, indirectness, and distancing.

Avoidance

Fictional examples like those above suggest that older adults are especially adept at avoiding negative memories—that they limit their expression of feelings to the "good times." Indeed, this is true for many writers, regardless of race, class, or gender. Unless prompted, taught, or required, many older adults avoid the public display of negative emotions, including expressions of fear, anger, jealousy, envy, anxiety, insecurity, and feelings of dependence. They admit to editing out the "bad parts" and offer good reasons for doing so. What some psychologists would consider an act of repression, older adults see as a means of staying healthy and maintaining social harmony: avoiding the expression of negative feelings is a personal coping strategy and an approach to protecting the feelings of others in the writing group and the family circle. As one woman told me, "Some things are just too hurtful to tell." This is true even in the urban centers, where members have experienced poverty and considerable hardship. Writers still choose not to "dwell on the negative," and they are supported by their peers in making this decision.

An illustrative discussion occurred during a meeting of a writing group at an urban Detroit center. During this session, Annie, an African-American woman of seventy-seven, is explaining to the group why she has not written much about her husband, now dead: "This part on the marriage business—I stopped because I started getting mad," she says. All of the women around the table that day (except for me) are African Americans; they all are widowed or divorced; and they all support Annie's avoidance of this charged topic through a humorous exchange of stories that challenge the sanctity of marriage. Florence laughs and tells about a woman at the center whose blood pressure shoots up every time anyone even mentions her husband. "I learned some sense with the second one," she says of her own two marriages. "I kept me a little change on the side. I had me an account at the credit union. We had some savings bonds, and I put my name on 'em and down at the bottom, his." Annie and Ella nod and confirm that husbands can't be trusted. Ella says she stayed with hers and buried him on their thirty-fifth anniversary, but he still took her money and cashed in their savings bonds without her knowing it. Annie suggests a reason for women's foolishness around men: "I think they stay in these bad marriages for so long because they're afraid to be on their own. I think I was *hypnotized* or something." Florence counters, "I wasn't afraid, because I worked, but I just didn't want to be married a lot of times, so I stayed with one." Florence then tells a story about a friend of hers who met a man three months ago and has already married him. "She was talkin' to me on the phone late last night, and I said, 'Well, shouldn't you go upstairs and see about your husband?' And she said, 'He's up there snoring. I can hear him all the way down here' [group laughter]. And I wanted to say, 'I *told* you so!' But she's the type that likes to be married. This is her third husband."

The conversation, besides entertaining everyone present, confirms that narrative evasions are perfectly all right. A few days later, when I interview Annie, she explains further why she has left the details of her marriage and other troubling times out of her life story: "I says [to myself] some of the things in there—when I start thinking about other things I could have put in there—I just say, 'Well, now, Lord, what's the use of upsettin' myself?' 'Cause upsettin' myself, I'm the one who got to pay for it. I'm the one whose blood pressure's gonna be goin' up."

It is useful to consider here the differences between ordinary life-story telling and literary memoir. Most older adults write in order to understand the meaning of their lives *for themselves*, and to pass along this knowledge, selectively, to younger generations. Their stories are written within a complex matrix of family relationships. Professional authors, in contrast, write memoirs and autobiographies in order to project a public, rather than familial, identity. The best memoirists, according to literary critics, use language and memory as creative devices to engage in a personal reckoning, which is often painful to family and friends. Though intimacies are betrayed and wounds displayed, professional writers justify these acts in the name of art. But the narrative strategies of literary authors are quite different from those of the writer in a life-story group. Phyllis, a member of a group at the geriatric center, explains to me that there are some things—"intimate things"—that she will not share, like her mother's suicide. Why? "It would be too painful. I'd break down. It would not only be painful for me, it would be painful for others to hear." To expect Phyllis or any other member of her writing group to engage in a painful reckoning of the past through autobiography is to impose a concept of narrative "truth" that is literary rather than familial. This is why the fictional figures at the beginning of this chapter are in some sense unfair characterizations. They are representations of old age as seen through the assessing eyes of professional writers—writers more likely to criticize the evasions of everyday people and to privilege the artistically done confessional.

Although the desire to spare people's feelings exerts a powerful influence on older adults' life stories, this is not to say that these writers would not like to be more forthcoming, or that they do not admire those who are. Phyllis, for example, greatly respects Jean, a fellow group member who has written extensively about the emotional traumas of her life, including the loss of her husband and two children in a car accident; her subsequent miscarriage, nervous breakdown, and hospitalization for severe depression; and psychiatrists' diagnoses during the 1950s that she would never again lead a "normal" life. Although she is not as "courageous" as Jean, Phyllis feels she gains a lot just being in a group with her: "With Jean to be able to philosophize about, talk about how she emotionally came to be the woman she is today, what she has gone through emotionally from a young woman to where she is today, I can learn from her experiences and integrate them into my own life. . . . And therefore it expands my world. It broadens my life. I guess that's what writing groups are all about."

Phyllis herself has come a long way in learning to express feelings through writing. When she first joined a writing group at the geriatric center, about a year prior to our interview, she was unable to write anything at all because she "wasn't emotionally ready." Deeply depressed at the time, Phyllis was seeing a psychiatrist, had begun taking antidepressants, was meeting with counselors at the geriatric center, and had joined a women's support group. Gradually, she began to write short pieces for the group, concentrating exclusively on the happier memories of her childhood. She says of the other memories, "There's a lot there that I probably never will write about, and then I may. I don't know, because there's a lot I need to write about, but I'm not ready for it yet." Sharing the good times with the writing group is what she needs to do right now:

> The release I get is the positive feedback. I think I'm looking for somebody to say, "Gee, you've done a good job, Phyllis." And whatever level it is, there's always a comment, and it's a polite comment: "Well, that was really a good piece." We support one another and give positive feedback. I've been evidently hungry for support. . . . I came from a very quiet family. What's the term? I can't think of the psychological term right now, but there wasn't any communication. Silent meals, you know. We just didn't visit a lot, and I think it's what I've been looking for all my life—somebody to talk with, to visit with, to share experiences with. And I think that's what the writing group has brought to my life.

That Phyllis has reflected on and talked about many of her feelings in therapy but has not written about them is significant. She reminds us of the role language and culture play in a person's willingness and ability to display emotions publicly: we all have to be taught that it is all right to reveal emotions, and we each need to learn the language of emotional expression. One of Phyllis's deepest regrets is that she did not have this vocabulary at an earlier time in her life when she most needed it. Neither she nor her husband, who died at fifty-eight of lupus, were ever able to express their fears about his declining health and approaching death:

> When the doctors came in and told him he had lupus, that he was the twenty-second patient at Henry Ford Hospital to have ever been diagnosed with lupus, he asked what happened to those twenty-two people, did they all die? And they told him yes. So that's when he learned he was going to die. But we didn't talk about it. We didn't talk about it at all, even the day he died. I think he wanted to spare me that knowledge. And I didn't talk about it because I didn't believe it, because he had never been sick, never, ever before.

Phyllis mentions that she would do things differently now, because she has learned how to "cope with terminal illness," both emotionally and linguistically, through subsequent volunteer work with a hospice group:

> Oh, I learned so much. And it's probably been one of my big regrets, both for my sister and my husband. My sister died in the same corridor, right across from the room where my husband died. She died in 1962, and he died in 1968. And I treated her the same way. I couldn't bear to hold her hand or talk to her, because she was getting cold, and I just couldn't. But through

hospice I learned all of these wonderful skills about how to relate to people who are ill and with their families. So I learned there is a whole—it's another language. It's just like learning French and Spanish, or astronomy. It's another skill that we all need to develop in ourselves, how to relate to given situations in a caring, supportive way. That's what hospice is all about.

Rhetorician Judith Summerfield offers further insight into the nature of writing about emotions. She explains that learning to write autobiographically involves a slow process of bringing one's life to language. Many memories are recalled from a liminal state, where they "are not yet easy in language." These experiences are still "raw" and have not been "cooked into a story."[7] On the other hand, narrative researchers Gary Kenyon and William Randall would explain the differences between Jean and Phyllis in terms of the *loss* of story. Sometimes when we lose key people in our lives, namely those who held, reinforced, and evoked a certain version of ourselves (good daughter, loving spouse), we can become temporarily "de-storied" until we reidentify ourselves. Jean has worked hard to establish a new story: she has become the heroine in her own survival narrative. Through Jean, Phyllis is engaging in what Kenyon and Randall call "biographical learning"; she is discovering new possibilities for identifying herself by listening to Jean's narratives. This, in fact, is the basis of adult development from a narrative standpoint—being open to "what, amid *our* lifestory, we can learn from [others] amid theirs, and what we can learn from *their* restorying as we, presumably, continue ours."[8]

Self-Censoring

Another strategy for dealing with negative emotions is to write them privately but not to reveal them publicly. A time-honored practice for women is to keep a personal journal. Feminist critic Margo Culley has traced the gendered uses of journals and diaries, concluding that American men have been unused to probing and expressing their inner life in any but religious terms and are thus unlikely to use journals for emotional release. Men typically pursue public forms of discourse, whereas women pursue private forms.[9] Still, the narrative stance of the journaling woman is often one of censorship, if not before or during the act of writing, then after the fact.

Mary, sixty-two, has kept a private journal for many years. She records aspects of her life that she does not tell to anyone, including her writing group. After a while, she tears the pages out that she does not want her kids to see. Mostly, she wants her family to know how she felt about things at the time and to remember "what a great mother I was." The writings she throws away are "therapeutic" and for her eyes only.

Other women keep a journal that they feel comfortable sharing with the writing group but not their children. This is the case with Catherine, sixty-eight, a mother of five, who says that many of the things she writes about are more meaningful to her peer group:

> I know one time . . . I wrote about the mother/daughter relationship, which I see as very complex and not always loving, like we like to portray that relationship. And when I finished, Mary [a fellow group member] really responded to that. She had tears in her eyes, and she told me about an experience that she had recently had with her daughter. . . . And so that would be an example, if you got into an area like that—that isn't resolved and that won't be resolved until one of you dies actually—probably something like [I wouldn't share with my kids].

Journal keeping is always defined by these writers in the context of familial relationships, as is *not* keeping a journal. One woman told me, "I never kept a journal very long; I was afraid someone might find it." Mary is careful to destroy the parts of her journal that might cause pain to her children or cast her in a negative light, and Catherine shares her journal entries selectively with age peers only. The appeal of journal keeping is the personal act of languaging emotions, not the public display of these emotions. Women writers, especially, have felt heavily censored in their public expression of strong feelings, especially those arising from the family. To represent any part of daughterhood or motherhood as anything but nourishing and benevolent is to write against the socially sanctioned scripts for women: "Good mother, in [American] culture, is selfless, cheerful, and deodorized. It does not include resentment, anger, violence, alienation, disappointment, grief, fear, exhaustion—or erotic pleasure. . . . Our culture does not give us images of a daughter desperate for a mother's love, or desperate to escape it, or contemptuous of the mother, nor do we have an archetype of the Prodigal Daughter who escapes and returns." [10] The tropes for the "good daughter" and the "good mother" often function as censors in older women's journal writing, as well as their public expressions of life story.

Indirectness

A third strategy for dealing with emotions is to write about them indirectly by zeroing in on a period from the past that is troubling. To paraphrase Emily Dickinson, the writer tells the truth but tells it slant. She details the events and activities that occurred during a period of conflict or turmoil, circling around the emotions associated with these events without naming them.

Sue, seventy, retired from kindergarten teaching after twenty-two years and has spent the past year writing exclusively about the time in her life between kindergarten and the sixth grade. Sue has never told the writing group exactly *what* is so compelling about this period, but she has written several life stories that center around the small injustices of childhood, particularly those in which adults (parents, an aunt, a friend's grandmother) behaved immaturely or unfairly toward her. Sue's re-creation of events is primarily descriptive; she focuses on the activities of the adults and the consequences to the child (being forced to do the work of an adult, being misunderstood or falsely accused) without revealing the inner state of the child. Sue's fascination with her own childhood has manifested itself in various forms of writing throughout her adult life. She once spent an entire summer vacation working on a children's book, which she eventually abandoned after it was rejected by two publishing houses. Now, she is not able even "find the darn thing," and she wonders if losing it has some deeper meaning: "I have lost it. I felt sure when I moved, I would find it, but I didn't. I don't understand it. I keep thinking, is it something psychological, did I lose it on purpose, or what?"

In our interview, Sue mentions that there are still segments of her childhood that she has not written about, and probably won't:

> I have been very aware that I have not written about some of the really bad experiences where I feel that my parents let me down. That type of thing. And I seem to put off doing them. There are a few incidents that I really remember very well that I still feel were quite unfair and not good parenting. And I may never write them. I've been thinking lately, maybe that is not important. Maybe I don't need to put that in there, even though it's part of life, and everybody has some of those. I'm not sure it's going to hurt me or anybody else for me to just keep it private. Or I could tell it to somebody. But I don't know why I need to have it in print.

At the end of our interview, Sue comes to articulate at least one of the reasons why she is writing about her childhood. We have talked about the fact that she still identifies strongly with the little girl she used to be and that her first ten years constituted the most formative period of her life. She has also asked me what I am going to do with all the interviews that I am conducting. I tell her that I am interested in how people "construct the self" in their autobiographical writing and how they structure their narratives—where they start and stop and how they decide what to include and leave out. She responds by elaborating on her own motivations:

> Just about as you started talking there, my mind was kind of going, and just before I asked you this question—and I think that's partly why I asked you the question—is it suddenly came to me why I am only interested in writing about my childhood. I think it's because my children didn't know me

then. They don't know the little girl I was. My grandchildren, of course, don't. Nobody except my contemporaries would know me and remember me in that period of life. That's why I want to tell that part of me.

This desire to reclaim a lost part of herself is a revelation to Sue, and she repeats it a week later in our second interview: "I'm writing mostly about my childhood, and I'm so glad that last week I realized exactly why. It's because nobody has known me all that length of time. . . . And everybody else is gone. I feel like that's a part of me, and nobody else knows it."

Sue's attempts at personal reclamation through writing are not, of course, unique to her. There is a growing body of literary scholarship that explains how professional authors use writing throughout the life course, but particularly in later years, to work through concealed, repressed, and unresolved feelings about earlier periods in their lives. Literary gerontologist Ann Wyatt-Brown reads Elizabeth Bowen's last two novels as "a battleground where she could struggle with her unruly emotions," a fictional place where "at long last she confronted more openly than before her suppressed feelings about her mother and her often mixed emotions about her husband." [11] Brown and other literary critics direct us to Kathleen Woodward's *Aging and Its Discontents,* which suggests, among other things, that artists (including professional and nonprofessional writers) occupy a creative space between mourning and melancholia where they work through the pain of various losses. [12] Women writers may be especially positioned by society, upbringing, and temperament to make personal writing "do the work of aging." In reviewing the writings of contemporary women poets on the subjects of memory, mortality, and aging, Diana Hume George concludes that the poetry of women, unlike that of many well-known men, "records the process of confronting their fear rather than the accomplishment of having defeated it. Theirs are poems of death and loss, and they would permit me no wishful projection that mature poets of demonstrated achievement, and presumably personal wisdom, had come entirely to terms with mortality or aging." Instead, "such poets use their fears, deliberately and creatively." [13] I suspect that fear—the fear of being forgotten or, even worse, never having been known in the first place—is also what motivates a great many everyday writers in senior centers.

Distancing

A fourth strategy that older writers use is to recognize and distance themselves from negative feelings, assuming the narrative stance of a "wise elder" looking back on earlier conflicts now resolved, or at least better understood. Most of these conflicts involve parents and siblings.

Selma, introduced in a previous interchapter, recalls differences in opinion between her and her sister Idella, who was eleven years older and stepped into the shoes of their father after his death. Selma describes Idella as "knowledgeable about a lot of things," but strict and controlling. She did not allow other family members much input: "Mostly what she would suggest, like a father would, we followed those instructions." Selma disagreed with Idella on a number of things, one of the most important being how to respond to racial discrimination. Idella kept her mouth shut, while Selma was likely to speak out. Today, Selma interprets their differences in a larger social and historical context:

> I think she was a person who in her day had to accept things the way they were. Her focus was on moving ahead with her life, trying to get ahead with her life, and whatever it took to get there, she was willing to do that. And she couldn't change segregation, so she had to adjust to that. . . . Her focus was on her goal, and she was not going to let segregation keep her from her goal. And she managed to accomplish those things, too, in her lifetime. She saw to it that all of us got an education, just as my father [would have]. . . . She was a real responsible person, and once he died, she just moved into that position and she had her goals for all of her sisters and brothers. She knew that my mother was limited about things in this country. My mother was set in her own old-time [Bahamian] ways.
>
> So [Idella] just took over, and she saw to it that all of us got an education. She decided, *she* decided I would be a nurse, because there would be a job for me when I got back. I had wanted to be a home economics teacher, but she told me there would be no job for me, "So you go into nursing and I know there'll be a job for you." And our other sister, she told her to be a teacher because there would be a job here for her. . . . She decided, when one of us got out of school, [that one] sent the next one to school. Then when that one finished, she had to send the next one, and so forth. When I graduated from school, she told me, "Now in September, your younger sister will be going to school, and her room, board, and tuition will be sixty-three dollars and sixty cents. And as you start on your first job, every month that comes off the top. You send that one to school. Sixty-three dollars and sixty cents, I've never forgotten that. And I did, until such time as a change was made.

Selma's narrative persona is that of mature older women; having assisted her siblings and raised her own two children, she now sees the wisdom in Idella's ways. She sympathizes with and even appreciates the responsibilities her sister shouldered on behalf of the family. Selma ends her narrative by describing the long-term benefits of Idella's strict requirements and controlling behavior:

> And we built a house for my mother the same way. Idella told me that we were gonna build a house for my mom, and it'd be a family house, because

until then we were renting. And she said that they had bought this land, and the man was going to start building. But they needed *X* number of dollars, I don't even remember what they needed. But my share was five hundred dollars, and [I was to] get that down there by such and such a date. And I didn't quite have that in the bank at the time. Remember, now, I'm making like a hundred and sixty dollars a month. So five hundred dollars was a lot of money, and I'm not living at home, I'm away. So I borrowed the last—I think I had four hundred—I borrowed the last hundred dollars. And in those days, blacks couldn't even borrow money from banks and things, like you couldn't walk into loan companies. I mean, you weren't even considered. So I borrowed this from a person, and I had to pay it back at the interest of twenty-five percent. And I didn't even know that was a lot. To me, I thought, "Oh, wow, good! I'll get that hundred" [she claps her hands], I can make my five hundred and send it to her.

And she bought that house, they built that house. That house cost eight thousand five hundred dollars, after the land. And my mom lived in it for thirty-some years until she died. She was almost one hundred. She was right there, and they just took her to the hospital the last week or so. And when that house was sold, which was interesting to me, because there's five of us and the [amount] was divided up equally, we each got eight thousand five hundred dollars. Isn't that neat? The first buyer that saw it, bought it. So we probably could have gotten more, but that's what it amounted to. I thought that was kind of God's way of telling us we did the right thing for our mom, because she was really secure after that.

In this story, Idella's character is redeemed over time through the sale of their mother's house and the return (times seventeen) on each sibling's original investment. In the end, Selma tells a spiritual narrative about the benefits of personal sacrifice and the acceptance of responsibility for one's own.

There is, of course, considerable narrative difference between writing about sibling rivalries that have been overcome and writing about relationships that still evoke strong feelings. Through their talk around a life story, writing-group members often help each other gain the larger perspective needed to reinterpret negative feelings and move into the "wise elder" position.

In one exchange around a sibling story, members of Margaret's group assist Eileen, seventy, in a subtle rethinking of her past. In the story she reads to the group, Eileen describes a conflicted relationship with her older sister Lillian:

My older sisters were two years years apart. I was seven years younger than Martha, the third sister. I'm sure my sisters were friends and played together when they were growing up. When I came along, they were too old to be my friends and play with me. They were my babysitters, my teachers, and my counselors. They helped me with my homework. . . . Whenever I had trouble in school with the Polish classes, my sister Martha would intercede for me with the nuns. Mother never went to school on my behalf. Mother always sent me to my oldest sister Lillian for advice. When I started menstruating, mother sent me to Lillian. Lillian was in nursing school at the time, so I guess mom thought she would explain things better.

Eileen goes on to explain how difficult Lillian's life became in adulthood and how their parents tried to help, to the exclusion of the other children. Although Lillian was a "religious fanatic" and wanted to be a nun, her parents opposed this vehemently and paid for nursing school so that she would have a career.

> While Lillian was in nursing school, the whole family catered to her. We finally got a phone in our house so Mom and Dad could keep in touch with her. She often complained about the food. Mom cooked and baked, and Anne would take the packages to Lillian, by bus, in all sorts of weather. Many times Anne would freeze waiting for a bus or get soaked by a drenching rain. All was done to keep Lillian happy and in school. Mom and Dad, who had very little education, were so very proud to have a daughter in nursing school.

In her late twenties, Lillian married and had two boys. When her husband came home from World War II, "he drank quite a bit," and "when Lillian found evidence of adultery, she packed his bags and left them on the front porch." Lillian moved into a flat downstairs from their parents and continued to work while her mother cared for the boys. For her part, Eileen "was expected to babysit at the drop of a hat. I had to go downstairs after school, and I was expected to cancel dates and arrangements with friends. I resented it very much. Mom always made me feel so guilty when I voiced my objections. After all, family always helped each other." Besides that, Lillian "never had a good word to say about men. In her opinion, all men were alike: *Bad*. Her attitude about men made it very hard for me when I was dating. Here was this person I used to go to for advice that I couldn't talk to anymore. She never saw any good in any boy I dated."

When she has finished reading, Eileen asks the group for their reactions to the emotional display in the story, and group members, including Selma, draw on their own experiences to assist her in considering more fully the nature of sibling rivalry:

Eileen: From what I've written, what kind of feelings do you get between my sister and me?

Lorraine: Well, I get a lot of the same kind of resentments in your family that I felt in mine, but I didn't have sisters, I had brothers. And I felt that they were favored. Now, my older brother was raised just like your oldest sister.

He was next to a god because he was a violinist. And everybody sacrificed to his education. He was sent to New York to study with the finest teachers, and we were living on a dollar a day. So—

Margaret, looking at me and raising her eyebrows, suggesting that I should take note: There's a trend in this.

Lorraine: Yes.

Eileen: You know, when I say these packages to Lillian, I mean my mother would buy fruit out of season. We never got to taste one of 'em. You know, they'd all go into a package for her.

Lorraine: Yes, that's the way my older brother was treated, just like that. Does she now—

Eileen: Well, she's dead now.

Lorraine: Oh, is she? Well, as an adult, as an older adult, did she come to any understanding of how she was favored and have any feelings about it?

Eileen: No, she didn't. No.

Lorraine: No?

Eileen: No.

Selma: Being the oldest one, she may have—and I'm basing this on my own sisters—she may have felt it was her due, because she started out being the first child, is that right?

Eileen: Yeah. Yeah, maybe a lot was expected of her that I don't know about.

Selma: And not only that, with the first child, you are an only child, and so everything comes to you, and maybe—

Eileen: It was only for two years. There was two years difference between those three girls.

Ginny: Well, even two years makes a difference.

Margaret: There's only one year between my—

Lorraine: Well, my older brother now realizes that much of the problem that he's had with relationships in his life and with adjusting to life was the favored treatment he received. He said he was led to believe that he was better, better than anyone else. More important than anyone else. And he understands that. It doesn't change his behavior, but he understands it.

Ginny: Maybe that's my husband's problem.

Selma: It seems like whatever is fed into them under age five, just stays there. You cannot get that out.

Margaret: Yeah, it never goes away.

Eileen: Well, you know, with Lillian, being separated from her husband, she always felt that her boys were missing something, okay?

Lorraine: Well, they *were.*

Eileen, conceding: Yeah, they were.

Lorraine: Sure they were.

Eileen: But then she catered to them. I mean, you know, she'd bring them home something everyday from work. You know, some little thing.

Margaret: But they were spoiled rotten!

Selma: But what I'm thinking is maybe she should have been a nun. She wanted to be a nun in the first place [several voices at the same time, including Eileen's, agree with this]. She should have been left alone to make that decision.

Eileen: Because all through her adult life, she was a member of some religious group or organization, had meetings at home and stuff like that.

Ginny: Yeah, it sounds like she was meant to be a nun and just got side-tracked.

Here the group discusses possible reasons why the elder child is often the favored one and leads Eileen to consider the negative effects of these family dynamics on her sister, as well as herself. The family may have helped Lillian extensively, but for this she paid a heavy price; she was expected to give up her own desires and pursue her parents' goals for her. The group, in its response, offers new ways of interpreting this sibling rivalry and helps Eileen distance herself from the resentment she still feels toward her older sister.

Another member of Margaret's group provides an interesting twist on the wise-elder tale of sibling rivalry. Cecille has written a life story in which she exercises a quiet revenge on the favored sibling and the favoring parent. Cecille's story serves as a kind of trickster tale in which the narrator, through harmless deception, narratively sets things right in the family.

Cecille begins the story—titled "Reginald's Birthday Cake"—with a description of the family hierarchy: "I am the oldest of four children. My brother Reginald is the youngest and only son. My sisters Frances and Shirley maintain that the double advantage of being the baby and only boy has given Reginald privileged status in our pecking order." Cecille goes on to prove Reggie's favored status by noting the many years their mother has baked him a special birthday cake, which "followed him to Mississippi, Japan, and Texas during his stint in the air force." Mother even paid the postage to send the pineapple upside-down cake *in a skillet* to Japan. The girls in the family, however, receive only cards and telephone calls on their birthdays. "Naturally, mother vehemently denies any differential treatment on her part, alluding to the fact that my brother was always made to share equally in household chores. However . . . of twelve grandchildren, only two receive cakes on their birthdays. We have not decided if the pair are so favored because they are grandsons or because they are Reginald's sons. In any case, the daughters do not receive cakes."

Having established the family dynamics, Cecille subtly subverts them in the proceeding narrative. In the spring of 1968, her mother is hospitalized with a pinched nerve and is unable to bake for Reggie's thirty-fourth birthday. She entrusts the preparing of the "ritual cake" to Cecille, the oldest daughter:

> At each visit [to the hospital], I received detailed instructions as to where and in which cookbook she had written her own special recipe for the cake. Drain the juice from the pineapple and substitute this for milk, I was directed. Use butter, not margarine, pecans, not walnuts. And I was given the location of the pan in which the cake was to be baked. On subsequent visits, I was further cajoled to follow her recipe carefully and re-create her cake following the directions. . . . I promised to buy and whip heavy cream. No artificial or prewhipped concoctions would be tolerated. This cake must be as near perfection as possible without her loving hands and protection. . . .

The day of the baking arrives, and Cecille picks up the specified pan, the cookbook, and the ingredients, including "a secret ingredient of my own—two boxes of Duncan Hines yellow cake mix."

> I proceeded to make all the alterations to the cake mix my mother had indicated in her from-scratch cake recipe. I carried the cake to Reggie's home, where I whipped cream and decorated the cake, carefully following my mother's instructions. The family raved about the cake, and Reggie, after extracting my promise never to tell my mother, declared it the best cake he had ever eaten. Swearing my sister-in-law to secrecy, I shared the cake-mix conspiracy.

When her mother is released from the hospital, she asks Reginald if the birthday cake was satisfactory. When he assures her it was, she "preens" and says, "Of course it was good. She followed my recipe. Cecille has always been very good about doing as I ask. I knew I could depend on her."

For many years after, when presenting the birthday cake to Reginald, Cecille's mother reminds the family that she has never failed to come through with this special "offering," except when hospitalized, at which point she appointed her good and reliable daughter as a stand-in. Twenty years pass before Cecille shares the secret with her mother ("but not the fact that we all considered the cake superior to her efforts"). The family has a good laugh about the oldest daughter's "treachery," and everything comes out all right: "Since that time, the cake has been prepared à la Cecille, with cake mix, which my mother has pronounced almost as good as her recipe, and much less time-consuming." In this story, narrator Cecille distances herself from lifelong inequity in the family through humor and one-upmanship. Since all family members are now "in" on the story, no one's feelings are hurt in the telling of it, and Cecille gets the satisfaction of continuing to challenge, in story form, her mother's authority and her brother's privileged status.

One of the most respected "wise elders" in my study is Jean, a member of a group at the geriatric center. Jean is able to distance herself enough from early traumas to frame them in terms of her own emotional development. "Growth" and "emotional honesty" are signature traits of her writing. For this reason, Jean's stories, like Jean herself, are praised and admired by writing-group members. Nearly everyone names Jean as an inspiration and a role model, noting her ability to confront emotionally difficult topics and to illustrate positive change, despite devestating personal crises. Jean represents someone who can write about the "intimate" and "painful" experiences of life without breaking down and losing status in the group—a serious concern for most older writers. Maintaining dignity and not "making a fool of yourself" is a recurrent theme in groups at senior centers.

Jean herself sees writing as a form of therapy and values "honesty" above all else. Many years before she joined a writing group, she kept a journal and shared it only with her therapist. Among her volunteer activities now, Jean, at sixty-seven, leads self-help groups, including one patterned after Robin Norwood's *Women Who Love Too Much*. She sees her life-story writing as a mirror image of her personal growth:

> Most of my writing, if it had anything to do with people, was not particularly honest when I was growing up. I had a sort of—I should be embarrassed saying this, but for some reason I'm not now—I had a chameleon-type personality. I could be anything anyone wanted me to be. Which is why I tried acting for a while, I guess. And I never was terribly happy because I was never pleasing me, and I couldn't please me because I didn't even know who the heck I was or what I wanted. And so honesty is very important to me today, for me today. And I think that's the big difference, is that I have become

an honest person, and I never was. I'm a product of both my parents, like most children. My father was definitely the more honest of the two. Mom was just—everyone loved my mom. They didn't really love Dad. But mother denied an awful lot. And I did, too. Whatever anyone wanted me to be, I was able to be. And I didn't see—at the time, it didn't seem dishonest. And that was hard because then it was hard for me to really know what was honest and what wasn't. I'm talking about healing.

Though, like most women who keep journals, she values writing honestly for *herself,* Jean does not always share this writing publicly. She has learned from experience what to tell and what to keep to herself:

I wouldn't share anything that would hurt anyone else. I started writing a book once, my experiences, and I shared that with my family. I'd bring different chapters and read it at Christmas time when we got together, and they got very, very upset about it. Everyone did. Because it was honest. It was beginning honesty. And they said, "You're not going to use names, and you're not going to . . ."—I had disguised the names but not terribly. You know? And I just, I thought, I was doing it primarily for myself, then. It was something I felt I had to do. And I got it out of my system. I never finished it. I got it out of my system and then one day—I don't know, I'm sorry I did this—I tore it all up. I'm sorry I did it, really, because I think it would have been good for me to keep and look at, even if I chose not to do anything about it or disguised it completely. I don't know, I didn't want to hurt them in any way. . . . But now, I think I would focus more on me. I don't have to bring out—I'm not writing a biography of them. So I could do it differently, and I would definitely do it differently. I don't know why I did it that way before.

Jean goes on to say that she did this revelatory writing in her thirties, largely through the urging of her therapist, "but I don't think I need to do that now. That's not where I'm at. That was a long time ago." I ask her if she ever thinks about how her writing will affect members of the writing group, if they will be offended:

I don't think I write anything that's offensive. No, I'm sure I haven't. Some of it has been sheer fantasy, you know? But I think the best kind of writing that I've done has been just about my feelings and my growth through the years. And a lot of them have told me afterwards that they could identify with that. Some of them fairly closely. And two or three have said after the class, "Gee, you know, you're really a role model for me because it's something I wanted to do, and I've never been able to do it." So no, I don't think I've offended them.

Jean's presence in the writing group affirms, among other things, that positive interpretations of negative events are always possible. Thirty years ago, Jean was a very different person emotionally than she is now in her late sixties, and she writes in order to reflect on and make public that change. She uses writing to articulate, analyze, and even celebrate her emotional growth, offering her life stories as an example to others.

This variety of narrative strategies for dealing with strong emotions is best understood—and appreciated—in the context of social-constructionist theories of emotion. Scholars working in narrative psychology and the sociology of emotions claim that feelings are in large part discursive practices established relationally through language. Our experiences of the world, ourselves within the world, and our feelings toward ourselves and others are limited by our abilities to describe them. Emotionally "we can only do what our linguistic resources and repertoire of social practices permit or enable us to do." [14] Feelings, then, are not "substances to be discovered in our blood, but social practices organized by stories that we both enact and tell. They are structured by our forms of understanding." [15] This is not to deny the bodily states of emotion, but to emphasize that physical sensations are mediated by language and culture, by what philosopher Rom Harre calls "the local moral order," [16] including the historical period in which we are socialized, the general culture or ethnic group with which we identify, family beliefs and values, institutional norms, and our own personal tendencies, as well as race, class, gender, and cohort group. In short, society influences "what we think we should feel, what we try to feel, and sometimes what we feel." [17]

To understand the implication of this theory, let us consider the examples of Phyllis and Jean, women of the same age cohort who use drastically different narrative strategies for dealing with negative emotions. The two women's lives are similar in many ways: both are middle-class, white women who grew up in families that did not talk about feelings; both describe themselves as shy and introverted children who became more extroverted in later life; both say they have had serious weight problems because they "eat down their feelings"; both came to language their emotions only after the untimely death of loved ones; and both have developed new patterns of emotional expression through cognitive therapy and women's support groups.

Yet the two approach their life-story writing quite differently. The suicide of her mother and her own insecurities led Phyllis to pursue a traditional marriage oriented around home and family. The death of her husband and a comfortable lifestyle came in middle age for Phyllis, but she did not seek therapy at the time. Only recently, in response to the onset of debilitating depression, has she begun to address the emotional consequences of earlier losses. Unlike Jean, Phyllis has not chronicled her feelings in a journal and is therefore not used to expressing them. She also has children and grandchildren whom she does not want to "hurt" through her life-story tellings. Jean, on the other hand, lost her husband and family earlier in life, retreated for a time into mental illness, and through a long process, including many years of psychotherapy, group therapy, personal journaling, and participation in women's suppport groups, she has come to articulate and understand her feelings. Jean has no children or grandchildren whom she feels she must protect from hard times. A primary difference between the two women, then, is their discursive repertoire: Jean has more experience trying to language her feelings, has developed a larger emotional vocabulary, and has found an empowering way to describe her losses in terms of adult development.

Jean's willingness to write about all apects of her life, even the traumatic ones, shows how therapy itself constructs a person's life story. What cognitive therapy does, in effect, is teach different communicative practices and alternative frameworks for interpreting the world. In fact, narrative psychologists describe psychotherapy as a "form of education" that "differs from other educational ventures mainly in terms of the nature of the curriculum and the arrangement of the student body. . . . [T]he focus of the tutoring is on living arrangements and life satisfaction," and its medium is language: "Words represent a relatively stable— and sometimes painful—set of practices. However, few [people] explore all aspects of the verbal terrain that are potentially available to them, and that is where a therapist may be of use." [18] Therapy groups model multiple perspectives on life, different ways of bringing life to language, and the relativity of life's meaning. Through group interactions, people in therapy learn to tell alternative life stories that include elements they have previously avoided, denied, trivialized, or otherwise censored. [19]

Gender and Narrative Strategies

The narrative strategies above have been illustrated with reference to older *women's* talk and writing. The small group of men in my study typically avoid writing directly about emotions. The choice is understandable, given the ways this cohort of men has been socialized into manhood. Current research on gender and emotion indicates that, while men and women experience the same emotions, they express them quite differently. Women typically internalize and contemplate their feelings, while men externalize and act out their feelings, divert their attention through physical activity, or suppress feelings altogether. Women are more verbally expressive of feelings and receive more social support for these expressions (female friends, for example, encourage each other to "talk through" their feelings). Current thinking holds that "although sex similarities far outweigh differences in the experience of emotions, women appear to have a wider latitude of emotional expression than do men." [20]

Differences in emotional expression are, of course, socially acquired and re-inforced. Sociologist Arlie Hochschild defines feelings within an interactionist model involving four elements, usually experienced simultaneously: appraisals of a situation, changes in bodily sensations, the free or inhibited display of ex-pressive gestures, and application of a cultural label describing specific constel-lations of the first three (that is, "anger," "happiness"). Hochschild suggests that the expression of any given emotion is culturally constrained by "feeling rules," which dictate how we are "supposed" to feel in a situation or setting. She pro-poses that the "emotional management strategies" we use to negotiate these rules are gendered, as are "feeling expressions." Men and women subscribe to different feeling rules: they learn different "lines of feeling and action through which [they] reconcile [their] gender ideology with arising situations." [21] Thus, expres-sions of emotion "are not randomly distributed across situations and time; they are guided by an ideologically informed aim. The aim is to sustain a certain gendered ego-ideal, to be, for example, a 'cookies-and-milk mom' or a 'career woman,' or some mix of the two, or neither." [22]

Hochschild acknowledges that much more is known about the emotion-management strategies of women than men, since women, lacking the kind of power in the external world that many men wield, rely on emotion management as their primary resource. [23] American culture has assigned women the role of doing the "emotion work" within relationships, and they have willingly accepted this role; consequently, women reflect on their emotions more consistently and verbalize their feelings more readily than do most American men. Older-adult writing groups, however, provide a unique environment in which men are sup-ported in doing more extensive "emotion work" around their life stories. The women serve as informal tutors, assisting men in the developmental process of learning to express feelings through personal writing.

Most of the older men in these groups come to the public expression of feel-ings slowly and reluctantly. Bill, seventy-five, is an exception. As a scholar and poet, he embraces the idea that writing can be an expression of emotion and has engaged periodically in what he calls "carthartic writing" throughout his life, primarily during times of crisis. Raised overseas by missionaires and educated by Quakers, Bill is a sensitive, introspective man who made his living before retirement as a professor of comparative literature at a small Quaker college in the Midwest. In our inteview, he informs me that he has discovered, just since taking a writing class a year ago, that "there is a well of experience inside of me which I have not expressed. . . . And I just feel like bringing that well out. Bringing the water of that well out." Prior to his foray into autobiographical writing, Bill had not written much about his personal life except for a period between 1975 and 1979, when he wrote religious poetry. During this time, Bill had a brief nervous breakdown, the second of his life, occasioned by his youngest son's leaving home for college and the decline of his marriage. His first nervous breakdown had occurred during the early days of World War II, as he struggled with the moral decision to claim the status of conscientious objector.

Although writing has been an emotional release for Bill, he acknowledges that, still, he does not express many "negative emotions"—namely, anger or fear—in his life stories for the writing group. Why? "Oh, they're too personal. I don't want to tell fifteen or so people what I feel." Of most concern to Bill are the other men in his group. Bill is quite aware of the feeling rules for men of his generation, as well as the gendered strategies for managing emotions publicly. He explains his perceptions about emotional display during a writing-group session in which he reads a life story called "Party Time." The story covers his fraternity life from 1936 to 1940 at a college on the East Coast, where "if you weren't a man's man in your fraternity, you were nothing." Bill describes himself as "a man's man from my hips downward to my loins, but a woman's man from my hips up," suggesting that, despite raging hormones, he behaved in a gentlemanly manner toward all his fraternity dates. Bill's writing—as well as his talk around it—reveals desire, frustration, and a longing for his former sexual self. The writing consists primarily of descriptions of the young women he dated. He reads aloud to the group:

> In mid October of 1938, I was rejected by my Mount Holyoke girl, who I heard later went to Dartmouth for a fall house party date so that she could be invited to the Dartmouth winter carnival. She loved skiing, and I never could ski. So I tobogganed my way to a town girl [he says as an aside: I figured out a name, an apocryphal name, Leona. Let's call her Leona]. Five foot seven, curly black hair, rosebud mouth, full pointing breasts, broad enough hips, and very long, slender legs, as I furtively diagnosed one day when I had to look up something in the catalog room [Bill snickers, and there is general laughter from the group]. The catalog room, incidentally, is where my erstwhile wife Nancy worked from 1949 to 1986, when she retired. Oh, well. Leona brushed occasionally against my thighs in the stacks [he laughs]. I was shelving books. I always experienced a strange but gratifying feeling at the time. I went on shelving, and she went on cataloging for two years. So anyway, I asked her in mid-stack if she wanted to be my date at the eclectic ball. The party was in October. Her rosebud lips parted, and she murmered, "Yes, Bill" in the stacks. Boy, was she ever stacked, I thought. So I spent that fall partying with Leona, five foot seven, curly black hair down her gorgeous neck, and dressed in a white satin formal gown, which set off her bounteous hair and black, shiny,

leather stiletto-heel pumps. Boy, was she ever formal [general tittering and laughter from the group]! Boy, were we ever informal! We necked in the dark, in the library, and with all the rest of the fraternity. Even while the music was on, and then while we watched other nondancing neckers in the library on the couch (it was a leather couch).

My next prom date, in spring of 1939, was a Jewish girl from Smith. And in my senior year, I was stag two times out of three parties because of senior comprehensives and preparation. I spent all of my time with that in the stacks, until, of course, my graduation girl Debbie from Waltham, Massachusetts, with her own generous loving on the living room chair at her home.

After finishing this reading, Bill engages the group in a discussion of his decision not to write any more about the women in his early life. All present are women, including Bill's wife Jean:

Bill, finishing reading: The end. The real end [group laughter]. I won't be writing about anymore girls!

Lee (facilitator): No?

Bill: I mean, there aren't any! Oh, yes [looking at Jean]. What I mean is, I think you're getting bored [Jean's reply is unintelligible, but she is laughing].

Lee: Well, I love the graduation-girl story.

Bill: Yeah, the graduation girl. That was better.

Lee: Yeah, that was good. Maybe you're losing your enthusiasm.

Bill: Yes, you see I'm in the confessional mode, but I'm really not a Catholic, and I don't really have to confess every Saturday, I mean every Thursday, and talk about all the women whom I've ever gone with, do I?

Lee: No, but it must be something you need to investigate [group laughter] because it does come up quite a bit, which is fine.

Bill: I know this is no great ancient, classical tragedy as catharsis. You just drain it out of your system, and it never comes back, except on Thursdays [general laughter].

Bill then reads a brief poem he has written about a boyhood memory of Greece and mentions he is joining another writing group, where he plans to concentrate entirely on lyric poetry.

Mary: You do a good job. We'll miss your stories.

Bill: Well, I don't have any humor left [general laughter]. I'd have to invent girls.

Lee, as the others laugh: Well? You can put anything you want on paper.

Bill: I'd have to use my fantasy. One should never use one's fantasy. I will not use my fantasy. I mean, I have been educated by none other than Immanuel Kant [general laughter].

Lee: Fantasy's not a dirty word here.

Bill: For some reason, it is more with men than women, I think. I mean, men may have fantasies, but they'd never experience them with men. I mean, many, many men would not share them with men. See, there are no men in the room. [general laughter].

Lee: So you're saying—

Bill: I mean, if Bob Charles [a former group member] was here, I wouldn't write about my, uh, 1938 house-party girls. He would be, WHAT! He, he would look with a serious look down at his paper.

Mary: I thought all men talked about those, uh, adventures.

Lee (and others), laughing: I did, too.

Bill: But Bob Charles hasn't told Bill. I'm waiting [much laughter]. Let's say, if he talks about one of his old flames, then—

Mary: You'll reciprocate?

Bill: I'll reciprocate. We will have a little battle of old flames.

In terms of Hochschild's interactive model of emotions, prior to his marriage, Bill had trouble maintaining the gendered ego-ideal defined by his fraternity brothers of a "man's man" (a sexually active man), given his moral principles. He was never able to talk about this at the time, and he wants to talk about it now, but ambivalence around sexuality is not a sanctioned subject of conversation among most heterosexual men. The writing group offers a relatively safe space for Bill to express these feelings and to explore their role in the making of his sexual identity *now*.

I get more insight into Bill's motivations for writing about early girlfriends during our first interview, which occurs two months after the session above. Bill has written at least two other life stories on the subjects of dating and sex, and I ask him about this recurring theme:

Ruth: And why have you chosen to write about those topics?

Bill: Well, there it's a matter of catharsis also, in looking back at those experiences, because I am a divorced person, and the first marriage was 1951 to

1987. I came to [the Detroit area] in 1986, so there was a year of separation, and then dating here through what is called "Sincere Singles," a group for professional dating. And I did that for a whole year, and then in November 1987, I met my present wife, Jean.

Ruth: So, the writing about the women was your way of maybe understanding your divorce, or—

Bill: Well, not exactly—Oh, I see what you mean. Yes, yes, one of those— that's true, yes. In one of those essays—one of those persons in "My Grad Girls" lived in Michigan, and I came out here to visit her, and that was the one main cause of my divorce. My wife divorced me.

Ruth: So would you say through your writing about girls and women and your relationships that you've come to a better understanding of that aspect of yourself?

Bill: Yes, I have. I've always had doubts about—as some men do—my virility, and I sometimes express an over-machoism when I don't have to.

In "My Grad Girls," Bill tells of several girls he dated during graduate school, creating the persona of an intense and shy young man still restrained by the values of his religious upbringing and the sexual mores of the time (the "quote of the day" was "no intercourse before marriage"). Of the woman from Michigan, whom he met in 1949, Bill writes of nothing but refined behavior: "Both of us were naive and tentative. Nothing like tentativeness for romantic arousal. We were both highly cultured; she and I spoke French fluently. We went to many cultural events and held hands tentatively. Again, no introit and no inflammatory crescendos. All innuendos." In our interview, Bill characterizes "My Grad Girls" as an expression of long-felt emotions, particularly his ambivalence toward sexual relations with women and concern about his slow sexual maturing; he mentions that, at the age of twenty-nine, he was still not ready to marry the woman from Michigan.

Bill is unique among older men who attend the writing groups I have known. Though guarded, he is much more expressive of his feelings than most. In two other groups I observed, women worked consistently to get the men to open up. The effect of these emotion-management strategies, over time, was a change in the men's writing toward fuller description of relationships. Charles, for example, came to express his sorrow over the death of his first two wives and the joy in his third marriage. Phil came to see that, by focusing on his earlier identity as a military officer, he was leaving his wife and kids out of his life stories. He also began to analyze his current dreams and nightmares, which often center on feelings of displacement.

Madeline, eighty, the facilitator for Phil's group, works to encourage everyone "to reveal themselves more than they're likely to do." During our interview, she talks about the role of emotional expression, as she sees it, in life-story writing:

What's interesting about autobiography—is where the person is. And sometimes, some of the people have been very reluctant to reveal anything of how they feel. And yet my feeling is that if I'm reading about somebody else's life, I want to know how he felt about what was happening to him. And I think their childrem are going to want to know that. And that's the hardest thing for them to get at sometimes. Some of them are self-conscious. Some of them have been taught in a way not to reveal themselves. Some don't feel that it's safe or proper to reveal themselves. I think it depends a lot on how comfortable they are with themselves. And how comfortable they are in the group. And I think as they get better acquainted with each other, they loosen up.

Madeline has noticed marked gender differences in older adults' writings: "Women are more willing to talk about themselves and probably more willing to write about themselves, and probably more willing to be approached by their children to write down something about their lives," she offers. "The men are more likely to be expository and write about external things. . . . It depends on the person. But I think Robert and Phil and Frank [a former group member]— they're telling us *about* themselves rather than revealing themselves."

Gender Influence, Emotional Expression, and Adult Development

Older women have considerable influence in persuading older men to write more about their feelings. Why might this be? Aside from the fact that they dominate writing groups by sheer numbers, older women draw on a lifetime of experience verbally managing their own emotions and the emotions of others—experience that begins very early in life. Many years of social and linguistic research on same-sex play groups have confirmed what is in fact an everyday perception— that little girls learn to negotiate power and authority through verbal strategies, while little boys influence one another through physical manipulation—rough-housing and physical competition. Asking "how do you *feel*?" is a gender strategy that little girls learn very early to establish connection and build relationships.[24] Boys adopt these communication strategies more slowly and usually through interactions with girls. Emotional vocabulary, too, is learned through adults' interpretations of children's behaviors and is also gender-biased: in U.S. culture, little girls who act out their feelings (rather than talk them out) are often described negatively as "impetuous" or "willful," while boys are more positively described as "active," "boisterous," and "all boy."[25] Children come to understand (and talk about) their emotions by assessing how adults *expect* them to behave according to their age and gender. Older women in writing groups therefore have considerably more experience talking about feelings, managing emotions in male/female relationships, and responding publicly to others' feelings.

Why older men in writing groups respond to women's prompts for more emotional expression is an open question. We do know that men of all ages report feeling better "understood" by women than men and consider their opposite-sex relationships (both platonic and sexual) more intimate and thus more conducive to personal revelation than platonic same-sex relationships. Additionally, when heterosexual men equate the public expression of feelings with femininity, homophobia may discourage them from confiding in male friends.[26] In a writing group in which they are surrounded by supportive females, older men are more likely to experience and express what they consider the "feminine" aspects of identity and life story.

The fact that older men are in the minority in a writing group may actually work in their favor in terms of personal development. I see these groups as being similar in many ways to courses in women's studies, at least in the sense that they are women-dominated and largely focused on women's experience. It is well known in feminist circles that power and gender dynamics change markedly in women's studies courses: women talk more, whereas men talk less (even lapsing into long periods of silence), and women sometimes confront men with expressions of strong feeling. Gail Griffin, a scholar of women's studies, asserts that in these "womanly contexts" a man "is the Outsider, for once, and this role is profoundly educative"—for men *and* women.[27] A writing group for older adults is a site where men are in some ways marginalized and made vulnerable. From this position of vulnerability (if they do not leave the group), they become more open to change.

For the older women in these groups, the men become figures they react to and against. In most of my interviews, the women talked about the men, usually in terms of their early limitations and their change over time, while the men *never* talk about the women in evaluative terms. Emily, for example, mentions her pleasure in seeing the men grow through the writing group: "I'm tickled to see the way the men are emerging—really, they're opening up." Emily's fellow group member Charlotte claims to have had a direct influence on at least one man in her group. In our interview, she focuses on Robert, who initially brought several lists, rather than personal narratives, to the group sessions. Charlotte and the other members suggested ways he could expand on these lists, writing about the memories they elicited. Charlotte considered the lists to be "quite contrary to writing group" and one day brought Robert a huge history book comprised of nothing but lists. Months later, in my interview with Robert, we discuss his writing process, and he mentions the impact of this gesture:

Robert: I like to get something down, like a list or some starting point. When I did this, Charlotte criticized me in the class. She said, "You've got to develop—you know, you can't just get by with a list." And she brought me this book, *The History of England* or something, with all these—you know, it was boring, just this list. [he laughs.] It was terrible.

Ruth: Is that why she gave it to you? So you could see how boring it was?

Robert: Probably. She showed me, but she didn't tell me [he laughs]. So, yeah. Then the second time I did that in the class, she really got on me again.

Older women in writing groups are more likely to assess other members and to take on an educative role, especially in their interactions with men. Psychologists who study women's conversational practices have documented their tendency to make men's experience the center of attention in both one-on-one and group interactions. Women ask more questions than men do, and these questions reflect their curiosity in mens' interiority—an interest that many men do not share in regards to women, or at least do not express.[28] Women seem to feel comfortable with their questioning role in the conversational enterprise and gain satisfaction in assuming it. This is one example of indirect conversational style with an instructive intent. As Robert indicates, Charlotte did not directly *tell* him how boring his writing was; she *showed* him.

Older men sometimes gain a better perspective on their own lives—and their relationships with women over their lifetime—through the narrative examples older women bring to the group. Robert describes a time when facilitator Madeline read part of the biography of Margaret Bourke White, whose new mother-in-law accused her of stealing her only son and vowed never to speak to Margaret again. The scene struck a chord in Robert, who was himself an only child:

I realized that a similar thing had happened when I got married. I came home on leave from the navy and then, you know, went right back. But after I left, there was something that happened between my mother and my wife, where she was in the same kind of situation where she was accusing my wife of taking me away from her. And so they never got along. Ever. And yet maybe I wasn't sensitive enough to that. I sort of put it aside and out of mind, you know, 'cause I was overseas, and maybe that's one thing that led to the end of love—this wife didn't love me anymore at some point. And maybe that's one factor that maybe I wasn't sensitive enough to, or whatever happened because of that.

Margaret's selection of a passage illustrating the emotional impact of power and gender dynamics between mother and daughter-in-law initiated a new direction in Robert's own self-understanding. He now realizes that the emotional conflicts between his wife and mother may have had long-term effects on his marriage that he did not (or could not) see at the time. Through the biography of Margaret Bourke White, Robert experienced what feminist psychologist Judith Jordan calls "empathy across difference," which she considers "one of the most compelling paths to personal and relational growth": "While some mutual empathy involves an acknowledgement of sameness in the other, an appreciation of the differentness of the other's experience is also vital. The movement towards the other's differentness is actually central to growth in relationship and also can provide a powerful sense of validation for both people. Growth occurs because as I stretch to match or understand your experience, something new is acknowledged or grows in me." [29] In Robert's case, the Bourke narrative helped him see (and, more to the point, *feel*) the difference between his experience of relational conflict and his former wife's experience.

Recently, psychologists have asserted that the ability to experience and express a range of feelings is essential to human development. In his book *Emotional Intelligence*, Daniel Goleman claims that "emotional life is a domain that, as surely as math or reading, can be handled with greater or lesser skill, and requires its unique set of competencies. And how adept a person is at those is crucial to understanding why one person thrives in life while another, of equal intellect, dead-ends: emotional aptitude is a meta-ability, determining how well we can use whatever other skills we have, including raw intellect." [30] Goleman argues for the importance of "multiple intelligences" in human development and claims that emotional intelligence has been minimized and trivialized in Western culture, despite the fact that it is a key predictor of success and overall happiness in life.

Lifespan-development psychologist Gisela Labouvie-Vief offers a similar conclusion. In her critique of the philosophies underlying traditional cognitive psychology, she shows that Western culture has priviledged logos (the realm of logic and objectivity) to the detriment of mythos (the realm of emotion) in its concepts of mind and development. The bifurcation of these two modes is especially troublesome when considered in the context of later life, where Labouvie-Vief directs her own research. Although the view of development as the "ascent and onward rush of logos" powerfully describes many changes from birth to young adulthood, it is woefully inadequate when applied to the total of the human life course: "When examined from the perspectives of logos, later adulthood seems to be a dark period indeed. . . . How are we to reconcile the disappointments of adulthood, the painful reminders of our organic limitations, with the view of an onward rush?" [31] In answer, Labouvie-Vief offers a conceptual model of development that integrates logos and mythos based on an understanding of the *gendered mind*, a symbolic structure that holds powerful sway in Western culture, where logos is identified as masculine and mythos as feminine. Labouvie-Vief argues that "the potential of later life development is a healing and bridging of the split introduced in early development." [32] This is accomplished, on both cultural and individual levels, through a decoding of gender imagery underlying conceptions of mind and development and a reevaluation of all that has been systematically devalued. Thus, "the primary issues of identity and development for men revolve around a sense of loss and disempowerment as they upgrade modes of knowing and ways of being that they previously experienced as 'feminine.' In contrast, the main focus for women's development is a deidealization of the 'masculine' as they struggle with issues of personal empowerment." [33]

In this chapter, we have seen evidence of such growth through subtle alterations in the "gendered mind" and its narrative expressions. Older women assist men in embracing mythos, and, through this teaching role, they are able to work through their own issues of empowerment. In evaluating the logos-oriented writings of male group members, women are also exposed to alternative ways of talking about personal accomplishments and one's place in the world. In some ways, however, the older men in writing groups reflect more narrative change than the women. Shirley, who has spent two years in the same writing group with Phil, still has not moved beyond the first ten years of childhood to chronicle her growth as an adult, while Phil has moved considerably from his initial (and exclusive) focus on his twenty years in the military. Charlotte, a member of the same group, stays focused on her British childhood, despite observing Phil's and Robert's ever-widening avenues for life-story telling. She expresses no interest in writing about her adult life as a successful child psychologist at a major research university.

In my future research on narrative development, I will be looking for situations that prompt major changes in women's narratives. Initial research by scholars of women's studies in Australia suggests that critical interventions focusing on feminist strategies for writing the body have worked to alter older women's self representations and to promote feelings of liberation and empowerment through narrative change. [34] In any case, anyone looking to understand the emotional experiences of later life can learn a great deal by closely observing the gender dynamics of writing groups for seniors.

Negotiating Normal

IT IS THE FIRST DAY for the writing group at the Northside Senior Center. The center is located in the northern regions of metropolitan Detroit on a four-lane stretch of highway amid three automotive world headquarters and a power-train division. A United States flag waves atop the low building of the senior center. A sign in the entryway says, "Welcome. Thank you for joining us." Today there are odds and ends stacked along the walls of the hallway, garbage bags full of clothes, and stacks of dishes—items for the upcoming rummage sale. The center director is sick, so her assistant shows me to a long table in an empty room adjoining the main community area. She tells me that not many have signed up for the group, advertised as a "Write Your Life Story" class on colorful flyers posted around the room. "You'll just have to go around and ask people," she says.

"Since there are so few of us, can we sit at one of those tables in the main room?" I ask, eyeing one of several round tables that look considerably more inviting.

"No, because people will be playing cards there," she says firmly.

I get the impression that the writing group is not on anybody's priority list. There are not more than ten people in the main area, which looks like a converted banquet hall: tables and folding chairs, florescent lighting, an expanse of tile flooring, a coffee urn. A pool table sits in one corner. A few tattered couches are arranged to the side, forming a conversation area. Four or five women sit on the couches, drinking coffee and gazing into space.

"Will you be joining us in the writing group?" I approach one of them hesitantly. Her response is a blink. The others merely stare at me. I walk toward two men playing pool.

"No," says the man in a red-plaid shirt in response to my invitation. "I don't want anyone knowing about my life. After seventy years, there's a lot to tell."

"Besides, your wife might find out," says his companion.

"Oh, I'm not worried about *her*," the man in plaid says, laughing.

A woman is now playing "Fur Elise," slowly and haltingly, on the upright piano. The assistant tells her she will have to stop when the class starts.

"Are you going to join the life-story group?" I ask the piano player, hopefully.

"Oh, *no*," she says, and hurries away.

My mood is sinking fast. I am beginning to think a writing group might not be such a good idea here. I roam around, reading the bulletin boards and trying to get my courage up to approach the others: "Saturday. Pancake brunch. $1.50, Includes sausage." I walk into a small room off the hallway where five women are sewing cancer pads—large squares of fabric handstitched over padding and sheets of plastic, which I later learn are used as bedliners by the Michigan Cancer Foundation. To my relief, three agree to try the class. With some prodding from one of the sewing ladies, whose name is Ella, a few others join us, including two from the couch.

By 10:40, we have gathered—seven women, ages sixty-one to seventy-five, all white except for Ella, who is African American—around the long table with pencils and paper before us. We introduce ourselves, and I ask people why they have come.

"To have a group experience," says a woman named Lynn, enunciating each word very carefully.

Another woman with a soft accent, Dee, begins to cry. "I'm writing for my family down South. I don't see them much. I just want 'em to want me, yes I do, I just want 'em to love me," she says. Her voice is barely above a whisper.

Others are reluctant to speak at all. I introduce today's topic: grandparents. Several murmur doubts. They don't know anything about that. Long periods of silence are broken, briefly, by someone summarizing the past in a single sentence: "All I know is my grandfather was a farmer." The group, as a whole, seems stricken by a profound inertia. The one exception is Netty, a quiet woman with a sweet smile, age seventy-one, who offers detailed accounts of her family.

"Well, OK," I say, moving on to the topic I had planned for next week: "How about your own childhood—can you write about that today?"

A woman sitting next to me, named Sue, says, "I'm from a group home. I don't remember much. I can't write."

"I'll help you," I say, not knowing what "from a group home" means, exactly. A woman named Lorna offers that she grew up in an orphanage. "All right, then, let's all start with your childhood home," I say.

I begin asking them questions, with short intervals between for writing. (What type of house did you live in as a child? Did you have a room of your own? A bed of your own? What were the other rooms in the house like? Did your family congregate in certain places in the house? How was the house heated? Did you have indoor plumbing and electricity, running water? Did your family can or otherwise preserve food?) I suggest that they respond in paragraph form. The questions are arranged so that inexperienced writers do not have to worry much about structure: if all are answered in order, the result will be a fairly coherent, descriptive paragraph that evokes a time and place. Netty sets out at a fast pace, writing easily. The rest begin cautiously. Some ask me how many questions there are going to be and number their papers accordingly, as if preparing for a test.

We do not get very far before the interruptions start.

"What's the date?" Sue says. "How do you spell September? See, I forgot already!" Her voice is frustrated.

"How do you spell *gazebo*?" Lorna asks. I spell it, but she decides to leave the word out.

"How do you spell *Tennessee*?" Ella asks, and repeats every letter I call out.

I want to tell them what I say to my college students—that spelling doesn't matter, at least not yet—but to these women, it obviously *does* matter.

Ella begins reminiscing aloud. I keep telling her to "write that down," but she seems more interested in talking. Then Lynn looks up at the clock and shouts, "It's ten after eleven!" Suddenly, chairs scrape against the floor and people shove their papers toward me.

"You keep them," says a tall, thin woman named Gert.

"Diabetics eat at eleven," Sue says to me, as if by way of explanation.

"What do you mean?"

"We have to eat on time," Sue says, getting up to go.

"Let's just take another five or ten minutes," I say weakly, to anyone listening, "for people who want to finish." That leaves only two—Netty and Dee. The rest have moved to a table nearby, where they are pulling sandwiches and drinks out of a big red cooler.

"You're a nice lady," Dee says, handing me her paper. "We like you. That's unusual."

"That wasn't so bad," Netty says. "I was scared at first. But it's good to remember."

I walk away with mixed feelings—glad anyone came at all, but unsure about the possibilities for this group. What constitutes the "life story" for someone who is not able to remember? Why write at all? I am beginning to suspect, though, that "I can't remember" means many different things: "I never knew," "I don't *want* to remember," "I'm not sure I *can* remember," "I'm afraid my memory is wrong," or "I *might* be able to remember if someone gives me a good reason and shows me how." What will be their response to my repeated requests for writing in the coming weeks? Will they resist? Get mad? Stop coming? My original goal for the group—each person creating a version of her "life story" that at least hits the conventional high points, including family, childhood, marriage, work, and reflections on what it all means—seems unlikely at this point. Judging from the wildly inconsistent spellings and unconventional syntax, I surmise that some in the group—at least Dee, Sue, and Ella—have never written much in their lifetimes.

As I pull out of the parking lot, I realize I am exhausted. Too many surprises today and a gnawing sense of my own inadequacies. Who are these women? [1]

Lynn's Writing

1. We moved two or three places and one had a out house which is the bathroom.

2. A garden, no fence yard had dirt on it. We had corn and potatoe's and green bean.

3. We moved all the time closer to his work that is my Dad work and school for us work for my Mom.

4. I had to share a room with my Mother and Dad a bed in the corner of the room, I had a bed of my own.

5. I ate in the dining room with my brothers and Dad and Mom we ate cereal & milk egg & brown bread.

6. Front room, dining, kitchen, bedroom two, and six kids, Mom & Dad and then my sister was born.

Dee's Writing

1. A board house

2. My house was made a building of paste & boards. It was painted out of wite paint and some times red & black paint, had pretty flowers.

3. Moved 3 times one house into the other, until we made a new house.

4. I had a room shared with my sister, at one time I shared my own room, I have to younger sisters, Ruth & Sue. Had my own bed.

5. In the kitchen, we had gravy, chicken, and my Dad was a coal miner. He drew a pension, we got our living cheap, and I had homemade clothes, we mad a garden.

6. We had a house that had all one room, we put petition and made a kitchen and, we couldn't all sleep in one room.

The following week there is hardly anyone at the center. The same two guys in plaid shirts are playing pool. Another man is watching them and drinking coffee out of a travel mug. He says hello to me.

"Do you want to join our class?" I say in my bright, visitor's voice.

"What class?"

"A writing class—tell your life story."

"I don't know how to write. I only make *x*s and *o*s." He grins.

"Free pencils," I say, holding out the florescent collection, newly sharpened, as a bribe.

"I'll take one of those," he says, slipping one into his shirt pocket. "I can use it for pinochle."

"I thought you said you didn't write."

"Well, I let the other players keep score."

"And you just pass the pencil around, is that it?" He grabs my hand and squeezes, laughing. His name is Bernard.

The center director is here today, and she is trying to round up volunteers for the class. She has been on the phone: Where's the van? Aren't they coming today? Why not? She tells me everybody on the class list from last week lives in group homes, and the van is off schedule. "One day they'll be here at nine, the next at quarter to eleven," she says. "You never know. Sometimes the caregivers are running late. Sometimes the van doesn't come at all. That's the way it is." The news unsettles me. *Everyone* is from a group home?

Our fledgling writing group convenes anyway, with four new people encouraged by the director. All are reticent, except for Ann, a talkative blonde woman. I read a couple of selections on family and early childhood written by people from other senior groups, hoping to motivate everyone to write.

Sarah, who tells me she is "eighty years young" responds: "I didn't know my parents or grandparents. I was raised by foster parents. It was a terrible time. I don't want to write that down."

"Well—anything about your childhood that you *would* like to write down?" I ask.

"No, nothing. I don't want to remember it. Why do we have to write about the past?"

"Because this is a life-story class."

"Well then, I'm not in it. I don't have a life story."

Despite the finality of her statement, Sarah stays and even writes something as I ask the questions that had not worked the preceding week about parents and grandparents. (What were the names of your parents and what did they do? What were the names of your grandparents on each side and what did they do? Do you have any personal memories of them? When and where were they born and where did they live? Are there family traditions passed on by grandparents that you still practice? If you *didn't* know your grandparents, how do you feel about that? If they were here now, what would you ask them?)

After a few minutes, Sarah confidently slides her paper over to me: "Want to read it?" she asks. Before I can read, she tells a version of it aloud: "I don't know anything about my grandparents. I was married at seventeen. It was a beautiful wedding. We were blessed with three lovely sons. I worked in the beauty business and then at the GM plant during the war. I had a good life."

"That's great!" I say, scanning the paper as she talks. She smiles broadly. "But I'd like to know the names of your sons."

"Oh, I don't want to write *that* down!" she says, her expression changing.

"Well, how about work? Can you say more about your life at the plant?"

"Oh, I was very good at it. I got written up in the newspaper."

"Well, write that down! That's great!"

She goes out for a cigarette, instead. When she returns, I ask her if she would like to read aloud. As she reads, her voice gets softer and softer until she's almost speaking to herself. "I had a good marriage until something broke us up," she tells us when she's finished. "It wasn't our fault. It was my stepparents. That's the way things were back then. They shouldn't have stuck their noses in, but they did. It was all brainwashing and propaganda. Just like this here," she says, tapping her paper.

Val, another new member, listens quietly. She looks different from the other women, more pulled together. She is wearing blue eye shadow, red lipstick, and a silky dress. The other women are wearing sweatpants. Val, I learn, was the woman playing the piano last week. At first, she told the director she did not want to come to the writing group today, then changed her mind. She writes "grandparents" at the top of her paper, stops, folds her arms, and watches the others. "I don't remember my grandparents," she says, matter-of-factly.

After the group ends, Val asks me questions.

"What's—how do you say—when? That war that was in 1915, World War II?"

"No, that was World War I."

"When was World War II?"

"1940 to 1945."

"I think it was 1915, my grandparents died in that war. Istanbul—Turkey. Did it have another name?"

"Istanbul was Constantinople," I say, remembering the phrase from an old song. "Are you Armenian?" I have heard a lot about the Turkish-Armenian War just this week from a woman at another senior center.

"Yes, part Armenian. I don't know what to write. I need to find out about that war. There was a baby, something about a baby."

"Well, maybe you can write down some questions you'd like the answers to as part of your life story," I suggest. She walks away.

Rose is very quiet. Although it is early September and the temperature is in the eighties, she is wearing a winter coat with a fur collar. She writes half a page in tiny script, dutifully answering all my questions. "It's not as interesting as the ones you read aloud," she says apologetically.

Ann is the only one who appears to be enjoying herself. Her writing is very detailed, including first, middle, and last names of great aunts and uncles and humorous anecdotes.

"Isn't that cute?" Sarah says when Ann reads about an uncle who made a squeaking noise every time he pulled her ear.

"That was really good," Sarah says enthusiastically after Ann has finished reading.

Because of the brevity of people's writing, the entire session is over in fifty minutes, compared with the usual one and a half hours for a group this size.

"That was fun," Ann says with animation.

"Yes, it was," Rose says quietly.

"Thanks for telling about your life today," I say.

"Thanks for asking," Val says.

Ann's Writing

My actual grandparents lived at a distance, so I was very close to my great-aunt and uncle. Aunt Dada (Daphnet Pritchert Smith) was a very creative person. She painted—watercolor scenery, flowers on china—and wrote poems and stories which were published. She was a woman of dignity and style. She had been a postmistress. She and Uncle Leon lived in a modest house in the woods. She had a garden with all kinds of flowers. She was a campfire girl leader. I still have her Indian dress and a lot of pictures she painted.

My sisters and I would visit there weekends and when my folks would go on vacation. I remember Aunt Dada setting up easels and showing us how to paint water color flowers. We would go to the movies and eat popcorn.

Uncle Leon had been an optometrist with his own store upstate. He was a very kind man who would tweak my ear and pretend it squeaked. He worked at the wheel company in Detroit, where he was time control person. My Dad got him the job during the Depression. My Dad was chief metalurgist there.

My mother's mother (also named Ann) was married to a dentist, but they were divorced. Mother said he was a philanderer, but who knows. She answered a personal ad and ended up married to "Uncle Ben," a sheep rancher in Montana near Billings. When I was ten, we went there and drove across the prairie watching the prairie dogs. We had a canvas water canteen in the car. The ranch was on a flat prairie surrounded by mountains. I think it was the only one there—it was 5,000 acres. We saw the sheepherder with a huge flock. There was no electricity. They had a well. My mother's sister's (Aunt Evelyn's) boy, Lynn, was visiting. He had straight blond hair and was four years old. They had a small herd of goats who would chew on my cloth belt. They could jump over the cars, which were high (1939–40 vintage). They had a few half-wild horses. I flew off the back of one, which was OK. We went up to a lake in the mountains. Saw a stag, trout in a clear lake. Grandmother Ann came to visit once. She was plump and nice and made homemade noodles.

My Dad's father had a horse farm, but beyond that I know nothing. Dad was raised by his grandparents in his teen years. He was one of five children. His mother was very religious and favored his oldest brother, who she lived with in California until her death in her 80's. She came to visit once, and Dad took us all for a ride in a motorboat up at Eight-Point Lake. After she died, Dad put her picture out as a young woman. She was a very attractive brunette.

Week Three, and the community room is buzzing. Everybody is here for the writing group from the first and second weeks, plus a couple of others I have seen previously snoozing on the couch.

"Are you coming to the group today?" I ask Lorna as she draws a cup of coffee.

"Yes, there's nothing else to do," she says, putting her broad face real close to mine and smiling. "That's not an insult to you."

"I don't feel good today," Sarah calls from the couch.

"Would you like to come and just listen?" I ask.

"No."

Bernard is sitting at a table with Ella, Netty, Gert, Dee, and Sue.

You're going to have to help me," Sue reminds me.

Netty, the quiet woman with the detailed memory, explains why she missed last week: "I fainted and had to go to the hospital. I'm still a little dizzy when I bend over."

Bernard grabs my hand. "I'm not coming. I don't write, only *x*s and *o*s, re-member?" But he follows us into the other room and sits at a nearby table, trying to get my attention. He begins to clip his fingernails.

"This is not proper etiquette, I know," he says, looking over at me. "I thought I knew etiquette pretty well until I was in the hospital. I was sittin' at a table with a couple of nurses. They were drinking coffee, and I started to clip my nails. You know, when you do that, you never know where they're gonna fly. They told me not to do that. I didn't know. Can I call you honey?"

"Your wife won't like it," Netty says.

"She doesn't care," Bernard replies.

"She does too," Netty retorts, laughing. "He likes all the ladies," she tells me conspiratorily.

"Can I get you something?" Bernard asks. He doesn't wait for me to answer but brings a styrofoam cup full of bright yellow drink. "Is it cold enough?" he asks. He pulls a piece of hard candy out of his pocket and offers it to me. As the others amble in and take their seats at the table, Bernard tells me his story: "My father was an alcoholic. There were five kids. My mother had to leave him, even though she still loved him. He didn't abuse her or anything, he just didn't have any money for the house when he was drinking. All the kids were split up to foster homes. This was in Illinois. I went to a farm, played alone. You know what my favorite sport was? They had those trains with the open cars. I'd throw rocks at 'em. Got pretty good. I was tough. See, you don't want to know my life story. There isn't much to it." He returns to his seat at a nearby table and watches the others, sliding his travel mug around in circles.

I get the group going with a few opening remarks, reminding them what we have written so far and what we're doing today. Sarah walks in. "I believe this room is warmer than the other room," she says off-handedly, taking a seat at the table. One of the new people from the couch—Dorene—asks if she can pass out the paper and pencils while I'm talking. When she has completed the task, she leaves, muttering, "It's none of their business." The other new member—Jan—tells me she is here just to listen. "My mind's not working," she says. "It's the medication. I'm all fuzzy, and my hands don't work."

"If you have something to write down, I can do it for you," I suggest.

While the others write, Jan talks to me about her childhood.

"Can I put that down for you?" I say, taking the opportunity to initiate some writing.

We get a few lines, which I later read aloud for her. She seems pleased to have generated something for the group.

Everyone else writes a little more this week. Most read aloud, but not Sue.

"I don't want to read mine," she says, leaning over to whisper in my ear.

At eleven o'clock Bernard interrupts and addresses the group, "Are you going to eat?"

"Yes, in a minute," someone says.

"Do you want me to lay it out for you?" he offers.

"No, I'll do it," Sue says. She gets up to open the cooler.

Several leave, find their lunches, and sit around adjoining tables, eating and listening to the remaining group members.

Ella is very talkative today, telling about a family ranch in Mississippi, seven boys and seven girls in her mother's family and a grandfather who was white. She talks much more than she writes, but she speaks with enthusiasm.

"He dictated that all the boys marry white girls and all the girls marry black."

"Why did he treat the boys and girls different?" I ask.

"I never could figure that out. But my Daddy was black. We got lots of white cousins. Martin Luther King came and asked us to ride with him, and that lady on the bus . . ."

"Rosa Parks?" I say, wondering about the nature of her associations with these famous activists.

"Yeah, that's it. We was in on all of that." She eats an egg-salad sandwich as she talks.

"Ella, don't talk with your mouth full," Bernard reprimands.

She keeps talking.

"Ella, don't talk with your mouth full!" he repeats. "She's ignoring me," he says, looking my way.

"Yeah, you got that right," Ella says.

At the end, they give me their papers to keep, except for Ann, who folds hers neatly and puts it with the other one she has brought from last week.

"Thank you," several say, and scatter away.

Ella's Writing

I was born in Atlanta. I lived in Alabama when I was a small child. I lived there until I was 12 years old. I moved to Tennessee when I was 12 years old.

The house in Alabama was a ranch house. I had two sisters. We had a bedroom together. We had three meals together a day. My sister and I would take baths together. The house had 6 bedrooms. The hired help would keep the work done. The bathroom was outside. We had lamps for light.

My grandfather was a white man. We loved him very much. I loved my mother and father very much. I cared for them above all the friends. I had teachers and church people that I loved very much too. Others I've liked in my life are Mrs. Rosa Parks and Mrs. Erma Henderson. When I grew up I wanted to be a good mother and look after my kids and other kids. (I was a mother and looked after my kids and other people's kids. My kids would not break no rules.)

I was the oldest child in the family. My sister was the youngest in the family. I was married when I was 14 years old. I had 2 kids while I was married the first time. The 2nd time was when I was 26 years old. Then I had 5 kids by my 2nd husband. I went to high school and finished high school. My mother passed away in Dayton, Ohio.

We have a small group the following week, because the van is running late again and many people have doctors' appointments scheduled at the same time. There is only Val, Netty, Ann, and Sarah.

Sarah seems distressed. "Oh, I can't do this. I don't want to do this," she whimpers.

"That's OK, you can just listen," I say. But she walks away, a little unsteady on her feet. Rose passes down the hallway several times, bundled in her winter coat, but she does not join us. Val talks a lot about her school memories (the topic of the day) but does not want to write anything down. She is especially dressed up today, with a treble clef on the end of a chain around her neck.

"I didn't like school," she says. "Do I have to say why? I don't want to write that."

She tells of getting Ds and Es, not being motivated, even getting Cs in music, her favorite subject, which she hoped to teach.

"But I went to the hospital and that was the end of that. I was irresponsible. I ended up in Clinton Valley. You know where that is, don't you?" she says, referring to the local mental hospital.

"Doesn't she look pretty today?" Ann says, smiling at Val.

"Thank you. My sister gave me the necklace—fourteen carat gold. I've lost weight. Otherwise, this skirt would be skin tight, and it wouldn't look right."

"She's the resident musician around here," Netty tells me.

"I played 'Happy Birthday' for Bill this morning with one hand."

"Why one hand?" I ask.

"Oh, I play by ear and by music."

I remember, then, that she and some of the others have trouble with *why* questions. I bring up the 1915 Armenian war again to see if she has learned anything more about it. She seems to have forgotten our earlier conversation.

"Was that a world war?" she asks. "Who else was affected? A baby, there was a baby, and taxes. My mother says that war started because they didn't pay their taxes. I have a book on it at home written by a German. I'm not prejudiced. I still like Germans."

"There was a German lady in my neighborhood when I was a kid," Netty says, getting in on the conversation. "Boy, are they neat and clean! You could eat off their floor. My mother kept a clean house, but she said she couldn't keep up with the German lady. That lady used to bake cakes and put coins, nickels and pennies, in them. She'd scrub those coins until they were shiny—you didn't get shiny pennies then like you do now. Whoever got the coins in their cake would buy candy with them. Penny candy. Remember those Mary Janes?"

"Caramel and peanuts," Val nods. "Oh that baby, I hated to see it. But it wasn't my fault. These wars are not my fault."

"No, there's nothing much we can do." Netty says.

Val ends up writing something today—a list of places where she went to school. Netty and Ann, as usual, remember early childhood and school in great detail.

"I was a lot happier back then," Ann says. "I just realized what a privileged childhood I had. I was lucky, in most ways anyway." I learn that she is an employee at the center, a senior aid under training with the Area Agency on Aging. Her jobs include keeping the center log, typing, running errands, socializing with the seniors, "telephone reassurance" (making biweekly calls to the homebound), and calling bingo. She has also taken an interest in assisting the residents of the group homes. She reveals that she has a bachelor's degree and once worked toward a master's in psychiatric social work, before dropping out in the 1950s to join her husband stationed in Texas. The group members did not know any of these things about her, and they are impressed.

"So *that's* why you're so nice to all the people around here," Netty says, looking at her carefully.

"Oh, I forgot all of that. I just like people," Ann says, shrugging off the compliment.

Today Netty writes about a police dog that guarded her baby carriage on the front porch. She remembers his "woof, woof" when the postman came.

A man comes in while we are writing and sits down at a nearby table with a piece of cake. He is lanky and weather-beaten. He lives in the same home as some of the writers. (I also learn today that the writing-group members come to the center every weekday morning from three local group homes.)

"Chocolate," Val says. "I see you got the kind of cake you wanted."

"That's Bill," Ann explains. "It's his birthday."

"You don't look sixty-nine," Ann says to Bill.

"Yeah." He grins and holds his fork over his head.

"Happy Birthday, Bill," I say. He holds his big hand out for a shake.

The lady in the kitchen says she got the cake for free along with the usual bakery goods today. On my way out, I notice the party makings: a fresh pot of coffee, donuts, something homemade under tinfoil, and the cake.

It is Indian summer in Michigan—eighty breezy degrees in October. The whole crowd is at the center, and everyone is feeling fine. Bill waves to me from the couch. When I stop by the little sewing room, Sue, Netty, and Ella greet me warmly.

"We were talking about you, wondering where you were," Netty says.

"Heavy traffic this morning on the freeway."

"How many classes do we have left?" she asks. "I'm going to move in three weeks to another group home. At this one, they won't cook for diabetics. And there's too much salt and processed foods. I'll be closer to my daughter, but I'll miss the center and the people here. I don't know what I'll do if I don't have a place to go." She seems most concerned about the social aspects of the move. I am confused as to why she even lives in a group home, but I don't ask.

"I'm not coming today," Sue says. "I just don't feel like it."

"You *can't* not feel like it," Ella counters.

"I don't want to come today," Sue repeats.

"Well, that's OK," I say, keeping my voice light. "Maybe we'll see you next week."

A few minutes later, she joins us at the table. "I decided to come," she says simply. I think Ella must have persuaded her.

Today we are writing about role models and early influences.

"I'm in the wrong class," Lorna says when I introduce the topic. "No offense to you. I can't think of anything. My mind is blocked."

"Well, just listen then," I say.

"I hope it's not too much information," Lorna says with a big smile. "My head might blow off."

Jan, who is with us for the second time only, sits next to me and talks while the others write. "I got hit in the head with a rock when I was a kid," she says. "And I can't remember anything. It's like I'm looking from a spaceship. I just remember walking with my brother and this shower of rocks. I thought I was going to die. I couldn't learn things, like social relationships." Her smile shows she is missing several front teeth. "Are you from Clinton Valley?"

"No, I'm from Wayne State. I'm an English teacher."

"Is it hard there?"

Two or three times during the class, Dee pushes her paper my way. "Do you want to read this?" she says, eager for my response.

"That's great," I say each time. She smiles back, pleased. But she does not want to read aloud to the group.

Val talks out loud while the others write. "I wanted to be a policeman. I never did, though. I wanted to be a piano teacher and an office worker. I used to get the hymn book and pretend I was a piano teacher, and I did become one. I became an office worker, too."

"Put that down," I say.

"Really?" She seems amazed that anyone would record such things.

I ask a question about family beliefs (Did religion play a part in your upbringing? If so, how?) and Val says, "My mother made me afraid about religion."

"How did she do that?" I ask.

"It's personal. I don't want to say. But I told my doctor about it."

"Oh, OK," I say, dropping the subject. But I note that Val writes more of what she says today, and she reads aloud for the first time.

Something else remarkable happens. Just before 11:00, Lorna mentions lunch for the diabetics, but nobody gets up. Then a visiting nurse begins to set up a table in the main room. Sue notices and reminds the others that flu shots will be given from 11:00 to 1:00 today. She takes this to mean that everyone has to get their shots at eleven sharp. Sue walks over and gets a stack of forms from the nurse and begins passing them around to the writing group. Everyone but Ann immediately stops writing about role models and starts filling out the forms.

Well—at least they're writing, I think, trying to fit this behavior into my idea of what we are supposed to be doing. They talk through the whole form-filling process.

Sue cannot remember her zip code or telephone number, and the others help.

"Am I Medicaid or Medicare?" she asks. "Do I check it or write it in?" "Now

I don't get this," she says about the race question: "Asian, African-American, Caucasian, Native-American, other. It doesn't say white."

Netty, Ella, and Sue get a big laugh out of the "Are you pregnant?" question.

"I haven't been with a man in twenty years." Netty says.

Sue pulls her sweater out at the stomach. "Let's see, am I pregnant?"

When the forms have been completed, I manage to convince them to wait a few minutes for their shots, at least long enough to read their stories aloud.

Netty tells about how unhappy her parents' marriage was and begins to cry. "I didn't think I'd cry when I read this," she says, apologetically.

Ann rubs her back. "That's OK," she says with a sympathetic look.

"That's why I didn't write about my mother passing, my father passing," Ella says. "I just wanted to put down the happy things."

Ann tells of an active childhood, her mother a Christian Scientist and teacher, her father an engineer, both major influences.

"I liked yours," Ella says, when Ann has finished. "And hers, too," she adds, motioning to Netty, already on her way out the door.

"And I liked *yours*," Ann replies.

I give everyone a brightly colored paper folder for their accumulated writings. I have gotten ten different colors so that each can choose a favorite. They are surprised and pleased by the gesture.

I notice for the first time today, as I walk out, that nearly everyone at the center on Thursday mornings is now in the writing group. The only nonparticipants I see are a man playing solitaire and, on the couch, two people I don't recognize.

Val's Writing

I admired
  My oldest sister Alice, and my cousin Harry.
  My doctor said that I was like a female Tom Sawyer.
  When I was young I wanted to be a police woman. I worked in a office and I use to play office. I use to play like I was a piano teacher and I really became a piano teacher.
  I had to follow the rules in my house or I would hear about it
  My mother scared me about religion
  I usually stayed by my mother and she had her friends too and I had to call them Aunt.

Netty's Writing

I went to business school after high school (1943). My first job was in an office as a bookkeeper and all-around office clerk. I was trained by a very nice lady, Mary Coleman. She was head of the office. I worked with another girl Hazel, and we worked in a train depot station for the L. H. Cole Oil Company.

My next job (1945) was for the navy Department in a gun factor. I ran a copy machine and sorted mail and was a file clerk. My salary doubled in 2 years and I was happy there until the war was over. Then I transferred to the Pontiac Motor Administration building until my husband returned from the Army. Then I quit to become a housewife and mother.

I held my last job in the 1960's (at age 45) after my children were in school. I was a dining room hostess, cashier, and part time bartender for the Detroit Gun Club for 3½ years. I really enjoyed the work and the training of younger waitresses for the dining room of the club.

After an operation, I stayed home full time and was a full time domestic engineer, Girl Scout leader, Brownie and Cub Scout leader. I belonged to a Methodist church and helped with the youth (teenage) group.

My years of working taught me to handle money, be more organized, and appreciate other people. I had a lot of friends at work, which helped my times of loneliness until my husband's return. I learned to be more patient with others, as I was always somewhat a perfectionist.

Although I never became an art teacher, my interest in art never left me. I did office murals, painted basement play rooms, and went on to a year of human anatomy at the Detroit Art Institute. I still sketch and paint.

At the present, I try to keep busy and help whenever I can. I do dishes, keep my room neat, dust, and take care of my grandchildren, 8 months and 2½ years, when I get the chance.

I've never lost my love for children!

Ella, Sue, and Lynn have been anticipating today's class.

"She's here!" Sue says, as I walk by the sewing room.

"We'll be right there," Ella hollers.

Sarah, sitting at a table in the main room, perks up. "Are you meeting in the back?" she asks. "Count me in!"

She is talking continuously today. "My doctor changed my medication from evening to morning. I don't stick my leg out anymore. And I can sit just as quiet . . ." But her eyes are red-rimmed, and she gets up from the table often to move around.

Sarah talks all the time she is writing: "Oh I was selling china at Kresge's and they made a story of it and put it in their paper because I was such a good salesgirl. Well, why wouldn't I be? I was a closet child. Oh yeah, they put me on the hosiery counter, too." She is also among the first to volunteer for reading: "I want to be next!" she calls out, excited. Her script, a combination of cursive and print, slides down the page in a list of lifetime occupations.

Sarah's Writing

(I was a baby)
cometology and academy
woolworths
hosetry counter
Im anspector
our mgr. under Det.
I worked at home
traveley bussised
I got married
I was a guard in
Rodchter Mich.
all winter

Everyone seems more interactive today. For the first time, Sue volunteers to read, and Dorene—who has attended only once before and stayed just long enough to pass out pencils and paper—says she is only going to watch but ends up writing about her job for an optical shop delivering eye glasses. She even reads aloud.

When Dorene has finished, Lynn says in her carefully enunciated way, "That was very nice." Lynn herself is very anxious to read her paper, especially the last line, which she tells me "everyone is gonna love."

Lynn's Writing

My first job was housework. I spent some time there. Later on, I did clerk work at a department store. My mother taught me how to do housework, and the sales girl (clerk) taught me how to do that. I had a natural gift of doing clerk work.

About the clerk work (sales girl), we dressed very fine and were very well behaved.

I had about five jobs before I married. One of them was a job as typist. The typing jobs, I typed envelopes and enclosed advertising. During this job, we'd type an enormous amount of envelopes.

The job I'd like to do would be a movie job in which I would be seen on the screen in movie houses.

A few smile at the last line, and Ella says, for emphasis, "Mmm*HMMM*!"

The group's liveliness seems spurred along by several factors. There's the topic of work, which inspires feelings of pride and accomplishment, and the colorful folders holding everyone's writing to date—visible evidence of progress. (Those who missed the preceding week and did not get a folder specifically ask me to bring more next time.) And then there is the presence of the center director, who has returned from an illness and has been talking up the group all week. She is sitting in today, encouraging people.

"Ella, tell about your work with children," the director says. And to the rest: "Don't forget all the work you do around the center—making coffee, washing dishes, cooking, secretarial jobs."

"Taking out the trash?" Sue asks.

"Yes, that's work."

"How do you spell *trash*? With a *c*?"

Even Lorna seems more confident today, finally getting a topic she can write about without feeling her head is going to blow off.

Lorna's Writing

The very first job at one day before my sixteenth birthday they hired me at Sanders as a basement jack of all trades, self serve and big coffee urns, two of them the size of barrels, bussing, and then I got to take care of registers, and it lasted two years. That was in the 50's. One day I missed my transportation, so I called in and they told me they didn't need me any more. My 2nd job was Stouffers. I spent all my salary for 3 weeks and worked 9 months, no tipping either. 6 months at Awreys and Ann Page or Ann Jane, for me it was a skill and acquired a talent or knack. It all boils down to experience I gained. If I had it to do over again, I would help to better myself.

At the end of the read-aloud session, Gert observes: "Everyone's was different."

The director smiles and says to me, "It's going well, isn't it?" I nod, thinking of the changes in the group over the past six weeks and what I have learned about these women. Most lack formal education, have divorced or never married, and have endured a long life of economic and emotional troubles. They are well acquainted with helplessness and loss, chronic mental illness, and lifelong submission to the medical system. Netty told us this morning about going to the psychiatrist yesterday only to find him out of the office. "He never even bothered to call me or my daughter," she said, indignant. "Oh, one of *them*," Sue said knowingly.

They are, however, kind, and treat each other with respect. Sue, the better seamstress, finished Lynn's cancer pad this morning so she would feel free to attend the group. (They take their work on cancer pads very seriously, setting weekly quotas for themselves.) Dorene listened patiently to Sarah's incoherent ramblings. They are unfailingly polite to outsiders (Dorene asked my name today and said very carefully, "Do you mind if I call you Ruth?" And Jan, who does not remember my name from week to week, still thanks me at the end of every session.) They take great pleasure in small things. (This morning Sarah sipped slowly from her Styrofoam cup and said with relish, "Boy, that's good coffee!") Many claim this is the happiest time of their lives.

"What's the topic today?" someone asks as I walk into the main room of the center.

"Love and romance."

"Ooo, hot stuff!" says Bernard from the sidelines.

As the rest of the group begins to write, Val sits with her arms folded and watches. But she helps Ella with her spelling of "two" and "separated."

Sue says, "I loved my puppy and my mother.

"OK," I say. "Write about your mother and why you loved her."

"Oh, there's that *why* question again," she says, exasperated. She writes about the dog instead, and later reads aloud.

(Reading): "Micky was bit by a rat—"

"Oh, *my*," Sarah comments, on her way out the door for a cigarette.

"and had to be put to sleep. I cried and cried."

"Why, of course you did," Sarah says, soothingly.

Several people show me their writing before they read aloud to assure that it "makes sense." Everyone who has written volunteers to read.

Ella brings up her friend and fellow writing-group member Dee in her writing:

My First Love

Mr. John Wesley Hutchinson. He was 18 years old, when we got marriage. I was 14 years old. We had two kids before I was 20 years old. He is living in Alabama. We separated when we were 24 years old. We had 2 kids. It was a boy and girl. It was 11 mounths differance in there age.

I live in Alabama. I live in Dayton Ohio. I also live in Chattanooga Tenn. Then I live in Detroit, Mich. I was married the second time there where I got married. Indiana. I live in Detroit, Mich 60 years. I have lots of friends. I love them all, Dee is one of my friend.

When Netty reads, she tells of forty-two years of marriage to the same man, forcing herself to slow down and push out the last few lines. "I didn't think I'd do that," she says, sniffling. "I didn't when I *wrote* it."

Everybody assures her that the writing is very good.

The center director has gotten several of the group members together before my arrival to make up the memories exercise they missed the week they had doctor appointments. Their papers and pencils are all laid out on the long table.

Everyone is in the main room, taking a break before the second round of writing. Jan, Dorene, and Rose are on the couch; Lorna and Val are sitting at a table with another woman I have not seen here before. Ella, Sue, Gert, Dee, Ann—everyone is here but Netty, who has moved to a group home that does not have a van service to the center.

The director tells me the new home is not very good. "We tried to intervene," she says, "But her daughters wanted this place because there's a doctor on the premises." The director has called Netty to see if she wants a ride to the center today, but Netty says she is not feeling well. The director thinks she is depressed.

By way of greeting, I tell Sue she gave me her cold last week, and she responds with the details of her own recovery.

"I still have mine, but I feel better. Marie—she owns our group home—gave me some Vicks to put on my nose and chest so I could blow it all out in the morning."

Lorna tells me she had a caramel apple yesterday and just licked the caramel off.

The topic for our final meeting is one that I have used with other groups to initiate self-reflection.

"Today we're going to talk about your philosophy of life," I say, trying to sound matter-of-fact, although I know they will find the topic difficult.

"I don't have any philosophy," Sarah immediately says.

"Philosophy of *what*?" Dorene says.

"What does philosophy mean?" Sarah asks.

"Oh, it's like what life means, what's important in life," I explain.

"Oh, just like with the psychiatrist," Lorna responds. "I *still* don't know about the meaning of life."

"Oh, I can't write *that*," Sue says. "I wouldn't know where to begin."

"Well, I'll ask you some specific questions," I say. "That'll show you where to start."

"Oh, OK," Sue says, congenially.

"All right, let's just start with this general question," I say, indicating that they are to begin writing. "The question is, 'What do you think are the most important things in life?'"

"Children," Sarah says promptly.

"OK," I say. "That would be one place where Sarah would start. One of the most important things in life is children."

"Yes," Sarah nods firmly.

"Now the rest of you—what are the most important things in life to make a happy life?"

Despite general confusion and many questions, several begin to write. Minutes pass in relative silence. Then Sue whispers to Jan.

"I'm not writing anything, are you?"

"Why not?"

"I can't think of anything to write about even though she asked a question."

Ella reads aloud what she's got so far: "The most important thing in life is food."

I sit next to Jan and write for her, because she says her eyes are tired from writing earlier about school. She has broken her glasses and cannot see well without them. Our conversation is interrupted frequently by my general questions to the group and others' running commentary.

"OK, Jan," I say. "What are the most important things in life to make a happy life?"

"Faith," she mumbles, barely audible. "OK, well I had fai—well, I never lived alone since that, uh, I learned some things earlier, earlier in my life, like . . ." She trails off.

"What are those things you learned?"

"Um, that God loves everybody, God loves everyone and us, um, I can't think of anything else."

"OK, well—"

"At our church," Jan says suddenly, as if struck by an idea, "We always say you're already forgiven, that uh . . ." She pauses, having lost the thought.

Sue, who has been watching from across the table, says. "I forgot about that woman. The one that sat there. Her name was—?

"Netty?" I say.

"I was thinking about her. She moved, didn't she?"

"Yes, she did," I say. "And she was going to come and join us today, but she's not feeling well."

I turn back to Jan. "This is what you've got so far." I read it back to remind her.

I raise another question for both Jan and the group: "Are there any teachings or biblical sayings that express your philosophy of life that you think are important?"

"I can't write such big words," Lorna says.

"That's all right," I say. "You don't have to write big words."

"What was the question again?" Jan asks.

"Are there teachings or biblical sayings, or—?"

"Um, I really don't know much about, that much about—but I, years ago I used to believe in God *so* much, but I never had any teaching that I remember, but I'm not sure. Probably with my parents, but I can't remember that. I don't know, I learned something about . . ." Her voice fades away.

"That's all I'm gonna write now," Sarah says, putting her pencil down. "I have to think about it some more." She goes out for a cigarette.

A man walks in and says, to anyone listening, that he spilled coffee. Lorna tells him where to find a rag, then gets up to do it herself.

I ask the group another question: "What do you think about all the changes that have taken place in your lifetime? Changes in society, for example? We now have computers, televisions, many technological breakthroughs. What do you think about all that?"

I return to Jan. "So do you have a response to that one?"

"Um, different changes? TV and radio and—"

"Computers and calculators."

"Yeah, computers and, uh space exploration, and uh, I can't remember anything more. I can't remember."

"It's there and then it disappears, doesn't it?" Sue says, listening to Jan. "You think of it and the next thing you go to say it and it disappears."

"Mmmmhmm," Jan agrees, chuckling. "Yeah, I don't know what's wrong."

"She's thinking of too many things at once maybe, that's what," Lorna offers from across the table.

"Maybe that's it," Sue agrees.

"Yeah," Jan says. "Things are coming into my head, but—"

"How you doin' today, Sue?" I say, trying to draw her into the writing task. "You need some help getting started?"

"Yes, I can't write a thing," she says flatly.

"Maybe we could help you out," I say. "Let's see, the first question was, 'What are the important things to have a happy life?'"

"I don't know," Sue says.

"Would you say you have a happy life?"

"Being with the women? To me it is. But to others it might not be."

"We're just talking about you. Being with other women is an important part of a happy life for you, right? How about putting that down?"

"How can I start it off?"

"You could say, 'Being with other—"

"People," Sue provides.

Lorna calls from across the table, "Ann, what you writin' so much about?"

"About big brother," Ann says. "Big brotherism on the television and the media, creating anxiety." She laughs at her own intensity.

I address the group with another question: "I'd also like you to tell what events have caused you concern in your lifetime. These could be social events, you know like race relations, or relations between the sexes, or violence, or crime, anything of that kind. What events have caused you concern in your lifetime?"

Sarah returns to the table. "What do I write about now?" she asks.

"The last question was, 'Are there any events that have caused you concern in your lifetime?'"

I turn to Jan with the question.

"Concern?" Jan says, unsure. "No, no, uh, I don't know about that."

"How about you, Sue?"

"What? No, not that I know of," Sue says.

"O-K," I say slowly, trying to think of another approach.

"You know what?" Sue says, thinking aloud. "People don't talk to me about anything, so how am I to know? I don't know. A lot of things I should know, I don't know."

I try to reorient Sue to the experiences she does know about. "Well, let's see, you've got your first line there, which is 'Being with people is important for a happy life.'"

"And the women I'm with," Sue continues. "And being with family."

"OK, OK," I say, writing that down. "That's good. Anything else?"

"No, nothing I can think of."

"How about social changes during your lifetime? How do you feel about those?"

Sue laughs. "I don't know. I got no social."

She pauses to think some more and then adds, "Oh, you mean going to these affairs and that? That's social?"

"It could be, it could be," I say, glad for a response.

"Going to the mall is social."

"That's another kind of social."

"Different kind?"

"Mmmmhmm."

"Ohhhh!" Sue says, as if experiencing a revelation.

I raise another question for the group: "What do you consider your most important achievements during your life?"

"Woooo!" Sue says. "I've never had any. Not that I know of."

"Achievements can be many things, " I say. "Like becoming a certain kind of person, becoming a kind person or—"

"Oh, whether I'm liked or not?"

"Mmmhmm. Being liked by others, learning how to get along with others. Those are achievements."

"Oh, " Sue says, pausing to think.

"So Jan," I say, returning to her. "What were you going to say now about your achievements?

"Oh, I don't know—achievements—" Jan says, thinking aloud. "I suppose graduating from high school. And, uh, being accep—. I was accepted to go to college, but I didn't—I thought I'd get too homesick . . ." Her voice thins to a dangling thread.

I write down everything she says, as closely as possible to the way she says it. "Anything recently?"

"I don't know, recently, I don't know about recently," Jan mumbles.

I turn to the group. "My last question is, 'What advice would you give to future generations for a happy life?' Pretend you're talking to kids or grandkids. What advice would you give?"

"Ooooo! These are hard ones," Lorna says.

"Yeah, these are the hardest ones we've had," I agree.

"I haven't answered any of them yet," Lorna says.

"Well, some people have. Maybe when they read, you'll get some ideas."

Someone who is not in the group begins to play the piano in the corner of the room.

"Jan, got any advice?" I ask.

"Uh, just to love your kids, um, make sure that you talk to them when they're little, talk to them a lot when they're little." Her voice is clear on this point. "I can't think of anything else."

"You've got a *lot* here," I say encouragingly and give it back to her.

"Does that give you any ideas, Sue?" I ask.

"No."

"What advice do you have for the younger generation?" I persist.

"I don't. I don't. 'Cause they wouldn't listen to me."

"Let's pretend they would. If they'd listen to you."

"What would I say then?"

"Yes, what would you say to them?"

"I can't even think of anything to say, I mean, about that."

"*Love!*" Ella calls out. "Regardless of what. Love. One. Another." She separates each word for emphasis.

Lorna gets up from her seat. "Is there anything we can get you?" she asks me, smiling.

The group is quiet for a few seconds as people finish writing.

"Is this your last time?" Sarah asks me.

"Mmmhmm."

"Is it?" Sue says.

"Guess what I'm gonna say?" Dorene poses.

"What?" I say.

"Thank you very much."

"Oh, thank *you*."

"For being, I mean, for helping us. I had trouble getting started, but I did OK."

"You did very well. Once you got started you wrote a *lot*."

"It's nice having you here," Sue says.

"Oh, it's been nice, nice to be here," I reply. "It's been a lot of fun for me to do this."

"I know one thing," Sue says. "You're *educated*."

"Mmmhmm," Ella agrees.

"Did you go to college?" Dorene asks.

"Yes, I did."

"I thought so," Dorene says confidently. She tells me her brother went to college and now has a real good job as a stockbroker.

I announce that it is time to read, and Dee begins immediately.

Lynn offers to read next, and when she's finished, Lorna responds that her advice is "sensible."

Sue and Dorene both want to read next. Sue selects her school-memories piece.

Lorna says, "Want me to read mine?" and shares her school writing.

Ella, Sara, Rose, Val, Gert, and Ann read their philosophies.

I read Jan's for her, and it elicits several positive responses. ("That's true. That's good," many say.)

It is the first time people have expressed such enthusiasm for reading aloud, and this despite the difficult topic.

"Are you going to print this?" Sara asks when we are finished.

"Yeah, I'll type it up if you want me to," I say. Earlier I have announced that I will type anyone's completed life story who requests it.

"I want you to," Sara says, brightly. "Including [supplying] the paper."

"What's your name again?" Dorene asks.

"My name's Ruth."

"Ruth, thank you very much."

"It was, ah, nice, and I was looking forward to seeing you," Val adds.

"Thank you," I reply. "I'm going to miss you all."

"Yeah, I'm going to miss you, too," Val says.

"I'm glad you joined us, too, Lorna," I say.

"I tried. I wasn't a party pooper," she says, good-naturedly. "Want an apple?"

Val's Writing

Everything is psychological and philosophical. My husband and my doctor are enough to make me happy and family too.

The most important achievements was being able to be a good piano player and also being a piano teacher.

The advice I give to young kids is listen to your parents and teachers in school.

Dorene's Writing

I'm glad I got such a nice family, they are very good to me, that's the first on my list. I live in a fantastic group home. The girls are good to me. There are 12 girls that live in the home including myself. I'm glad to say I'm in good health. My family is in good health and that is very important to me. My daughter Lou Ann is a wonderful girl. Her and her husband get along great together. When my parents were living, I had a good home life. My father died in 1974 and my mother in 1977. I had nice working jobs through the years. My job working at the bank was the best job I ever had. I worked at the bank for four years. The girls were very nice to work with. Graduating from high school was quite an achievement to me.

Ella's Writing

The most important thing in life is food and the right kind of food. The church is very important. They taught me and my kids religion all through life.

I have been taught about the change. My kids, 3 mens, are married to white girls. My kids and I all worship with different churches. They taught us to love one another, be understanding.

Lynn's Writing

Most people say money is the most important. I can't think of any biblical saying concerning money, but good can come of it. With an excess of money many people are made happy when receiving gifts of money.

Television gives many sad incidents, but after thinking that they were only make believe the air cooled and you were no longer sad.

Sarah's Writing

Joe was born Feb. 20, 1934. He was my first born. He was a little man when he was born. The most important things in life. So my husband and I raised three children. We had it rough but we made it just the same, til we were divorsed. My step mother saw to it that we wer seperated. And I had it real bad. I looked for a church that I could belavied in. I think we have gone from bad to worse. I have been taking for a fool. I did get a beauty coarse at 36 years of my life so my children would love me. One of the most of my life was bringing into life. I lived at the Barlow home for 28 days and was treated royal did I think I was cured but do you know I had wonderful treatment there. I am mature.

A week later, I return with typed versions of everyone's life stories, only slightly edited for spelling and punctuation, organized and paragraphed around the major themes we have addressed.

The group members crowd into the main room like schoolchildren waiting for the teacher to pass out treats. The director says they are "geeked" today:

"When I came in this morning, I reminded them you were coming, and they were, like, 'Oh yeah! She's going to type that up for us!'" She makes her voice breathless and laughs. I find out later that the director has made the group-home people her special project, her goal being to "include them in everything and exclude them from nothing."

The room gets quiet as everyone reads their writing. Most say they are going to share their stories with family and friends.

Val says, "I told her about this. My sister."

"Oh, did you?" I ask.

"They said that was nice. They asked what subjects you taught. My niece [her sister's daughter] is an English teacher, English and American lit."

"Oh, really? Well, she'll enjoy reading that."

"Yeah," Val says, laughing a little. "She graduated summa cum laude."

"Oh, she did? From where?"

"From Mercy College."

"Ah-h-h-h. And now she teaches where?"

"Uh, she was teaching at Lady Wood Catholic School, for girls? For years, and they wanted to make her a nun. Every day they would talk to her about it, she said. Then she got a job making seven thousand dollars more in a regular high school, so she says she's got to take that, it's time."

"So she's not gonna be a nun, then, huh?"

"No, she's not gonna be no nun, but they're looking for, all the time they're lookin' for people to be nuns."

"I'm sure they are," I say, laughing. "Well, that's good, I'm glad you've got somebody who's going to appreciate it with you." I try to bring the conversation back around to Val, but she continues to talk about her niece.

"Yeah. I was going to say something else about her. She ended up on the dean's list. As summa cum laude, you end up on the dean's list."

"Uh-huh. So she's a pretty smart person, huh?"

"Yeah, she is smart."

"Well, good."

"Oh, yeah," she says, remembering something else. "And she teaches Spanish, too, and speaks it fluently."

"How old is your niece?"

"My oldest niece is forty-seven, and the other one that graduated from that college is maybe forty, in the early part of her forties."

"Uh-huh, but you didn't have kids of your own, huh?" I assume this is why she is talking so much about her niece.

"No . . . I don't know," Val says, hesitating. "I guess not, but uh there was something that happened that makes me think that maybe I did, but I don't think so."

"Well, you didn't write about it, so I just figured you didn't have kids."

"Oh."

"Hmmm. Well, good, I was glad to work with you, Val. It was fun."

"It was nice working with you, too," she says. "Thank you for coming."

Our conversation reinforces what I have observed about many of the women: they have a much easier time talking about others' accomplishments than their own, and they remember them better, too.

I walk over to Dee, who is wearing a soft smile.

"So, what do you think, Dee? What are you going to do with yours?"

"Keep a memory of you, to remember you by," she says in her Southern accent. "You're a sweet person."

"Well—well, thank you."

"You're a very nice person," Dee continues. "I needed you. I need people like you. I never did realize it till I got this over with. But I feel a lot better since I was with you."

"You do?" I ask, not knowing how to respond. "I'm glad."

"I do, too. I think you're a nice person."

"Thank you. I'm going to miss you. I've gotten a lot from this group, too."

"I'm going to miss you, too. Yeah, I have, too. I feel a lot better, I feel straightened out. I feel nor . . . , more normal. I feel way better than I used to."

"Why do you 'spose that's so?"

"It's because we had someone to lead the way for us, we had our hand we couldn't reach out, we had to find you, we had to reach for, for outside, you know? We people are different persons, you know? It took you to straighten us out. It sure did."

"Good. It doesn't take much, does it?" I say, offering a little joke to deflect the gratitude.

"It doesn't take much," she repeats, chuckling.

As I am talking to Dee, I notice Sarah walk over to the garbage can and drop her folder into it.

"I don't have anybody to show mine to," Sarah says.

"You *don't*?"

"So I filed it."

"But—you might want to give it to the director to keep. How about that?"

"Well, I could do that," Sarah says, reconsidering.

"Yeah, why don't you give it to her? I know *she'd* like to see it."

"I will," Sarah says, and she retrieves the folder from the garbage can.

I interview the director the morning of my last visit. She says the group-home residents have very low self-esteem and various levels of social and intellectual functioning, but they are willing to try new things if repeatedly encouraged, and once they commit to something they stick with it.

"When they missed that second week because the van didn't get here, they were just crushed," she says. "They talked about it the next day, you know, 'We missed writing! We were supposed to be in the writing class yesterday!' But they need to be constantly prodded and reminded because they forget from moment to moment."

"Some people don't understand why they can't take it upon themselves to go and do things," the director continues. "They say, 'Well, all those group-home people do is sit there, all they do is sit there.' And I'm like, 'Well, no, that's not all they do!' But you have to ask them, you have to tell them. I had to tell Val every week, 'Val, it's time to go to writing class,' and she'd say, 'Oh, yeah.' Then she'd be psyched about it and she'd go in there, and it'd be great. But you have to remind them, and you have to tell them, and a lot of people don't want to do that. People think they're adults, they can do it on their own, but they can't."

"So what do you think they got out of the writing group?" I ask.

"I think they got out—they finally told a little bit about themselves that wasn't just where they're at in the group home. So many people think, 'Well, they've probably been living in this group home their entire life.' And in the writing group, they finally got it on paper that they *haven't* been living there their whole life and they *have* done other things, and they are just as normal as everybody else."

"Going through that school thing was great," she continues. "I mean, it was fun for me, too, because I did it with them and they were like, 'I don't have anything to say about school memories.' So then I'd ask them a question, and they were like, 'Oh, well, I went to blah, blah, blah' you know, and they remember all of that stuff. And it's just something that *they* did that they're very proud of. And I think that's the biggest thing—that they are recording what *they* did."

She then tells me a story about Dee.

"I found out that Dee lived right down the street from here her whole life until she went into the hospital, and her family has never acknowledged her at all. They sign her check, give it to her—that's *it*. The sewing people have grown attached to these group-home ladies. There's three or four sewing ladies in the community who come in, and they get all the cancer pads ready, and they get the girls in there on Wednesdays, because they know that as much as I would love to spend all my time with them, you know, I don't have any. Just look at my desk." With a sweep of her gaze, she invites me to survey the mass of paperwork. (With a bachelor's degree, she makes around $17,000 a year, having recently gotten a raise from her starting salary of $15,000.)

"You just don't have the time that you want to," she says. "So the sewing ladies will get them in there and do different projects with them, whether it be stuffing a teddy bear and letting them sew it up or making pillows, just doing anything. Well, one of those sewing ladies, whose name is Verna, lived across the street from Dee's mother and did not even know that it was the same connection until I drove Verna home one day. I was driving the big van, and Dee was sitting in the back, and as we drove down the street Dee said, 'I used to live there.' And Verna called me up later, and she was crying. She said, 'Is that little DeeDee?' She'd always heard of little DeeDee from the neighbors. And she said, 'Those people, her family, will never see her.' And they live right here in the neighborhood. And that is just the saddest thing to me. . . . But we keep 'em going here at the center."

The number of older adults with developmental disabilities in the United States has been estimated at more than one and a half million. Congregate housing for people with disabilities exists on a continuum based on the amount of care provided. On the lowest end of the care continuum are congregate apartments, which typically offer a meal plan only; on the highest end are nursing homes. In between are residential care facilities, also known as group homes, board-and-cares, adult foster homes, assisted or sheltered housing, rest homes, homes for the aged, or domicilaries, depending on the state in which they are located. Unlike nursing homes, group homes are not regulated by all states, and there is little reliable data on them. Some states, including Michigan, do not require licensing of homes serving fewer than six residents, and it is estimated that the number of unlicensed homes may far outnumber those that are licensed. Available statistics on licensed facilities in the United States indicate that in 1986 there were twenty-nine thousand that housed the elderly, with a total of more than 370,000 residents.[2]

Group-home residents typically have one or more disabilities. They are mentally impaired or confused; developmentally disabled (and lacking in personal, social, or interpersonal skills); survivors of stroke, heart attack, or some other disabling accident or illness (closed-head injuries, for example); and some have a major chronic condition (AIDS, arthritis, cancer). Most are single or widowed (women predominate) adults who lack enough income to support themselves in a privately owned home or congregate apartment.[3] Particular group homes may direct their services to a specific category of individuals, such as the emotionally impaired or developmentally disabled.

Despite physical, mental, and/or emotional impairments, most older group-home residents have led a relatively "normal" life, including school, jobs, marriage, and children, prior to entering the home in late life. They are usually white females of low socioeconomic status. A recent study of 177 group homes in Cleveland determined that the average age of residents was seventy-seven; they were predominantly female; 15 percent were African Americans (higher than the representation of this group in the U.S. population); and 16 percent had never married.[4] Mental-health professionals count group-home residents among the "forgotten aged" in terms of research and clinical practice in gerontology.

Because the rate of state and federal reimbursements to group homes is low, and because they rely for operating expenses on residents' incomes, which are also low (typically Social Security Disability Income or Supplementary Security Income), group homes offer little beyond shelter and basic physical care. As Janice Sinson notes in her study of group homes, most facilities "regard themselves as providers of a particular type of homely hotel service which ensures that their residents have a secure and sheltered life. They do not see their role as being concerned with individual personal development and consequently do not provide their residents with any opportunities for such development." [5] For this reason, as well as the desire to circulate more largely in the community and to approximate a normal lifestyle, older group-home residents will increasingly seek out social and educational stimuli provided by senior centers.

SEVEN

Learning from
Our Differences

The daughter's reactions at various ages represent one
of the greatest limitations if not tragedies of growing up
and growing old for many of us. As we move through
our lives, we seem so often to have so little
understanding for those who are younger and those
who are older.
—Kathleen Woodward

ONE OF THE GREATEST CHALLENGES for all of us throughout life is to
respect our differences and learn from them. Initially, North American feminists
worked to define gender differences and to overcome gender inequities; today,
we work with difference of many kinds—race, class, ethnicity, sexual orientation, nationality, religion—and we theorize about its effects on individual development and social movement. Surprisingly, within this landscape of feminist
excursion, age is largely unexplored territory. U.S. society at all levels suffers
from continued ageism and generational splitting, even among the very feminists
who champion diversity. This inattention to ageism, like inattention to sexism or
any other form of oppression, is a sign of unacknowledged privilege and is itself
oppressive in fostering covert participation in systemic neglect and internalized
domination.[1] For these reasons and more, we must examine feminists' avoidance
of age and its many meanings. Even feminist gerontologists have not fully explored or theorized the social and personal meanings of age, especially as they
affect the making of knowledge in age studies.

In previous chapters, we saw that gendered identities and generational identities were written into life stories, and we observed the effects of gender splitting—the separation of feminine and masculine aspects of self and society
through delineation of gender roles and the division of domestic and public
spheres. In this final chapter, I take up the question of "generational splitting,"
whereby generations are separated through age-graded social roles, assumptions,
and expectations about "age appropriate" behavior, and the unwillingness or

inability to associate and identify with generational "others."[2] Generational splitting results from unexamined ageism. From the standpoint of developmental psychology, maturity in later life involves full integration of these "split off" aspects of self. It is my belief that advancement of various social movements into the next century, including the feminist movement, also depends on the integration of such splits in both self and society. Feminists, for their part, must develop an awareness of age and an appreciation for age diversity.

What is the possible source of generational splitting and ageism within the women's movement? More than one feminist has proposed that unresolved differences between women are rooted in unrealistic concepts of mother—specifically, the mother/daughter relationship. Most women, at some time in their lives, are culturally assigned the role of "mother" (she who nurtures, takes care, supports, enhances, comforts, sustains, encourages, facilitates, moderates), whether or not they are biological mothers. American men (most of whom are still split off from the feminine aspects of themselves) often assign (usually unconsciously) the mother role to their girlfriends, wives, female lovers, friends, and women in the workplace. American women typically assign (usually unconsciously) the mother or grandmother role to any older woman. Older lesbians have been most observant of this tendency and its damaging consequences, because in patriarchal culture they are less identified with the role of woman as object of sex and reproduction.[3] The problem with assigning the mother role is that it creates a decidedly one-sided, nonreciprocal relationship in which the mother figure becomes a self-sacrificing "giver-who-does-not-get"; Baba Copper, a lesbian writing from "over the hill," notes that, although she may receive deference, she does not always receive respect, and "almost never do I sense that I am being approached by a younger woman in the spirit of acceptance, learning or wonder."[4] Instead, the younger woman approaches with the expectation of encountering a mother—someone who gives unconditional love, support, encouragement, and service but does not get angry, express needs, assert her own interests, or make demands. The younger woman expects to be nurtured by the older woman but does not expect to nurture her in return. Copper calls this one-sidedness on the part of young women "daughterism"; she equates it with the ageism found throughout the feminist movement and U.S. culture at large. Of course, a parallel "motherism" exists among older women who treat younger women as surrogate daughters in need of advice and guidance or as potential sources of unreciprocal care. In both cases, each woman's individualism is erased when former mother/daughter figure dynamics are projected onto the new relationship, because role-playing ensues, and the possibilities for real exchange are diminished.

These projections of the mother/daughter relationship have profound emotional and psychological consequences. The mother figure feels used, misunderstood, and unappreciated, while the "daughter figure" feels confused and angry "for being raised by her mother to fulfill goals that are largely in violation of her own self-realization," a situation that is compounded when the daughter is lesbian.[5] Psychologist Daniel Levinson confirms through large-scale research on women's life-course development that most daughters feel anger and ambivalence toward their mothers, due largely to the mixed messages that American mothers have been sending their daughters in the last half of the twentieth century. The official message is "be a mother and homemaker like me," and don't attempt to move beyond the Traditional Marriage Enterprise. The unofficial, muted message, founded on the mother's unrequited desire to pursue her own goals, is "escape as best you can, learn to be independent, and create an alternative life, although I don't know what that will be or how to help you." Copper offers a sobering description of traditional mothering:

> It is the mother's *job* to prepare the daughter for the use of men. She must teach her, by example, how to assume the terrible responsibility for maintaining the center—the stabilizing core of family and the private world. She must instruct her in the self-defeating standards of taste which will govern the daughter's attitudes toward her own body and face, her personality, and her choices of life adventures. Successful mothering is still measured in terms of the daughter's attractiveness to men, her success in a male-controlled work world, and her reproductive capacity. These successes depend to a large degree upon the daughter's ability to assimilate into male culture. She must learn to conform to the aesthetic rules which deify female youth and teach allegiance to a hierarchy which will forever divide her from other women.[6]

The daughter who identifies strongly with this teaching works hard to be a "good girl," a "good woman," and a "good wife." The daughter who identifies more with the antitraditional message works hard to become her *own* woman through self-exploration, work, and gender equity. Today's middle-aged career women and feminists are, not surprisingly, antitraditional and have often defined themselves *against* their mothers. Entering adulthood, they knew what they did *not* want in terms of gender roles and life structure, but not always what they *did* want, or how to get it, having had few successful role models or mentors. Levinson concludes that the challenge now for careerists and feminists in midlife is to integrate the internal figures of the traditional and antitraditional female in order better to understand and appreciate themselves *and* their mothers.

Through my life-story research, I have found that this challenge actually extends throughout the second half of life and well into old age. The life stories of women in their sixties, seventies, and eighties show that they are still reacting to and against their mothers, while simultaneously engaging in a similar dynamic with their daughters, who may be repeating the patterns with *their* daughters.

The cycle of projection, reaction, rejection, and ageism continues until it is broken through new awareness and deliberate efforts to change. Copper believes that true reconciliation between women of all ages is impossible until "daughter-rearing goals are radically modified" in U.S. culture. For her, "the betrayal of the Daughter by her loving Mother poisons the relationships between all women, but most clearly those between young women and old women."[7] Put in developmental terms, what is needed is nothing less than a new psychology of generational relations based on a respect for mother/daughter differences and an appreciation for age-related developmental issues.

A first step toward reconciliation, suggested by new work in feminist psychology, is for mothers and daughters to gain knowledge of their different collective and personal histories and to work actively toward empathy and understanding. Only then can women establish mutual growth-enhancing relations, as opposed to the unequal, patronizing dynamics that so often characterize intergenerational exchange. In her research on race relations among women, Cynthia García Coll finds that a major stumbling block to equality across diversity is the pull of collective histories, by which she means both collective experiences and "the prior and current history of power differentials and conflicts between the groups."[8] As we saw in chapter 2, generational culture pulls an individual in certain directions in terms of identity and life-course development. Generational culture entails shared beliefs, assumptions, and moral vocabularies, as well as a feeling of separation from other generations. Some generations, such as the one born prior to or during the Great Depression and the baby boomers born between 1945 and 1965, are "stronger" than others in terms of collective identity and cohesiveness and therefore react more strongly to other groups. Members of these two generations, for example, may experience specific conflicts rooted in the perceived "other centeredness" of the depression generation and the perceived "me centeredness" of baby boomers. In terms of power relations, members of each group may feel oppressed by the other: women from the Great Depression era feel blame from boomers for being self-sacrificing and putting everyone else's needs before their own, while boomers feel blame from the depression generation for being selfish and putting their own needs before those of others. When individuals react from feelings of group oppression, they assume power differentials that preclude mutuality, thereby limiting their potential for growth.

Personal history, as well as collective history, gets in the way of generational relations, as does denial or lack of awareness of either. Coll concludes that, as a first step, individuals have to acknowledge their collective histories and personal experiences; they have to both own them and share them in good faith with members of other groups, listen and learn from others' stories, and adapt to differences, realizing that this will involve risk to one's previous sense of self, and may cause emotional discomfort. Each of us must get beyond the self-serving attitude that "my way" through life is better than "your way"; we must advance emotionally to the point where we can see how each of us does the best she can with the knowledge, abilities, and opportunities available to her. Sharing life stories across the generational divide will help with this. Feminist gerontologist Collette V. Brown reminds us that women's sharing of life stories is, first and foremost, a declaration of women's *visibility,* which not only brings recognition of accomplishments and contributions, but also highlights women's strategies for resisting oppression across the life course; "By regaining their voices and history, women seek and share common experiences, and in this way, linkages to other women can be found."[9]

Of course, life-story patterns, as well as life experiences, differ across generations, and this understanding must be part of our growing awareness and appreciation for mother/daughter differences. As we saw in chapter 3, standard scripts for gender, race, and class shape individual life stories, although these change over time. The traditional romance plot that underwrote the lives of women from the depression generation has given way to an array of alternative lifestyle plots in response to the social critique and political movements of the boomer generation. In the late-twentieth century, men and women are writing new marriage plots that make way for gay and lesbian unions; nonmarriage plots that celebrate single life, multiple partners, alternative versions of monogamy, and the growth potentials in celibacy; and antimarriage plots, which challenge the whole concept of marriage on social, political, and personal grounds. The "happy family plot" has been exposed for its denials and aversions in new narratives of alcoholism, mental illness, drug abuse, sexual abuse, and incest.

The willingness to repeat conventional patterns in the telling of life stories is also a generational issue. As a baby boomer feminist comfortable with the protest mentality cultivated by my generation, I am much more likely than a nonfeminist from the depression generation to write a life story that pursues new, unconventional scripts and openly resists the old ones.[10] Most of the older men and women in my study follow the traditional patterns, a tendency that reflects not only their life experiences but also their rhetorical reasons for writing life stories. At the senior center, participants are mainly interested in fitting in with other members of their generation. The structure and content of their narratives reflect this purpose: while narrators adopt conventional patterning, demonstrating their acceptance of established generational norms, they also select unusual and interesting events to share, thereby distinguishing themselves from their cohort in acceptable ways through narrative content. It is significant, too, that older women's life stories typically function as examples and role models for the family. Older women often see themselves as chroniclers or upholders of their generation and its values and as keepers of the family legacy. Their adoption of conventional storytelling patterns is a key aspect of this cultural transmission.

Generational differences are also apparent in the ways older women present their stories to the family. Many want to leave their stories behind to be read *after* they are gone, but they do not want to discuss the stories with children or grandchildren while they are writing them. Some do not want to be questioned about events they have chosen not to discuss, and some anticipate a critical response to their interpretations of family experiences. In our discussion of whether a mother/daughter writing group would work, for example, Catherine, a mother of five, said "no," for reasons that speak to the core mother/daughter conflict: "What it might turn into would be—I see it as the daughters blaming their mothers for something and the mothers trying to explain why they did what they did. And I sort of cover that with one phrase these days: 'I wasn't a perfect mother, but I was a good enough mother.' And *you've* gotta work on the rest of it."

Neither I nor the older women in my study were fully aware of these generational differences in our storytelling patterns until I became a participating member of a writing group for seniors. As an English professor who has taught autobiographical writing for many years, initially I had no reservations about sharing my life stories with the group; I was, in fact, pleased that they asked me to participate in this way. I wrote enthusiastically and with little censorship on subjects I wanted to think about, including personal conflicts and highly emotional experiences from my present and past. After a few weeks in one group, however, it became apparent that my writing and my presence were making some members uncomfortable. Two incidents occurred on one particular day that made this discomfort apparent and brought generational conflicts to the surface. My re-creation of that day's events is based on notes I took at the time, a partial transcript of the group session, and subsequent interviews with members and the group facilitator. I offer the story here as a personal example of the need for increased awareness of age in feminist research.

The session in question occurred during the fourth week of my observations. It began as usual, with members sharing information and good-natured banter. Some of those present had been writing together for nearly a year, and they knew each other quite well; others were new participants. All present were white, middle-class women; all had graduated from high school and had some postsecondary education, if not college degrees. Aside from myself (age forty), Lee, the facilitator, aged fifty, was the youngest present. Four members had brought something to read that day: Mary had written about dangerous activities and close calls during her childhood and adolescence; Phyllis wrote about the time she got her tonsils out; Rosemary described her recent reaction to a mispronouncing newscaster on National Public Radio; and I wrote about my father's death.

Lee, not knowing the subject of my story, asked me to read first. My father had died nine months earlier, and at the time I was facing another imminent death. My boyfriend's father, Joe, was declining rapidly and had been moved to a nursing home. We had spent the summer cleaning out his home in an old Polish neighborhood of Detroit, where Joe had lived most of his adult life. We had sold a majority of Joe's things, as well as the house. The story I presented to the group was a cathartic jumble in which I described Joe's decline in health and the deterioration of the family home, intermixed with flashbacks to my own father's last days in the hospital. My description of Joe's final weeks prior to placement in the nursing home were graphic:

> David had found him wandering the streets at 11 o'clock at night. He wore filthy blue polyester trousers and a thin summer shirt. He smelled of shit and urine. David drove him to the emergency room. While waiting for admission, his father went to the bathroom, lost control of his bowels, and left his dirty underwear on the floor. It was the beginning of the end—late-stage liver disease accompanied by toxic dementia. Seeing him like that was a terrible blow. David and his father had shared many things, among the more positive being a partialness for good clothes and good grooming.

I also revealed that, during this time, David learned that Joe had been held up at gunpoint a few months earlier. A man had forced his way into the house, hit Joe on the head, tied him up, and stolen most of what he had of any value. The friend who informed David said she thought the violent intrusion might have had something to do with Joe's rapid decline and dementia.

I also described the time immediately after my father's death from emphysema—a time David and I had shared, visiting the hospital together:

> He looked very small and very old in the hospital bed, his arms deeply bruised from the IV's. "Touch his arm, he's still warm," my mother said, still holding on. The family left us alone with him. I tried to pray but could think of nothing to say except, "I didn't even get a chance to say goodbye." "He was a good man," David said. "He'll be with us at the lake next spring." David and I held hands and cried together a long time—for both our fathers.

Intermingled with these descriptions were small glimpses into my relationship with David, which was intimate. The story ends two days after my father's death. David and I are sitting on the couch in my mother's living room after everyone has gone to bed, reading the newspaper, eating macaroni and cheese from a casserole someone has left, and laughing at some absurd comic routine on television. The last line of the story is "Somewhere in the midst of it all, I felt a surge of joy at the possibility of such everyday intimacy during a time of chaos, crisis, and an uncertain future." Though not very well-written or particularly coherent, the life story I read to the group that day did accurately reflect the mire of complex, unresolved feelings I had about love and death.

The group's reaction to this story varied. At one point during the reading, Mary took off her glasses, looked away, and began to cry. When I finished, the group was silent at first, then began to talk about the emotions the story had raised. Mary talked about her own father's death and her impatience at the time with her mother's weak and confused response. She expressed feelings of guilt about that now. The others supported Mary and confirmed that no one knows how they will respond to death until it happens. Lee, a social worker, mentioned that to mourn the death of a parent is to mourn the loss of your own role as a child. And then we moved on to the other readings.

Rosemary read last that day. She had written about a radio announcer who did the morning news and commentary and who repeatedly mispronounced names and words: "Fort" Motor Company, "Bop Etwards," and the "UassA." Rosemary found the announcer grating and expressed concern that the standards of the radio station were being eroded. The group's response to this story was positive and encouraging. Comments centered around whether the announcer's continued presence on the air might have been a case of affirmative action. I listened and remained silent for several minutes, and then Rosemary and I had the following conversation:

Ruth: That's really into what I was going to ask. Why was this story so important to you? I mean, there's a lot of energy involved in hearing you.

Rosemary: Because I really don't like to have to decipher information. . . . And I found myself having such a barrier of trying to figure out what the word was, or the word was grating on my ear. Part of it has to do with the fact that my mother was a stickler on speech. Speech was the very backbone of the information of things. She didn't even like us to use slang. I mean, and she wanted the words to be pronounced correctly, not sloppily. . . . So I think what I was doing was I guess I had been imbued with this standard of how you speak, that you speak correctly, and your pronunciation is right, etc. etc. Now, it's interesting that I—of course, everybody has exceptions to the rule of knowing how to pronounce things. And I never realized that I have my own way of pronouncing certain words until people began kidding me about it. Because I always call the thing up above the top of the building a roof [she pronounces the vowel as in *ruff*], and everybody else seemed to be calling it a roof [she uses an *ooo* sound].

Ruth: That's a regionalism.

Mary: I say roof [Mary pronounces the *ooo* sound].

Ruth: It's both.

Rosemary: It's both. Well, I never learned it as roof [with an *ooo*]. I always said roof [pronounced as in *ruff*].

Mary: I had a coworker correct me on pronunciation of *route* [she pronounces it with an *ooo*] and *route* [with an *ow,* as in *out*].

Rosemary: Well, I think they're both correct, aren't they?

Mary: Well, she didn't think so. She let me know in no uncertain terms.

Ruth: Which did she prefer?

Mary: I don't know now.

We went on to talk more about regional pronunciations, and the session ended with a brief discussion of the time and place of the next week's meeting.

Although not immediately apparent in the words from the transcript, my questioning of Rosemary reflected my own discomfort: I was deeply offended by Rosemary's description of the announcer and the group's references to affirmative action, which seemed racist and classist to me. I kept wondering, "Would they be talking this way if someone from a different racial or ethnic group were present? Would Rosemary have even shared the story?" Trained in the liberal traditions of feminism (as well as contemporary sociolinguistics), I value diversity in all things, including speech patterns, and consider variations in the use of language natural and desirable in a global community. In fact, I have taught many classes based on these very principles. Yet the group's concept of language appropriacy was quite different from mine, following a more prescriptive ideology that values correctness and standard usage. Members were operating on the common assumption that "proper English" is objective and value-neutral. My response to this value conflict was to move into my English-teacher mode: I asked a probing question to get Rosemary thinking about why she had written what she did, and I provided information that suggested the inevitability of linguistic difference ("It's a regionalism"). By assuming this role, I separated myself from the group and evoked a discourse of authority, if not superiority, putting Rosemary in the position of defending herself.

The following week, Lee called me at home to say that the group needed to discuss at the next meeting whether to continue with the research. Some members had expressed ambivalence about further participation. Rosemary had mentioned that she felt "put on the spot" by my response to her life story. Someone else had brought up the language issue, expressing discomfort at my use of *shit* and asking Lee if I was writing in this way "just to get a reaction" out of them. Lee thought there were generational differences being expressed through our language and selection of topics: "They're not used to the stark realism of your writing," she suggested. "They tend to pretty things up." For my part, I began to question my motives: *Was* I writing about painful subjects to shock them? Subconsciously, was I making some effort to provoke? Could I perhaps be playing out some old psychological drama, maybe conflicts with my own mother? Otherwise, why had I gotten so offended by Rosemary's critique of an anonymous radio announcer's nonstandard pronunciation? Lee interpreted the dissention in terms of group dynamics and power struggles. She noted that Rosemary considered herself a founding member of the group and had made it an important part of her life; by questioning her, I had, in effect, threatened her identity and authority among her peers.

The day after Lee's telephone call, the group met. I attended without notebook or tape recorder. We talked about whether I should continue with the observations, how the group had changed since I had become a member, and what the others wanted from the group sessions. Mary asked me what I was looking for; did I have expectations about what I would find? I told her, honestly, that my perspective was evolving. Catherine, who had not been present for any of the previous meetings in which I had read, said she was not sure she wanted me to be a contributing member—she may not want to know what I thought and felt. The life story she read that day was about ageism and how mad it made her when people like her daughter (who is my age) tell older people who are perfectly capable of making their own decisions what they should do. She spoke of the writing group as a place where elders could speak and be heard, where their ideas, memories, and feelings would be shared, honored, respected, and not judged. We talked about whether I was old enough to be part of this group, and Lee raised the question, "Is it only age differences that the group is feeling?" Phyllis said she had learned a lot from me, even though she had only heard me read the previous week, but she did not feel comfortable with all aspects of my writing. "You write so beautifully. Last week—and this is just my personality, but I tend to back away from things—I was intimidated by your writing. What you wrote, once I got beyond the language, touched me to the core."

Rosemary, the member whom I had most directly offended, spoke of the group as an intimate circle of friends who had spent months getting comfortable with each other. She then read a piece she had written especially for this meeting: a parable about a small, primitive tribe on a remote island that got together to share its stories. Then an anthropologist came and asked to hear the stories. Then the anthropologist taped the stories, and some members began to feel uncomfortable. Then the anthropologist began to share her own stories, which made members feel even *more* uncomfortable. Everything changed. The group's focus began to shift to the anthropologist. The ending of the story was yet to be determined. Lee called a few days later to say the group had decided to withdraw from the study.

The conflict illustrates very concretely how differences in the use of language, in writing style, and in narrative scripting reflect generational differences in values, beliefs, and practices of self-representation. It also illustrates my insensitivity, at the time, to these differences and to group norms. In responding critically to the language of Rosemary's story and, indirectly, to her presentation of self, I violated the norms for encouragement and support so important to successful functioning of a senior writing group. As a result, I was removed as a noncomplying member.

The diverse responses to my own life story might also be considered in terms of generational differences. I suspect that members' discomfort with the language in my story reflects a more general discomfort with my worldview—how I talked about love, death, and intimacy outside of marriage. My writing style, which could in some ways be considered a generational style—singled me out among the other women; besides the directness of my language, I chose to write about highly emotional subjects, and I presented myself as still embroiled in turmoil and conflict. The pain in my story was still very much *present*. I have since come to think that these narrative differences reflect larger developmental differences between middle age and late life.

Certainly, my purposes for writing autobiographically differed from the senior writers' purposes. Besides the fact that I was writing as a temporary group member and a researcher, I wrote as a woman on the brink of middle age attempting to understand her present emotional life and the unresolved conflicts in her past. The older women in the group wrote from the distance of age and experience, usually displaying an acceptance that such broader perspectives bring. In their 1971 study of the function of reminiscence, psychologists M. A. Lieberman and J. Falk, in fact, documented that middle-aged adults are more likely to use reminiscing as a means to solve current problems, while older adults are more likely to use it as a means of looking back and "summing up" the life from a distance.[11] Psychologist Jeffrey Webster, discussing his own research on reminiscence in age groups ranging from teenagers to eighty-year-olds, lends qualified support to Lieberman and Falk's conclusion, noting that the use of reminiscence for problem solving was lowest among adults age sixty and over in his study.[12] These different purposes suggest a different emotional (and developmental) impulse behind reminiscing: problem solving is likely to be initiated by feelings of pain, discomfort, lack of understanding, or lack of control, while "summing up" is more likely initiated by a desire for acceptance and resolution. As Brian Connery explains, as we age "more than *narrative* coherence is wanted. . . . As we retell our stories, we make heroes of ourselves and thus give our pasts significance which thereby justifies our *lives*."[13]

Narrative researchers confirm that our position in the life course affects why and how we construct our life stories. Jan-Erik Ruth and Anni Vikko found that young children's life stories emphasize negative emotions toward parents and same-sex peers and avoidance of conflict; youth's stories emphasize value systems ("right" and "wrong" behaviors), gender roles, and intimacy; young adulthood stories center around power relations; middle-age stories show a concern with balancing individuation and commitment and establishing harmony; and older-adult stories emphasize compensation, reconciliation, and transcendence. There are also differences in emotional tone. Among older narrators, "the childhood memories tend to get a rather positive or nostalgic emotional tone, whereas the memories of old age sometimes are depicted in a more commonplace or emotionally flat way. The life stories told by middle-age persons, however, contain both critical commentary and vivid, dramatic memories, and the negative emotions are not avoided in the same way as they are for the aged." [14]

Cross-sectional studies of life-span development further support the claim that middle-aged and older adults tell life stories differently. In their study of self-representations across the lifespan, Gisela Labouvie-Vief and her colleagues asked a randomly selected sample of 149 people, ranging in age from eleven to eighty-five, to write a brief autobiographical paragraph including a description of the self and to complete a battery of psychological tests. Based on their analyses of the autobiographical writings, the researchers concluded that, over time, self-representations move increasingly toward individuation and differentiation from groups and institutions, toward awareness of complex interpersonal dynamics and subconscious processes of self-development, and toward a concept of the self as dynamic and changing. Preadolescents and the elderly performed similarly on the researchers' measures. Most interestingly, "transformational" thinking peaked between the ages of forty-six and fifty-nine, supporting psychological theories that propose that in midlife we reexamine the self and restructure our identities. After middle age, self-representation scores declined, indicating a move back toward continuity and stasis: "[T]he oldest groups appear to be much more conventional, displaying an orientation toward proper or [socially] desirable self-descriptions." [15] The researchers have not determined whether the differences in self-representations between middle-aged and older adults reflect developmental stages or a cohort effect (social influences and generational attitudes), but regardless, they are surely related.

Psychologist John Kotre suggests that these generational attitudes and narrative patterns provided by culture are useful and desirable for development in later life, for they provide unity and order at a time when elders are looking to find meaning that transcends the finiteness of their own existence. In this case, "culture turns out to be an ally" in providing "the enduring apparatus of meaning" to which older people can affix their lives, even if that "apparatus" admits few alternatives.[16] Why is it important for feminists to know that generations vary in their ways of telling life stories? Because this information offers hope, confirmation, and a basis for deeper understanding across the generational divide: it confirms that we are different people at different times in our lives, that we are capable of continual growth and development, and that we can learn through dialogue with diverse others.

Another important lesson in my own experience of generational difference is the necessity of developing reflexivity and sensitivity as a feminist researcher studying age. In reflecting on disagreements with her grandmother over the interpretation of one of her grandmother's life stories, folklorist Katherine Borland reminds us that "the performance of a personal narrative is a fundamental means by which people comprehend their own lives and present a 'self' to their audience"; researchers, therefore, must be sensitive and careful not to attack a narrator's carefully constructed self narrative.[17] We also must be careful, particularly when working cross-generationally, not to assume a "likeness of mind" between ourselves and those we study: while narrative researchers approach life stories as symbolic constructions full of dramatic characters, narrators see them as accounts of real experience with real people that are embedded in the context of their actual lives.

The time I have spent with writing groups of seniors has convinced me that understanding diversity in the telling of life stories is a crucial need in feminist studies of adult development. We must discover the array of life stories that reflect human differences of all kinds, and we must study a variety of mixed-age and similar-age groups to learn how people respond to and learn from these differences. Narrative psychologist Anthony Paul Kerby provides the rationale for this such research, claiming that "self-understanding rides tandem with an encountering of otherness, with an imaginative empathy for the other that in turn discloses or develops possibilities for oneself."[18] Anthropologist Mary Catherine Bateson agrees: "Part of the secret of continuing development . . . is the discovery through a variety of relationships that social expectations can be changed and that difference can be a source of strength rather than weakness."[19]

There are many kinds of difference that can be explored through narrative studies. In this book, I have focused on age and gender, with side glances to race, ethnicity, and class, understanding that these are "interlocking" forms of oppression.[20] In the interchapter "Negotiating Normal," I also explored informally how impaired mental functioning affects older women's willingness and ability to "write the life." Although I am reluctant to draw grand conclusions about the learning and growth I observed across writing groups for seniors, I can say confidently that it did occur in every group—subtly, gradually, and in small degrees—and that it is best observed through close examination of group dynamics over time; changes in the form and content of life stories; and the evolving attitudes of life-story tellers about themselves, their narratives, and others' narratives. I can recount specific scenarios in which older writers both learned from their differences and reflected on them, which readers will recall from earlier chapters: Cecille, sixty-four, and Helen, eighty-four (the age of Cecille's parents), acknowledging and accepting their conflicting beliefs about how parents should be represented in life stories; Alma teaching her age peers what it was like to grow up poor and black in the South and learning from them what it was like to grow up poor and white in the North; Phil and Robert beginning to write with "feeling," and the women experiencing their influence in shaping the men's life stories; and the many sessions in which group members at the geriatric center learned from Jean that writing honestly about personal traumas need not be debilitating but can, in fact, be positive and therapeutic.

My experiences with the twelve older women from group homes ("Negotiating Normal") were especially revealing in a number of ways. As a result of my interactions with this group, I began to think more deeply about the social functions of memory and resistance to storying a life. The fact that many of the women had been institutionalized during at least part of their lives and were now living in restricted communal settings designed for elders with "special needs" obviously affected their self-concept and their willingness to write autobiographically. As we know from the work of sociologist Erving Goffman, living communally with a socially stigmatized group can be enervating, and maintaining a sense of individual identity is difficult in these settings.[21] In addition to disability, the women in the writing group were experiencing the daily oppressions of gender, class, and age. What we have learned from gerontological research, too, is that the less socially and mentally active an older person is, the less she, or he, remembers; the social context of one's current life situation affects what a person remembers, as well as how much.[22] Most of the women in the writing group were not used to being asked to talk at length about themselves (in other than professional therapy sessions); they were not used to being listened to; and they were not used to having their words validated and formalized through writing. Many had limited literacy skills and feared criticism. On the other hand, they highly valued the written word, as was evident in their emphasis on proper spelling and their excitement and pride in their finished life stories, and they valued group interaction and an ability to connect with others verbally.

The social context in which this group operated at the Northside Senior Center, too, is important to our understanding of its members and their development. The director had been working hard to integrate group-home residents into the social structure of the center. She tried to include them in as many activities as possible, which took considerable effort, given their passivity and the prejudices of other seniors toward them. Yet it was clear that the group-home residents' functioning changed according to their social situation. In the writing-group sessions, they wrote together, read aloud, responded to one another, and demonstrated a developing self-confidence. Within the senior center, where they were sometimes avoided by the more "able" seniors, they became passive and unresponsive. These observations reinforce the truth of the argument made by disability activists: while disabilities are manifested physically, their meanings and significance are more importantly social. A disability, indeed any "difference," is always defined situationally.[23]

Scholars from the Stone Center at Wellesley College have been exploring just what it means for adults to develop in relationships of difference. In contrast to Freudian and Eriksonian theories, which define psychological growth and maturity in terms of autonomy and individuation of the self from others, Stone Center psychologists, inspired by feminist and social-constructionist theories, define growth and maturity in terms of our ability to connect with and feel empathy toward others. As Judith Jordan explains, the relational theory of self "emphasizes the contextual, approximate, responsive and process factors in experience. In short, it emphasizes relationship and connection. Rather than a primary perspective based on the formed and contained self, this model stresses the importance of the intersubjective, relationally emergent nature of human experience." [24] Within this paradigm, the goal of development is to participate in increasingly empowering relationships with one's self, as well as with diverse others. "Maturity," from a relational standpoint, entails "the capacity to integrate individual and relational goals and to deal with conflict within relationship." [25]

Following this research, how might feminists deal maturely with conflict across age groups? In Jordan's terms, how can women be "different and not alienated"? Stone Center psychologists suggest that women must openly discuss their differences, the feelings they generate (typically anger, guilt, and fear), and the inequities that arise from them. Three lessons are central for women, who are often socialized to deny and avoid conflict: difference need not mean deficit, the struggle with difference is inevitable in any relationship, and the conflict that arises from difference can be positive. When managed with developmental goals in mind, conflict expands awareness and initiates change. Such conflict management also includes understanding on the part of more powerful groups that their privileged status blinds them to the need for change and makes them more resistant to it. Young and middle-aged women, for example, may not see their own ageism toward older women (and their own aging selves) and will be reluctant to address it. Older women who speak from a more privileged position (white, educated, middle- or upper-class, physically and mentally able, living independently), may not see their own ageism toward less-privileged older women (minority, uneducated or undereducated, lower- or working-class, frail or disabled, dependent on others' care).

But we must also have compassion for ourselves and consider that the very *limits* of our vision may serve us developmentally. Age-studies scholar Kathleen Woodward observes that sometimes a certain blindness to others yields the best insight into ourselves:

> [The] assumption of our age at each point in time gives us a certain self-confidence, permitting us to focus on what needs to be done and experienced at the moment rather than losing ourselves in others—or, alternatively, losing ourselves in our past selves or future selves. We all have interests of our

own at different points in time. Does this not help explain why so few people would really rather be their younger selves again? Here we have yet again another form of the double bind of age.[26]

The lesson for feminists is clear: to deal successfully with conflicts across age groups, we must first deal with the conflicts in our aging selves. To recall the title of Gloria Steinem's book on feminist self-exploration, we must initiate a "revolution from within."

Having dealt with inner conflict, feminists can better address their social, political, and moral obligations to celebrate difference across and within generations. We can look for guidance to the courageous feminists who write from their identities as middle-aged and old women—Simone de Beauvoir, Betty Friedan, Gloria Steinem, Barbara MacDonald and Cynthia Rich, Baba Copper, Margaret Gullette, Carolyn Heilbrun, Kathleen Woodward, and Barbara Frey Waxman, to name only a few. Literary critic Carolyn Heilbrun tells us that "it is perhaps only in old age, certainly past fifty, that women can stop being female impersonators, can grasp the opportunity to reverse their most cherished principles of 'femininity' and write their lives differently." [27] Such words should encourage feminists of any age to learn from others' life stories, to write new stories, and to work toward improving the material conditions of everyone's life so as to inspire future generations to "write the life" in yet untold and unimagined ways.

Notes

Introduction

1. Woodward, *Aging and Its Discontents*, 97–98.
2. Ibid., 99.
3. Ibid., 101.
4. For a summary and critique of reflexive scholarship in literary studies, see Miller, *Getting Personal.*
5. Gullette, *Declining to Decline*, 14–15.
6. Behar, "Out of Exile," 2.
7. On the "mirror stage" of old age, see Woodward, *Aging and Its Discontents.*
8. Rich, "When We Dead Awaken," 35–38.
9. Behar, "Out of Exile," 6.
10. Ruth and Kenyon, "Biography in Adult Development," 4.
11. Stewart, "Toward a Feminist Strategy."
12. Ibid., 31.
13. Gullette, xx.
14. Cole, "What Have We Made?"; Katz, *Disciplining;* Moody, "Gerontology and Critical Theory,"; Moody, "Overview."
15. Gubrium, *Speaking of Life*, 62.
16. Griffin, *Calling.*
17. Myerhoff, *Number.*
18. Bateson, *Composing*, 101.
19. Culley, *A Day at a Time*, 3.
20. Ibid., 4.
21. Gannett, "Journals, Diaries," 115–16.
22. Helen Fielding, *Bridget Jones's Diary* (New York: Viking, 1998).
23. Tannen, *That's Not What I Meant!*
24. Griffin, *Calling*, 219, 77–78.
25. Linde, *Life Stories.*
26. Chanfrault-Duchet, "Narrative Structures."

1. Language, Narrative, Self, and Adult Development

1. Gergen, "Social Constructionist Movement," 267.
2. Berlin, *Rhetoric and Reality*, 17.
3. Fish, *Doing What Comes Naturally*, 345.

4. See, for example, Estes and Binney's critique of the scientific paradigm in "The Biomedicalization of Aging" and Lyman's "Bringing the Social Back In." See also Katz's excellent review and interdisciplinary critique of the construction of academic gerontology, *Disciplining Old Age*.

5. See Gubrium, *Old Timers and Alzheimer's* and *Speaking of Life*.

6. Featherstone and Hepworth, "Images of Positive Aging."

7. Cole, *Journey of Life*, xxii.

8. Coupland, Coupland, and Giles, *Language, Society, and the Elderly*, 21.

9. Sampson, "Deconstruction of the Self," 4.

10. Gergen, *Saturated Self*, 146.

11. Shotter, "Social Accountability and the Social Construction," 141.

12. Bruner, *Acts of Meaning*, 2.

13. Ibid., 101.

14. Ibid., 119.

15. Polkinghorne, *Narrative Knowing*, 50.

16. Schafer, "Narration in the Pychoanalytic Dialogue," 31.

17. Spence, *Narrative Truth and Historical Truth*, 62.

18. Hermans, Kempen, and van Loon, "The Dialogical Self," 28.

19. Ibid., 29.

20. Bordo, "Feminism, Postmodernism," 141.

21. Ibid., 137.

22. Probyn, *Sexing the Self*, 2.

23. Robinson, "Feminist Criticism," 146.

24. Gunn, *Autobiography*, 9.

25. Ibid., 31.

26. Jelinek, *Tradition of Women's Autobiography*, 19.

27. Smith, *Poetics of Women's Autobiography*, 5.

28. Shields, *Stone Diaries*, 340, emphasis added.

29. Shields, interview in Penguin Putnam Reading Group Guide.

30. Moore, "People Like That," 67–68.

31. Bergland, "Postmodernism and the Autobiographical Subject."

32. There are a handful of notable exceptions. See, for example, Bornat's *Reminiscence Reviewed;* several chapters in Birren et al., *Aging and Biography;* Wallace's "Reconsidering the Life Review"; and Luborsky's "Romance with Personal Meaning."

33. Butler, "Life Review," 66.

34. See Butler's foreword to *Art and Science of Reminiscing*, as well as the contributors' challenges to and extensions of Butler's original ideas.

35. Birren and Deutchman, *Guiding Autobiography*, 4–6.

36. Flax, *Disputed Subjects*, 49.

37. See especially Erikson, *Life Cycle Completed;* Levinson et al., *Seasons of a Man's Life;* and Levinson and Levinson, *Seasons of a Woman's Life*.

38. Freeman, *Rewriting the Self*, 224.

39. Ibid., 9, emphasis added.

40. Singer, "Story of Your Life," 443.

41. Ibid., 452.

42. Ruth and Kenyon, "Biography in Adult Development."

43. For research on the personal and social effects of writing groups, see Gere, "Kitchen Tables"; Hollis, "Liberating Voices"; Heath, "Finding in History,"; and Heller, *Until We Are Strong*.

44. Hollis, "Liberating Voices," 57.

45. Rosenwald, "Conclusion."

46. Freeman, *Rewriting the Self*, 225.

47. Kenyon and Randall, *Restorying Our Lives*, 162.

48. Kenyon, "The Meaning/Value of Personal Storytelling," 29.

49. Gullette, *Declining to Decline*, 65.

50. Ibid., 220.

51. The act of *reading* autobiographies and biographies also undoubtedly heightens a person's narrative sensibilities, developing in the reader a more acute awareness of the many interpretive possibilities for her own life story. Literary scholars Carolyn Heilbrun and Anne Wyatt-Brown, both longtime readers and critics of life writings, describe how casual questions posed by friends prompted them to reread and revise aspects of their own life stories that they had earlier taken for granted as established truths. It is no coincidence that such examples come from women, who may be more sensitive to narrative interventions, given their greater propensity to look inward and their tendency to approach life as an "improvisation." See Heilbrun, *Last Gift of Time*, 201–2; Wyatt-Brown, "Future of Literary Gerontology"; Bateson, *Composing a Life*.

52. Gergen, *Toward the Transformation*.

53. Gergen, ibid., 155.

54. McDermott and Varenne, "Culture, Development, Disability," 109.

55. Ibid., 113.

56. Shweder, "True Ethnography," 17.

57. Ibid., 18.

58. Myerhoff and Ruby, "Crack in the Mirror," 312.

59. This question for age scholars is suggested by Kathleen Woodward in *Aging and Its Discontents*.

60. Gergen, *Toward the Transformation*.

2. *Age and the Life Story*

1. Baker, "Search for Adultness."

2. The research on overaccommodation to the elderly is summarized in Coupland, Coupland, Giles, and Henwood, "Accommodating the Elderly." See also Coupland, Coupland, and Grainger, "Intergenerational Discourse."

3. Coupland, Coupland, and Giles, *Language, Society and the Elderly*.

4. McDonald and Rich, *Look Me in the Eye*, 75.

5. Rich, "Women in the Tower."

6. Hen Co-Op, *Growing Old Disgracefully*.

7. Hessel, *Maggie Kuhn on Aging*.

8. Woodward, "Tribute to the Older Woman," 86.

9. Wallace, "Reconsidering the Life Review." 124.

10. Waxman, *To Live at the Center.*

11. See Neugarten, "Age Groups in American Society," and Laslett, *Fresh Map.*

12. Ginn and Arber, "Only Connect."

13. Turner, "Aging and Identity," 255.

14. Barusch, *Older Women in Poverty.*

15. Ginn and Arber, "Only Connect," 8.

16. Uhlenberg and Miner, 210.

17. Ibid., 219.

18. McPherson, *Aging as Social Process.*

19. Newman, "Ethnography, Biography, and Cultural History," 374.

20. Ibid., 379.

21. Elder, *Children of the Great Depression,* 15.

22. Ibid., 295.

23. Ibid., 202.

24. Chanfrault-Duchet, "Narrative Structures," 90.

25. Coupland, Coupland, and Giles, *Language, Society and the Elderly.*

26. Kotre, *Outliving the Self,* 10.

27. Ibid., 14–15.

28. Ibid., 15.

3. Social Scripts for Gender, Race, and Class

1. The research on minority responses to survey and interview questions is summarized by Jackson, "Methodological Issues."

2. Etter-Lewis, introduction to *Unrelated Kin,* 8.

3. Smith and Watson, *Getting a Life.*

4. Gergen, "Life Stories," 128.

5. Smith and Watson, 11.

6. Smith, *Poetics,* 47.

7. Ibid., 48.

8. Jelinek, *Tradition of Women's Autobiography,* 104.

9. Gergen, "Life Stories," 138–39.

10. Wagner-Martin, *Telling Women's Lives,* 6.

11. Ibid., 19.

12. Ibid., 76

13. This comparison became apparent to me while rereading Griffin's interpretation of voicedness and silence in *Jane Eyre.* See her chapter on "A Good and Worthy Voice," in *Calling.*

14. Gergen, "Life Stories," 138.

15. Readers may be thinking that gender differences in writing are cohort-related— that today's young adults will demonstrate fewer gender markings in their discourse than older adults who have followed more traditional patterns of sex-role socialization. Current research on college students in their teens and twenties, however, shows continued

gender difference in men's and women's autobiographical writings. Male students write personal narratives of achievement, adventure, and mischief, characterizing themselves as competitive and autonomous; female students write personal narratives in which achievements are embedded in relationships, characterizing themselves as connected to others and open to exploration and experimentation, especially in terms of their relations with others. See, for example, Flynn, "Composing as a Woman"; Peterson, "Gender and the Autobiographical Essay"; Tobin, "Car Wrecks, Baseball Caps, and Man-to-Man Defense"; and McGann, "We Get into a Bunch of Mischief."

16. Johnstone, *Stories, Community, and Place*, 76.

17. Smith, *Poetics*, 51.

18. Higginbotham, "African American Women's History."

19. See Rosenblatt, "Black Autobiography" and Fox-Genovese, "My Statue, My Self."

20. Fox-Genovese, "My Statue, My Self," 65.

21. Waxman, *To Live in the Center*, 93.

22. Fox-Genovese, "My Statue, My Self," 71.

23. Ibid., 71.

24. Hill-Collins, "Meaning of Motherhood."

25. Ibid., 49.

26. Stack, *All Our Kin*.

27. Hill-Collins, "Meaning of Motherhood," 54.

28. Milligan, "Understanding Diversity," 122.

29. See, for example, Thomas and Eisenhandler, *Aging and the Religious Dimension;* Kimble et al., *Aging, Spirituality, and Religion;* and Bianchi, *Aging as a Spiritual Journey.*

30. For more on the role of religion and the church in the lives of African-American elders, see Chatters, Levin, and Taylor, "Antecedents and Dimensions"; Chatters and Taylor, "Age Differences in Religious Participation,"; and Jackson, Antonucci, and Gibson, "Cultural, Racial, and Ethnic Minority Influences."

31. Golden, introduction to *Skin Deep*, 3, emphasis added.

32. bell hooks, *Talking Back*, 208.

33. The phrase is from Anzaldua, "Haciendo Caras," 65.

34. Fox-Genovese, "My Statue, My Self."

35. Etter-Lewis, *My Soul Is My Own*.

36. Griffin, *Calling*, 88.

37. Ovrebo and Minkler, "Lives of Older Women," 293.

38. Barusch, *Older Women in Poverty*, 46.

39. Linde, *Life Stories*, 129.

40. Gutmann, *Reclaimed Powers*.

41. See, for example, Kerr Conway, *When Memory Speaks*.

42. Schachter-Shalomi and Miller, *From Age-ing to Sage-ing*.

4. Memory and Truth

1. Welch-Ross, "An Integrative Model," 350.

2. Gergen, "Mind, Text, and Society," 80–81.

3. Edwards and Middleton, "Conversational Remembering."

4. Fivush, "Constructing Narrative," 90.

5. Gergen, "Mind, Text, and Society," 90.

6. Fitzgerald, "Intersecting Meanings."

7. Whitbourne and Powers, "Older Women's Constructs."

8. Kotre, *White Gloves*, 116–17.

9. Personal Narrative Group, *Interpreting Women' Lives*, 261, emphasis added.

10. Myerhoff, "Life History among the Elderly," 240.

11. Spence, *Narrative Truth and Historical Truth*, 177.

12. Dillard, "To Fashion a Text," 71.

13. Neisser, "Self Narratives."

14. Ibid., 8.

15. Kerby, *Narrative and the Self*, 7.

16. See, for example, Thomas and Eisenhandler, *Aging and the Religious Dimension;* Koenig, *Research on Religion and Aging;* Kimble et al., *Aging, Spirituality, and Religion;* McFadden, "Religion, Spirituality, and Aging"; and Bianchi, *Aging as a Spiritual Journey.*

17. Moore, "Most Americans."

18. See Jackson, Antonucci, and Gibson, "Cultural, Racial, and Ethnic Minority Influences," and Chatters, Levin, and Taylor, "Antecedents and Dimensions of Religious Involvement."

19. Ross and Buehler, "Creative Remembering," 220.

20. In *The Saturated Self*, Gergen suggests that the preference for narrative over historical truths is what most distinguishes the postmodern condition. In this view, identity is created more through what we *say* about ourselves and how we read our lives as texts than through the material conditions of our lives. Many contemporary works of art, literature, and popular culture play with this concept of identity-negotiation through the blurring of lived experience and text, including Woody Allen's 1997 film *Deconstructing Harry*, in which the main character, a writer, ultimately "finds himself" in the fictional characters of his own novels and short stories.

21. Watson, "Ordering the Family."

22. Fowler, "No Snapshots," 50.

23. Spence, *Narrative Truth and Historical Truth*, 32.

24. Ross and Buehler, "Creative Remembering."

25. Kotre, *White Gloves*.

26. Ibid., 184.

27. Sherman, *Reminiscence and the Self*, 231.

28. Sherman, ibid., 232.

29. Myerhoff, *Remembered Lives*.

30. Rider, *Writer's Book of Memory*, 128.

31. Freeman, *Rewriting the Self*, 224.

5. Group Effects on Writing the Life

1. Bruffee, "Social Construction, Language, and Authority," 777.

2. Summerfield, "Is There a Life in This Text?," 189.

3. Gubrium and Holstein, "Analyzing Talk and Interaction," 179.

4. For a discussion of discourse communities in academic and nonacademic settings, see Bizzell, "Cognition, Convention, and Certainty"; Harris, "The Idea of Community"; Swales, *Genre Analysis;* Spilka, *Writing in the Workplace;* Geisler, *Academic Literacy and the Nature of Expertise;* and Clark, "Rescuing the Discourse of Community."

5. See Altacruise, "Stepford Writers."

6. See, for example, Flower and Hayes, "Problem Solving Strategies"; Flower, "Revising Writer-Based Prose."

7. Elbow, "Being a Writer vs. Being an Academic."

8. Summerfield, "Is There a Life in This Text?" 185, emphasis added.

9. Ibid., 188.

10. Birren and Deutchman, *Guiding Autobiography,* 1.

6. *Gender and Emotion*

1. Shields, *Stone Diaries.*

2. Lessing, *Diary of a Good Neighbour.*

3. Newman, "Letter to Harvey Milk."

4. Smith, "Happy Memories Club."

5. Labouvie-Vief, Hakim-Larson, and Hobart, "Age, Ego Level, and the Life-span Development"; Labouvie-Vief, DeVoe, and Bulka, "Speaking about Feelings"; Blanchard-Fields, Jahnke, and Camp, "Age Differences in Problem-Solving Style."

6. See Shields, *Stone Diaries,* 344–45 for the full list.

7. Summerfield, "Is There a Life in This Text?" 186.

8. Kenyon and Randall, *Restorying Our Lives,* 138.

9. Culley, *A Day at a Time,* 3.

10. Ostriker, *Stealing the Language,* 179–80, quoted in Jeanne Braham, *Crucial Conversations,* 10.

11. Wyatt-Brown, "Liberation of Mourning," 172.

12. Woodward, *Aging and its Discontents.*

13. George, "Keeping Our Working Distance," 314.

14. Harre, "Outline," 4.

15. Rosaldo, "Toward an Anthropology of Self and Feeling," 143.

16. Harre, "Outline."

17. Hochschild, "Ideology and Emotion Management."

18. Efran and Clarfield, "Constructionist Therapy," 211–13.

19. For a review of narrative therapies, see Atwood, *Family Scripts;* Parry and Doan, *Story Re-visions;* White and Epston, *Narrative Means;* Young, *Adult Development, Therapy, and Culture.*

20. Canary, Emmers-Sommer, and Faulkner, *Sex and Gender,* 46.

21. Hochschild, "Ideology and Emotion Management," 129.

22. Ibid.

23. For more on emotion as a social and economic resource, see Hochschild, *Managed Heart.*

24. See Maccoby, "Gender as a Social Category"; Swann, *Girls, Boys, and Language;*

and the discussion of gender, sex, and emotion in Canary, Emmers-Sommer, and Faulkner, *Sex and Gender.*

25. Armon-Jones, "The Social Functions of Emotions."
26. Canary, Emmers-Sommer, and Faulkner, *Sex and Gender,* 62.
27. Griffin, *Calling,* 113.
28. Bergman and Surrey, "The Woman-Man Relationship," 268.
29. Jordan, introduction to *Women's Growth in Diversity,* 3.
30. Goleman, *Emotional Intelligence,* 36.
31. Labouvie-Vief, *Psyche and Eros,* 2.
32. Ibid., 17.
33. Ibid., 18.
34. Kambler and Felman, "Mirror Mirror on the Wall."

Negotiating Normal

1. The writings that follow have been minimally edited—for readability only.
2. Gelfand, *Aging Network;* Moos and Lemke, *Group Residences for Older Adults.*
3. Down and Schnurr, *Between Home and Nursing Home,* 30–31.
4. Gelfand, *Aging Network,* 186.
5. Sinson, *Group Homes and Community Integration,* 65.

7. Learning from Our Differences

1. Coll, Cook-Nobles, and Surrey, "Building Connection," 190.
2. The term *generational splitting* comes from Levinson and Levinson, *Seasons of a Woman's Life.*
3. MacDonald and Rich, *Look Me in the Eye.*
4. Copper, "View from Over the Hill," 125.
5. Ibid., 128.
6. Ibid.
7. Ibid.
8. García Coll, Cook-Nobles, and Surrey, "Building Connection," 180.
9. Browne, *Women, Feminism, and Aging,* 270.
10. See the narratives from my generation discussed in Gilmore, *Autobiographics,* and the chapters on "different stories" and "grim tales" in Conway's *When Memory Speaks.*
11. Lieberman and Falk, "Remembered Past."
12. Webster, "Adult Age Differences."
13. Connery, "Self-Representation and Memorials," 156, emphasis added.
14. Ruth and Vilkko, "Emotion in the Construction of Autobiography," 176.
15. Labouvie-Vief et al., "Representations of Self," 413.
16. Kotre, *Outliving the Self.*
17. Borland, "That's Not What I Said," 71.
18. Kerby, *Narrative and the Self,* 63–64.
19. Bateson, *Composing a Life,* 94.

20. See Brown, *Women, Feminism, and Aging* on interlocking oppressions, 238–42.
21. Goffman, *Asylums.*
22. Harris and Hopkins, "Beyond Anti-ageism," 78.
23. McDermott and Varenne, "Culture, Development, Disability," 123.
24. Jordan, "A Relational Perspective," 15.
25. Jordan, "Do You Believe?" 30.
26. Woodward, *Aging and Its Discontents,* 96.
27. Heilbrun, *Writing a Woman's Life,* 126.

Bibliography

Altacruise, Chris. "Stepford Writers: Undercover Inside the M.F.A. Creativity Boot Camp." *Linguafranca* (December 1990): 18–30.

Anzaldua, Gloria. "Haciendo Caras, Una Entrada," introduction to *Making Face, Making Soul: Creative and Critical Perspectives by Feminists of Color*, ed. Gloria Anzaldua, xv–xxviii. San Francisco: Aunt Lute Books, 1990.

Armon-Jones, Claire. "The Social Functions of Emotions." In *The Social Construction of Emotions*, ed. Rom Harre, 57–82. Oxford: Blackwell, 1986.

Atwood, Joan, ed. *Family Scripts*. New York: Taylor & Francis, 1996.

Baker, Carolyn D. "The 'Search for Adultness': Membership Work in Adolescent-Adult Talk." *Human Studies* 7 (1984): 301–23.

Barusch, Amanda S. *Older Women in Poverty: Private Lives and Public Policies*. New York: Springer, 1994.

Bateson, Mary Catherine. *Composing a Life*. New York: Penguin, 1989.

Behar, Ruth. "Out of Exile." Introduction to *Women Writing Culture*, ed. Ruth Behar and Deborah A. Gordon, 1–29. Berkeley: University of California Press, 1995.

Bergland, Betty. "Postmodernism and the Autobiographical Subject: Reconstructing the 'Other.'" In *Autobiography and Postmodernism*, ed. Kathleen Ashley, Leigh Gilmore, and Gerald Peters, 130–66. Amherst: University of Massachusetts Press, 1994.

Bergman, Stephen J. , and Janet L. Surrey. "The Woman-Man Relationship: Impasses and Possibilities." In *Women's Growth in Diversity*, ed. Judith U. Jordan, 260–287. New York, Guilford, 1997.

Berlin, James. *Rhetoric and Reality: Writing Instruction in American Colleges, 1900–1985*. Carbondale: Southern Illinois University Press, 1987.

Bianchi, Eugene C. *Aging as a Spiritual Journey*. New York: Crossroad, 1995.

Birren, James E., and Donna E. Deutchman. *Guiding Autobiography Groups for Older Adults: Exploring the Fabric of Life*. Baltimore: Johns Hopkins University, 1991.

Bizzell, Patricia. "Cognition, Convention, and Certainty: What We Need to Know about Writing." *Pre/Text* 3 (1982): 213–43.

Blanchard-Fields, Fredda, Heather Casper Jahnke, and Cameron Camp. "Age Differences in Problem-Solving Style: The Role of Emotional Salience." *Psychology and Aging* 10 (1995): 173–80.

Bordo, Susan. "Feminism, Postmodernism, and Gender-Skepticism." In *Feminism/Postmodernism*, ed. Linda Nicholson, 133–56. New York: Routledge, 1990.

Braham, Jeanne. *Crucial Conversations: Interpreting Contemporary American Literary Autobiographies by Women*. New York: Teachers College Press, 1995.

Browne, Colette V. *Women, Feminism, and Aging.* New York: Springer, 1998.

Bruffee, Kenneth. "Social Construction, Language, and the Authority of Knowledge: A Bibliographical Essay." *College English* 48 (1986): 773–90.

Bruner, Jerome. *Acts of Meaning.* Cambridge: Harvard University Press, 1990.

Butler, Robert. Foreword to *The Art and Science of Reminiscing: Theory, Research, Methods, and Applications,* ed. Barbara K. Haight and Jeffrey D. Webster, xvii–xxi. Bristol, PA: Taylor & Francis, 1995.

————. "The Life Review: An Interpretation of Reminiscence in the Aged." *Psychiatry: Journal for the Study of Interpersonal Processes* 26 (February 1963): 65–76.

Canary, Daniel J., Tara M. Emmers-Sommer, and Sandra Faulkner. *Sex and Gender: Differences in Personal Relationships.* New York: Guilford, 1997.

Chanfrault-Duchet, Marie-Françoise. "Narrative Structures, Social Models, and Symbolic Representation in the Life Story." In *Women's Words: The Feminist Practice of Oral History,* ed. Sherna Berger Gluck and Daphne Patai, 77–92. New York: Routledge, 1991.

Chatters, L. M., J. S. Levin, and R. J. Taylor. "Antecedents and Dimensions of Religious Involvement among Older Black Adults." *Journal of Gerontology: Social Sciences* 47 (1992): S269–78.

Chatters, L. M., and R. J. Taylor. "Age Differences in Religious Participation among Black Adults." *Journal of Gerontology: Social Sciences* 44 (1989): S183–89.

Clark, Gregory. "Rescuing the Discourse of Community." *College Composition and Communication* 45 (February 1994): 61–74.

Cole, Thomas R. *The Journey of Life: A Cultural History of Aging in America.* Cambridge: Cambridge University Press, 1992.

————. "What Have We 'Made' of Aging?" *Journal of Gerontology: Social Sciences* 50B (1995): S341–43.

Connery, Brian. "Self-representation and Memorials in the late Poetry of Swift." In *Aging and Gender in Lieterature: Studies in Creativity,* ed. Anne Wyatt-Brown and Janice Rossen, 141–63. Charlottesville: University Press of Virginia, 1993.

Copper, Baba. "The View from Over the Hill." In *The Other Within Us: Feminist Explorations of Women and Aging,* ed., Marilyn Pearsall, 121–34. Boulder, CO: Westview Press, 1997.

Coupland, Nikolas, Justine Coupland, and Howard Giles. *Language, Society, and the Elderly: Discourse, Identity, and Ageing.* Oxford: Blackwell, 1991.

Coupland, Justine, Nikolas Coupland, and Karen Grainger. "Intergenerational Discourse: Contextual Versions of Ageing and Elderliness." *Ageing and Society* 11 (1991): 109–208.

Coupland, Nickolas, Justine Coupland, Howard Giles, and Karen Henwood. "Accommodating the Elderly: Invoking and Extending a Theory." *Language in Society* 17: 1–41.

Culley, Margo, ed. *A Day at a Time: The Diary Literature of American Women from 1764 to the Present.* New York: Feminist Press, 1985.

Dillard, Annie. "To Fashion a Text." *Inventing the Truth: The Art and Craft of Memoir,* ed. William Zinsser. Boston: Houghton Mifflin, 1987.

Down, Ivy, and Lorraine Schnurr. *Between Home and Nursing Home: The Board and Care Alternative.* Buffalo, NY: Prometheus, 1991.

Edwards, D., and D. Middleton. "Conversational Remembering and Family Relationships: How Children Learn to Remember." *Journal of Social and Personal Relationships* 5: 3–25.

Efran, Jay S., and Leslie E. Clarfield. "Constructionist Therapy: Sense and Nonsense." In *Therapy as Social Construction,* ed. Sheila McNamee and Kenneth J. Gergen, 200–217. Thousand Oaks, CA: Sage, 1992.

Elbow, Peter. "Being a Writer vs. Being an Academic: A Conflict in Goals." *College Composition and Communication* 46 (1995): 72–83.

Elder, Glen H. *Children of the Great Depression: Social Change in Life Experience.* Chicago: University of Chicago Press, 1974.

Erikson, Erik. *The Life Cycle Completed.* New York: Norton, 1984.

Etter-Lewis, Gwendolyn. Introduction to *Unrelated Kin: Race and Gender in Women's Personal Narratives,* ed. Gwendolyn Etter-Lewis and Michele Foster, 1–12. New York: Routledge, 1996.

———. *My Soul Is My Own.* London: Routledge, 1993.

Featherstone, Mike, and Mike Hepworth. "Images of Positive Aging: A Case Study of *Retirement Choice* Magazine." In *Images of Aging: Cultural Representations of Later Life,* ed. Mike Featherstone and Andrew Wernick, 29–47. London: Routledge, 1995.

Fielding, Helen. *Bridget Jones's Diary.* New York: Viking, 1998.

Fish, Stanley. *Doing What Comes Naturally: Change, Rhetoric, and the Practice of Theory in Literary and Legal Studies.* Durham, NC: Duke University, 1989.

Fitzgerald, Joseph. "Intersecting Meanings of Reminiscence in Adult Development and Aging." In *Remembering Our Past,* ed. D. C. Rubin, 360–83. New York: Cambridge University Press, 1996.

Fivush, Robin. "Constructing Narrative, Emotion, and Self in Parent-Child Conversation About the Past." In *The Remembering Self: Construction and Accuracy in the Self-Narrative,* ed. Ulric Neisser and Robin Fivush, 136–57. New York: Cambridge University Press, 1994.

Flax, Jane. *Disputed Subjects: Essays on Psychoanalysis, Politics, and Philosophy.* New York: Routledge, 1993.

Flower, Linda. "Revising Writer-Based Prose." *Journal of Basic Writing* 3 (1981): 62–74.

Flower, Linda, and John R. Hayes. "Problem Solving Strategies and the Writing Process." *College English* 39 (1977): 449–61.

Flynn, Elizabeth. "Composing as a Woman." *College Composition and Communication* 39 (1988): 423–35.

Fowler, Connie May. "No Snapshots in the Attic: A Granddaughter's Search for a Cherokee Past." *New York Times Book Review,* 1994, 50.

Fox-Genovese, Elizabeth. "My Statue, My Self: Autobiographical Writings of Afro-American Women." In *The Private Self: Theory and Practice of Women's Autobiographical Writings,* ed. Shari Benstock, 63–89. Chapel Hill: University of North Carolina Press, 1988.

Freeman, Mark. *Rewriting the Self: History, Memory, Narrative.* London: Routledge, 1993.

Gannett, Cinthia. "Journals, Diaries, and Academic Discourse." In *Feminine Principles and Women's Experience in American Composition and Rhetoric*, ed. Louise W. Phelps and Janet Emig, 109–36. Pittsburg: University of Pittsburg, 1995.

García Coll, Cynthia, Robin Cook-Nobles, and Janet L. Surrey. "Building Connection Through Diversity." In *Women's Growth in Diversity*, ed. Judith V. Jordan, 176–98. New York, Guilford, 1997.

Geisler, Cheryl. *Academic Literacy and the Nature of Expertise: Reading, Writing, and Knowing in Academic Philosophy*. Hillsdale, NJ: Lawrence Erlbaum, 1994.

Gelfand, Donald. *The Aging Network: Programs and Services*, 3rd ed. New York: Springer, 1993.

George, Diana Hume. " 'Keeping Our Working Distance': Maxine Kumin's Poetry of Loss and Survival." In *Aging and Gender in Literature: Studies in Creativity*, ed. Anne Wyatt-Brown and Janice Rossen, 314–38. Charlottesville: University Press of Virginia, 1993.

Gergen, Kenneth. "Mind, Text, and Society." In *The Remembering Self: Construction and Accuracy in the Self-Narrative*, ed. Ulric Neissser and Robin Fivush, 78–104. New York: Cambridge University Press, 1994.

———. *The Saturated Self: Dilemmas of Identity in Contemporary Life*. New York: Basic Books, 1991.

———. "The Social Constructionist Movement in Modern Psychology." *American Psychologist* 40 (1985): 266–75.

———. *Toward the Transformation in Social Knowledge*. 2nd ed. London: Sage, 1994.

Gergen, Mary. "Life Stories: Pieces of a Dream." In *Storied Lives: The Cultural Politics of Self-Understanding*, ed. George Rosenwald and Richard Ochberg, 127–44. New Haven, CT: Yale University Press, 1992.

Ginn, Jay, and Sara Arber. " 'Only Connect': Gender Relations and Ageing." In *Connecting Gender and Ageing: A Sociological Approach*, ed. Sara Arber and Jay Ginn, 1–14. Balmoor, England: Open University Press, 1995.

Goffman, Erving. *Asylums: Essays on the Social Situation of Mental Patients and Other Inmates*. Garden City, NY: Anchor Books, 1961.

Golden, Marita. Introduction to *Skin Deep: Black Women and White Women Write about Race*, ed. Marita Golden and Susan Richards Shreve, 1–5. New York: Anchor Books, 1996.

Goleman, Daniel. *Emotional Intelligence*. New York: Bantam, 1995.

Griffin, Gail. *Calling: Essays on Teaching in the Mother Tongue*. Pasadena, CA: Trilogy, 1992.

Gubrium, Jaber F., and James A. Holstein. "Analyzing Talk and Interaction." In *Qualitative Methods in Aging Research*, ed. Jaber F. Gubrium and Andrea Sankar. Thousand Oaks, CA: Sage, 1994.

———. *Old Timers and Alzheimer's: The Descriptive Organization of Senility*, Greenwich, CT: JAI Press, 1986.

———. *Speaking of Life: Horizons of Meaning for Nursing Home Residents*. Hawthorne, NY: Aldine de Gruyter, 1993.

Gullette, Margaret Morganrath. "Age Studies as Cultural Studies." In *Handbook of the Humanities and Aging*, ed. Thomas R. Cole, Ruth E. Ray, and Robert Kastenbaum, 2nd ed., 214–33. New York: Springer, 1999.

————. *Declining to Decline: Cultural Combat and the Politics of the Midlife.* Charlottes-ville: University Press of Virginia, 1997.

Gunn, Janet. *Autobiography: Toward a Poetics of Experience.* Philadelphia: University of Pennsylvania Press, 1982.

Gutmann, David. *Reclaimed Powers: Toward a New Psychology of Men and Women in Later Life.* New York: Basic Books, 1987.

Harre, Rom. "An Outline of the Social Constructionist Viewpoint." In *The Social Construction of Emotions*, ed. Rom Harre, 2–14. Oxford: Blackwell, 1986.

Harris, John, and Tom Hopkins. "Beyond Anti-Ageism: Reminiscence Groups and the Development of Anti-discriminatory Social Work Education and Practice." In *Reminiscence Reviewed: Evaluations, Achievements, Perspectives*, ed. Joanna Bornat, 74–83. Balmoor, England: Open University Press, 1994.

Harris, Joseph. "The Idea of Community in the Study of Writing." *College Composition and Communication* 40 (1989): 11–22.

Heath, Shirley Brice. "Finding in History the Right to Estimate." *College Composition and Communication* 45 (1994): 97–102.

Heilbrun, Carolyn. *The Last Gift of Time: Life beyond Sixty.* New York: Ballantine, 1988.

Heller, Caroline. *Until We Are Strong Together: Women Writers in the Tenderloin.* New York: Teachers College Press, 1997.

Hen Co-Op. *Growing Old Disgracefully: New Ideas for Getting the Most Out of Life.* Freedom, CA: Crossing Press, 1994.

Hermans, Hubert J. M., Harry J. G. Kempen, and Rens J. P. van Loon. "The Dialogical Self: Beyond Individualism and Rationalism." *American Psychologist* 47 (January 1992): 28.

Hessel, Dieter ed. *Maggie Kuhn on Aging: A Dialogue.* Philadelphia: Westminster Press, 1977.

Higginbotham, Evelyn Brooks. "African American Women's History and the Metalanguage of Race." In *We Specialize in the Wholly Impossible: A Reader in Black Women's History*, ed. Darlene Clark Hine, Wilma King, and Linda Reed. Brooklyn, NY: Carlson, 1995.

Hill-Collins, Patricia. "The Meaning of Motherhood in Black Culture and Black Mother-Daughter Relationships." In *Double Stitch: Black Women Write about Mothers and Daughters*, ed. Patricia Bell-Scott, Beverly Guy-Sheftall, Jacqueline Jones Royster, Janet Sims-Wood, Miriam DeCosta-Willis, and Lucie Futz, 42–60. Boston: Beacon Press, 1991.

Hochschild, Arlie Russell. "Ideology and Emotion Management: A Perspective and Path for Future Research." In *Research Agendas in the Sociology of Emotions*, ed. Theodore Kemper, 117–42. Albany: State University of New York Press, 1990.

————. *The Managed Heart: Commercialization of Human Feeling.* Berkeley: University of California Press, 1983.

hooks, bell. *Talking Back: Thinking Feminist, Thinking Black.* Boston: South End Press, 1989.

Jackson, James S. "Methodological Issues in Survey Research on Older Minority Adults." In *Special Research Methods for Gerontology*, eds. M. Powell Lawton and A. Regula Herzog, 137–61. Amityville, NY: Baywood, 1989.

Jackson, James S., Toni C. Antonucci, and Rose C. Gibson. "Cultural, Racial, and Ethnic Minority Influences on Aging." In *Handbook of the Psychology of Aging*, 3rd ed., ed. James E. Birren and K.Warner Schaie, 103–23. San Diego, CA: Academic Press, 1990.

Jelinek, Estelle C. *The Tradition of Women's Autobiography: From Antiquity to the Present*. Boston: Twayne, 1986.

Johnstone, Barbara. *Stories, Community, and Place: Narratives from Middle America*. Bloomington: Indiana University Press, 1990.

Jolliffe, David, ed. *Writing in Academic Disciplines*, vol. 2. Norwood, NJ: Ablex, 1988.

Jordan, Judith V. Introduction to *Women's Growth in Diversity*, ed. Judith V. Jordan, 1–8. New York: Guilford, 1997.

———. "Do You Believe That the Concepts of Self and Autonomy Are Useful in Understanding Women?" In *Women's Growth in Diversity*, ed. Judith V. Jordan, 29–32. New York, Guilford, 1997.

Katz, Stephen. *Disciplining Old Age*. Charlottesville: University Press of Virginia, 1996.

Kenyon, Gary. "The Meaning/Value of Personal Storytelling." In *Aging and Biography: Explorations in Adult Development*, ed. James E. Birren, Gary M. Kenyon, Jan-Erik Ruth, Johannes J. F. Schroots, and Torbjorn Svensson, 21–38. New York: Springer, 1996.

Kenyon, Gary M., and William L. Randall. *Restorying Our Lives: Personal Growth through Autobiographical Reflection*. Westport, CN: Praeger, 1997.

Kerby, Anthony Paul. *Narrative and the Self*. Bloomington: Indiana University Press, 1991.

Ker Conway, Jill. *When Memory Speaks: Reflections on Autobiography*. New York: Knopf, 1998.

Kimble, M., S. McFadden, J. Ellor, and J. Seeber, eds. *Aging, Spirituality, and Religion: A Handbook*. Minneapolis: Fortress Press, 1995.

Koenig, Harold G. *Research on Religion and Aging: An Annotated Bibliography*. Westport, CT: Greenwood Press, 1995.

Kotre, John. *Outliving the Self: Generativity and the Interpretation of Lives*. Baltimore: Johns Hopkins University Press, 1984.

Labouvie-Vief, Gisela. *Psyche and Eros: Mind and Gender in the Life Course*. New York: Cambridge University Press, 1994.

Labouvie-Vief, Gisela, Lisa M. Chiodo, Lori A. Goguen, Manfred Diehl, and Lucinda Orwoll, "Representations of Self Across the Life Span." *Psychology and Aging* 10 (1995): 404–15.

Labouvie-Vief, Gisela, Marlene DeVoe, and Diana Bulka. "Speaking about Feelings: Conceptions of Emotion across the Life Span." *Psychology and Aging* 4 (1989): 425–37.

Labouvie-Vief, Gisela, J. Hakim-Larson, and C. J. Hobart. "Age, Ego Level, and the Life-span Development of Coping and Defense Processes." *Psychology and Aging* 2 (1987): 286–93.

Laslett, Peter. *A Fresh Map of Life: The Emergence of the Third Age*. London: Weidenfeld & Nicolson, 1989.

Lessing, Doris. *The Diary of a Good Neighbour.* New York: Knopf, 1983.

Levinson, Daniel, and Judy Levinson. *The Seasons of a Woman's Life.* New York: Knopf, 1996.

Levinson, Daniel, C.N. Darrow, C. B. Klein, M. H. Levinson, and B. McKee. *The Seasons of a Man's Life.* New York: Ballantine, 1978.

Linde, Charlotte. *Life Stories: The Creation of Coherence.* New York: Oxford University Press, 1993.

Maccoby, E. E. "Gender as a Social Category." *Developmental Psychology* 24 (1988): 755–65.

McDermott, Raymond, and Herve Varenne. "Culture, Development, Disability." In *Ethnography and Human Development: Context and Meaning in Social Inquiry,* ed. Richard Jessor, Anne Colby, and Richard Shweder, 101–26. Chicago: University of Chicago Press, 1996.

McDonald, Barbara, with Cynthia Rich. *Look Me in the Eye: Old Women, Aging, and Ageism.* 2nd ed. San Francisco: Spinsters Book, 1991.

McGann, Patrick. "We Get into a Bunch of Mischief: The Personal Narratives of Male Adolescents and a Feminist Critique of Experience." In *Considering Women: Teaching Gender in Secondary and College English Classrooms,* ed. Susan Tchudi and Carol Harriman. Upper Montclair, NJ: Boynton/Cook, forthcoming.

McFadden, Susan H. "Religion, Spirituality, and Aging." In *Handbook of Psychology and Aging.* 4th ed., ed. James E. Birren and K. Warner Schaie. San Diego, CA: Academic Press, 1996.

McPherson, Barry D. *Aging as a Social Process: An Introduction to Individual and Population Aging.* 2nd ed. Toronto: Butterworths, 1990.

Miller, Nancy K. *Getting Personal: Feminist Occasions and Other Autobiographical Acts.* New York: Routledge, 1991.

Milligan, Sharon E. "Understanding Diversity of the Urban Black Aged: Historical Perspectives." In *Black Aged: Understanding Diversity and Service Needs,* ed. Zev Harel, Edward A. McKinney, and Michael Williams, 114–27. Newbury Park, CA: Sage, 1990.

Moody, Harry R. "Gerontology and Critical Theory." *Gerontologist* 32 (1992): 294–95.

———. "Overview: What Is Critical Gerontology and Why Is It Important?" In *Voices and Visions of Aging: Toward a Critical Gerontology,* eds. Thomas R. Cole, W. Andrew Achenbaum, Patricia L. Jakobi, and Robert Kastenbaum, xv–xli. New York: Springer, 1993.

Moore, D. W. "Most Americans Say Religion Is Important to Them." *Gallup Poll Monthly,* no. 353 (1995): 16–21.

Moore, Lorrie. "People Like That Are the Only People Here." *New Yorker,* 27 January 1997: 67–68.

Mor, Vincent, Sylvia Sherwood, and Claire Gutkin. "A National Study of Residential Care for the Aged." *The Gerontologist* 26 (1986): 405–17. Quoted in Rudolph H. Moos and Sonne Lemke, *Group Residences for Older Adults: Physical Features, Policies, and Social Climate.* New York: Oxford University Press, 1994.

Myerhoff, Barbara. "Life History among the Elderly: Performance, Visibility, and Remembering." In *Remembered Lives: The Work of Ritual, Storytelling, and Growing Older*, ed. Marc Kaminsky, 231–47. Ann Arbor, MI: University of Michigan Press, 1992.

———. *Number Our Days*. New York: Simon & Schuster, 1980.

Myerhoff, Barbara, and Jay Ruby. "A Crack in the Mirror: Reflexive Perspectives in Anthropology." In *Remembered Lives: The Work of Ritual, Storytelling, and Growing Older*, ed. Barbara Myerhoff, 307–40. Ann Arbor: University of Michigan Press, 1992.

Neisser, Ulric. "Self Narratives: True and False." In *The Remembering Self: Construction and Accuracy in the Self-Narrative*, ed. Ulric Neisser and Robin Fivush, 1–18. New York: Cambridge University Press, 1994.

Neugarten, Bernice. "Age Groups in American Society and the Rise of the Young-Old." *The Annals of the American Academy of Political and Social Science* 415: 187–98.

Newman, Leslea. "A Letter to Harvey Milk." In *A Letter to Harvey Milk: Short Stories*, 177–94. Ithaca, NY: Firebrand Books, 1988.

Ostricker, Alicia. *Stealing the Language: The Emergence of Women's Poetry in America*. Boston: Beacon, 1986.

Ovrebo, Beverly, and Meredith Minkler, "The Lives of Older Women: Perspectives from Political Economy and the Humanities." In *Voices and Visions of Aging: Toward a Critical Gerontology*, ed. Thomas R. Cole, Andrew W. Achenbaum, and Robert Kastenbaum, 289–308. New York: Springer, 1993.

Parry, A., and R. E. Doan. *Story Re-visions: Narrative Therapy in the Post-Modern World*. New York: Guilford, 1994.

Penguin Putnam Reading Group Guide to *The Stone Diaries* by Carol Shields. Penguin Putnam Inc. 27 Jan. 2000 ⟨http://www.penguinputnam.com/guides/⟩.

Peterson, Linda H. "Gender and the Autobiographical Essay: Research Perspectives, Pedagogical Practices." *College Composition and Communication* 42 (1991): 170–83.

Polkinghorne, Donald. *Narrative Knowing and the Human Sciences*. Albany: State University of New York Press, 1988.

Powers, Charles, and Susan Whitbourne. "Older Women's Constructs of Their Lives: A Quantitative and Qualitative Exploration." *International Journal of Aging and Human Development* 38: 293–306.

Probyn, Elspeth. *Sexing the Self: Gendered Positions in Cultural Studies*. London: Routledge, 1993.

Rich, Adrienne. *On Lies, Secrets, and Silence: Selected Prose, 1966–1978*. New York: Norton, 1979.

Rich, Cynthia. "The Women in the Tower." In *Look Me in the Eye: Old Women, Aging, and Ageism*, 2nd ed., ed. Barbara McDonald, with Cynthia Rich. San Francisco: Spinsters Book, 1991.

Rider, Janine. *The Writer's Book of Memory: An Interdisciplinary Study for Writing Teachers*. Mahwah, NJ: Lawrence Erlbaum, 1995.

Robinson, Lillian S., quoted in Catherine Stimpson, introduction to *Feminist Issues in Literary Scholarship*, ed. Shari Benstock, 1–6. Bloomington: Indiana University Press, 1987.

Rosaldo, Michelle. "Toward an Anthropology of Self and Feeling." In *Culture Theory:*

Essays on Mind, Self, and Emotion, ed. Richard Shweder and Robert Levine, 137–57. Cambridge: Cambridge University Press, 1984.

Rosenblatt, Roger. "Black Autobiography: Life as the Death Weapon." In *Autobiography: Essays Theoretical and Critical,* ed. James Olney, 168–80. Princeton: Princeton University Press, 1980.

Rosenwald, George C. "Reflections on Narrative Self-Understanding," conclusion to *Storied Lives: The Cultural Politics of Self-Understanding,* ed. George C. Rosenwald and Richard L. Ochberg, 256–89. New Haven: Yale University Press, 1992.

Ross, Michael, and Roger Buehler. "Creative Remembering." In *The Remembering Self: Construction and Accuracy in the Self-Narrative,* ed. Ulric Neissser and Robin Fivush, 205–35. New York: Cambridge University Press, 1994.

Roth, Philip. *The Facts: A Novelist's Autobiography.* New York: Farrar, Straus & Giroux, 1988.

Ruth, Jan-Erik, and Gary M. Kenyon. "Biography in Adult Development and Aging." In *Aging and Biography: Explorations in Adult Development,* ed. James E. Birren, Gary M. Kenyon, Jan-Erik Ruth, Johannes J. F. Schroots, and Torbjorn Svensson, 1–20. New York: Springer, 1996.

Sampson, Edward E. "The Deconstruction of the Self." In *Texts of Identity,* ed. John Shotter and Kenneth J. Gergen, 1–19. London: Sage, 1989.

Schacter-Shalomi, Zalman, and Ronald S. Miller. *From Age-ing to Sage-ing: A Profound New Vision of Growing Older.* New York: Warner Books, 1995.

Schafer, Roy. "Narration in the Psychoanalytic Dialogue." In *On Narrative,* ed. W. J. T. Mitchell. Chicago: University of Chicago Press, 1981.

Sherman, Edmund. *Reminiscence and the Self in Old Age.* New York: Springer, 1991.

Shotter, John. "Social Accountability and the Social Construction of 'You.'" In *Texts of Identity,* ed. John Shotter and Kenneth J. Gergen, 133–51. London: Sage, 1989.

Shweder, Richard A. "True Ethnography: The Lore, the Law, and the Lure." In *Ethnography and Human Development: Context and Meaning in Social Inquiry,* ed. Richard Jessor, Anne Colby, and Richard Shweder, 15–52. Chicago: University of Chicago Press, 1996.

Shields, Carol. *The Stone Diaries.* New York: Viking, 1993.

Singer, Jefferson A. "The Story of Your Life: A Process Perspective on Narrative and Emotion in Adult Development." In *Handbook of Emotion, Adult Development, and Aging,* ed. Carol Magai and Susan H. McFadden, 443–63. San Diego, CA: Academic Press, 1996.

Sinson, Janice C. *Group Homes and Community Integration of Developmentally Disabled People: Micro-institutionalization.* London: Kingsley, 1993.

Smith, Lee. "The Happy Memories Club." *Atlantic Monthly,* December 1995: 108–18.

Smith, Sidonie Smith. *A Poetics of Women's Autobiography: Marginality and the Fictions of Self-Representation.* Bloomington: Indiana University Press, 1987.

Smith, Sidonie, and Julia Watson, eds. *Getting a Life: Everyday Uses of Autobiography.* Minneapolis: University of Minnesota Press, 1996.

Spence, Donald. *Narrative Truth and Historical Truth: Meaning and Interpretation in Psychoanalysis.* New York: Norton, 1984.

Spilka, Rachel, ed. *Writing in the Workplace: New Research Perspectives.* Carbondale: Southern Illinois University Press, 1993.

Stack, Carol B. *All Our Kin: Strategies for Survival in a Black Community.* New York: Harper & Row, 1974.

Stewart, Abigail J. "Toward a Feminist Strategy for Studying Women's Lives." In *Women Creating Lives: Identities, Resilience, and Resistance,* ed. Carol E. Franz and Abigail J. Stewart, 11–36. Boulder: Westview Press, 1994.

Summerfield, Judith. "Is There a Life in This Text? Reimagining Narrative." In *Writing Theory and Critical Theory,* ed. John Clifford and John Schilb, 179–94. New York: Modern Language Association, 1994.

Swales, John. *Genre Analysis: English in Academic and Research Settings.* New York: Cambridge University Press, 1990.

Swann, Joan. *Girls, Boys, and Language.* Oxford: Blackwell, 1992.

Tannen, Deborah. *That's Not What I Meant! How Conversational Style Makes or Breaks Your Relations with Others.* New York: Morrow, 1986.

Thomas, Eugene, and Susan A. Eisenhandler, eds. *Aging and the Religious Dimension.* Westport, CT: Auburn House, 1994.

Tobin, Lad. "Car Wrecks, Baseball Caps, and Man-to-Man Defense: The Personal Narratives of Adolescent Males." *College English* 58 (1996): 158–75.

Turner, Bryan S. "Aging and Identity: Some Reflections on the Somatization of the Self." In *Images of Aging: Cultural Representations of Later Life,* ed. Mike Featherstone and Andrew Wernick, 245–160. London: Routledge, 1995.

Uhlenberg, Peter, and Sonia Miner. "Life Course and Aging: A Cohort Perspective." In *Handbook of Aging and the Social Sciences,* 4th ed., ed. Robert H. Binstock and Linda K. George, 208–28. San Diego, CA: Academic Press, 1996.

Wagner-Martin, Linda. *Telling Women's Lives: The New Biography.* New Brunswick, NJ: Rutgers University Press, 1994.

Wallace, J. Brandon Wallace. "Reconsidering the Life Review: The Social Construction of Talk about the Past." *Gerontologist* 32 (1992): 120–25.

Watson, Julia. "Ordering the Family: Genealogy as Autobiographical Pedigree." In *Getting a Life: Everyday Uses of Autobiograpy,* ed. Sidonie Smith and Julia Watson, 297–323. Minneapolis: University of Minnesota, 1996.

Waxman, Barbara Frey. *To Live at the Center of the Moment.* Charlottesville: University Press of Virginia, 1997.

Welch-Ross, Melissa K. "An Integrative Model of the Development of Autobiographical Memory." *Developmental Review* 15 (1995): 350.

White, Michael, and David Epston. *Narrative Means to Therapeutic Ends.* New York: Norton, 1990.

Woodward, Kathleen. *Aging and Its Discontents: Freud and Other Fictions.* Bloomington: Indiana University Press, 1991.

———. "Tribute to the Older Woman: Psychoanalysis, Feminism, and Ageism." In *Images of Aging: Cultural Representations of Later Life,* ed. Mike Featherstone and Andrew Wernick, 79–96. London: Routledge, 1995.

Wyatt-Brown, Anne. "The Liberation of Mourning in Elizabeth Bowen's *The Little Girls and Eva Trout*." In *Aging and Gender in Literature: Studies in Creativity*, ed. Anne Wyatt-Brown and Janice Rossen, 164–86. Charlottesville: University Press of Virginia, 1993.

———. The Future of Literary Gerontology." In *Handbook of the Humanities and Aging*, ed. Thomas R. Cole, Ruth E. Ray, and Robert Kastenbaum, 2nd ed., 41–61. New York: Springer, 1999.

Young, Gerald. *Adult Development, Therapy, and Culture: A Postmodern Synthesis*. New York: Plenum, 1997.

Index